The University in Transformation

THE UNIVERSITY IN TRANSFORMATION

Global Perspectives on the Futures of the University

EDITED BY

Sohail Inayatullah and Jennifer Gidley

BERGIN & GARVEY
Westport, Connecticut • London

Library of Congress Cataloging-in-Publication Data

The university in transformation : global perspectives on the futures
  of the university / edited by Sohail Inayatullah and Jennifer
  Gidley.
      p.   cm.
    Includes bibliographical references (p.   ) and index.
    ISBN 0–89789–718–8 (alk. paper)
      1. Universities and colleges—Forecasting.   2. Education, Higher—
  Aims and objectives.   3. Educational change.   I. Inayatullah,
  Sohail, 1958– .   II. Gidley, Jennifer.
  LB2324.U56   2000
  378′.01—dc21   99–16061

British Library Cataloguing in Publication Data is available.

Library of Congress Catalog Card Number: 99–16061
ISBN: 0–89789–718–8

First published in 2000

Bergin & Garvey, 88 Post Road West, Westport, CT 06881
An imprint of Greenwood Publishing Group, Inc.
www.greenwood.com

Printed in the United States of America

The paper used in this book complies with the
Permanent Paper Standard issued by the National
Information Standards Organization (Z39.48–1984).

10 9 8 7 6 5 4 3 2 1

Contents

1

Introduction: Forces Shaping University Futures

—— Sohail Inayatullah and Jennifer Gidley

INTRODUCTION

While it often appears to academics that the university is stable, looking back in history and forward to the future, the university is far more malleable. Just as in Western history where there were a range of possibilities—the Bologna student model versus the Paris university of masters model, or in recent colonial Indian history between indigenous traditions and modernist British models—the university stands at the gateway of a range of futures. Creating these futures are a number of trends and emergent issues, among others, globalism, multiculturalism (including indigenization), virtualization, and politicization. These promise to dramatically change the face of the university, in some ways taking it back to more ancient indigenous models, in other ways transforming it in ways that will make the future university all but unrecognizable to those of us in the 20th century.

This book is divided into four sections: Futures of Higher Education in the West (which, given the dominating positions of Western universities has direct and structural implications for the rest of the world); Futures of the University in the nonwest (these are not as representative as they ideally could be, still, modernist, scholar/activist, dissenting, and multicultural approaches are presented); Alternative Universities (these contest the foundations of the modern university and seek to offer disjunctive alternatives); and, Transformations of the University (our concluding chapters, where we summarize what has gone before and offer alternative futures ahead).

Authors range from varied disciplines: social and political science, political economy, futures studies, cultural studies, education, consciousness studies, and women's studies. All work, or have worked, as academics in the modern university to some extent, and all take a critical view of the current transformations that universities are undergoing. This book is not an apologia of globalization. Even if the scholars here are critical of current universities, they are more so of the commodification process universities are undergoing. None are Luddites, but they are cautiously optimistic about the role of the Internet, believing that while it may lead to increased interaction, it may also continue to distance teacher from student, knowledge from ethics. Some are more concerned about the content ("Does it dissent from current understandings?"), others more about the process of education, and still others about the political economy of knowledge ("Who gains and loses when structures of education change?"). All writers have a preferred future of the university. While assessing the trends creating the future, they have not shied away from explicitly stating the future they want, and in some cases, the future they fear.

Our hope for this book is that it impacts the policy debate on the futures of the university, particularly by contesting current assumptions of the future, and offering alternative future possibilities. We understand that the forces changing the university are often more than any particular university or nation can address, and yet, there are spaces for agency—whether it be ensuring that content is more multicultural, finding ways for faculty to show solidarity, better meeting the changing needs of students, or creating alternative universities. More significantly, the future undetected is a future given to us, and thus taken away from us. A future contoured, alternative futures mapped, means that the possibility of influence can increase, at the very least, it means that there is a possibility that the futures being shaped are done more thoughtfully, more creatively, and with more urgency.

A FORWARD GLIMPSE

Gaps and Imbalances

As with all such books, while the intention is comprehensiveness, complete representation is often not achieved. Gaps have remained. From a conceptual perspective, although the current corporatization of universities is mentioned in many of the chapters, in our seeking to access an author from within that framework, our contact with colleagues in one of the largest international corporate business degree providers was unfruitful. It became evident that they were too busy creating the future to write a reflective chapter.

The cultural and gender imbalance is particularly evident in the first section where we were seeking a range of critical views of shaping trends from the broad perspective of the Western situation. The perspective of students has only been addressed second hand by academics and this is indeed an oversight. The geographic/cultural diversity we sought became somewhat more limited when some of our prospective authors (from Nigeria, Hungary, Tibet in exile

[Dharamsala, India]), were unable to make the required commitment, mainly due to connectivity problems, as this book was edited largely through a continuous passing back and forth of e-mails, and partly because academics in these areas are already overly taxed with teaching and community/national responsibilities, and financial hardship. In addition, there were other alternative universities that could have participated, some of which are mentioned and others that are unknown to us. Perhaps this book will inspire other authors to develop a "Global Transformations Mark II," as undoubtedly the gaps we have left could fill another book.

We now summarize the main arguments made by the contributing authors in the context of the book's four sections. Following this, the drivers creating the future are explored.

Western Perspectives

A broad context is provided for this section by the first three chapters. Philip Spies presents a historical overview of the development of the traditional Western model of the university. Speaking of the university as both the product and coproducer of each age in which it exists, he looks back at such broad historical stages as the Renaissance/Enlightenment age, the Industrial age, and the present "Nomocratic" age. However, he places the deep roots of the university in much earlier classical Greek times. Spies' focus is the great liberal/classical tradition reminding us of the criteria for an education that develops the whole person through a search for welfare and freedom, as well as goodness, beauty, and truth. Decrying the current emphasis on quantity rather than quality in education, he calls for a new kind of intellectualism, which includes the five-fold breadth of the classics, as a means of acquiring context and systems knowledge capable of addressing the *global problematique*.

Peter Manicas extends the historical context into more recent developments in England, Europe, and the United States. Along with Deane Neubauer, he tracks the major forces of change today in terms of globalization, unaffordability, and computer-mediated technology. Manicas also describes who the survivor institutions might be, but places responsibility for survival and quality firmly back in the hands of faculty. Deane Neubauer focuses strongly on the impact of economic rationalism, as well as numerous other macro-forces, on the university sector. He further develops the survivor proposal with an examination of three types of new "convenience" institutions. Neubauer discusses the major institutional challenges, particularly for university managers, in the wake of these macro-changes. He also poses some dramatic future scenarios with far-reaching implications for universities: the 20–80 scenario where 80 percent have no work; and the 185,000,000 student scenario worldwide.

The virtualization of the university is taken as a given by Michael Skolnik and Jim Dator. Skolnik explores the major implications of this in terms of its impact on students and, particularly, faculty. He discusses the mixed responses of faculty, from organized rejection on the one hand to passionate "conversion" on the other.

Skolnik also fears the inevitable loss of jobs for faculty as in other mechanized industries. Dator's emphasis is more on the changes to the structure of university institutions once the bricks and mortar fall. He also bemoans the likely loss of academic freedom, and develops a brief charter for what needs to be learned in the universities of the 21st century if we want humans to exist in the 22nd.

Tom Abeles argues that it is time for the Academy to face its demise (and rebirth). In the massive competition of the marketplace for the production of what he calls short half-life knowledge (with a short use-by date), Abeles believes universities have lost the battle because of the infrastructure costs compared to costs of virtual space. He believes faculty need to ask the deep questions such as, "What is their purpose?" His own position is that there needs to be a return to the core business of providing long half-life knowledge, the ability to synthesize, and wisdom.

David Rooney and Greg Hearn, and also Paul Wildman, to an extent summarize some of the forces of change acting on universities, yet each from different perspectives. Rooney and Hearn discuss the commodification of higher education in terms of how inappropriate it is to attempt to use a linear industrial economic model to support a process that deals with educating the complex, nonlinear human mind. They present three scenarios for the future of university education—the do-nothing scenario, the commodified university, and their favorite one, the on-line learning community—incorporating their comprehensive typology of four types of knowledge, which goes beyond simple information gathering. Wildman looks at how emerging issues for future universities might look from the periphery. He discusses how fragmented futures might be for young people and how the idea of a "subversity" might appeal to the children of the alternative generation who seek an "alternative to the alternative" and yet can't fit back into the mainstream. He looks toward a "futures active learning system" that listens to the voices coming from the margins of society.

Nonwestern Perspectives

The five chapters in this section can give only a taste of the richness and diversity of views that exist beyond the paradigm of the traditional, Western university model and even beyond its critique of itself. Ashis Nandy's opening chapter sets the context for the others in the sense that he analyses the politics of the "knowledge" that is taught in universities, regardless of whether they be Western or their hybrid transplants into other cultures. He examines how the imported Western university system has worked at taming traditional knowledge systems and looks at how knowledge may truly be pluralized through the recovery and affirmation of indigenous knowledge systems.

Tariq Rahman and Shahrzad Mojab present completely different positions on the struggles within colonized or postcolonial cultures to develop quality, autonomous university education. Rahman tracks the colonial history of universities in India and Pakistan, leading to the present situation of government control, poverty, and lack of quality. He looks to three options for the future, and given the limitations he sees with both privatization and Islamization, he would prefer to see a modernization of the public universities as a necessary step toward Pakistan's transition to modernity, which he believes lags far behind its East Asian counterparts. Mojab discusses the difficulties in parts of the Middle East in creating genuine tertiary education in the context of education being seen by the political dictators as creating sites of dissent. She describes the various attempts to found an autonomous university in Iran, and of the elimination of the Kurdistan university by Khomeini on the eve of its inauguration. For Mojab, the idea of an autonomous university is inextricably linked to the idea of a civil society. She highlights the ongoing challenges for university futures in the Middle East and presents a fairly grim outlook for the likelihood of autonomous universities, let alone academic freedom.

Not surprisingly, university futures in the Caribbean are somewhat less disturbing, in the view of Anne Hickling-Hudson. Hudson looks to the "soul of the university," rooted in the Caribbean soil, as a source of vital scholar-activism. She points out that this tradition and flavor of university life has been flagging, and needs to be rebooted, in order to put "scholarship at the service" of the Caribbean people and the sustainable development of its culture. She presents some rich and colorful scenarios as to how this "scholar-activism" might be reawakened and used as a lever of change in the coming decades.

Patricia Kelly takes another tack again viewing globalization and the current "internationalization" of many Western universities to be about more than just an increase in numbers of international students. From her perspective and experience in academic staff development, she discusses the politics of language and teaching and the need for institutional support for cultural awareness among academics.

Alternative Universities

This section includes the two very different alternative university visions of Ivana Milojevic and Patricia Nicholson, and also two case studies of existing universities that radically depart from the traditional Western secular model. Milojevic discusses the two commonly occurring likely scenarios of the corporate university and the global electronic university in terms of their implications for women. Since, in Milojevic's view, women do not fare well in these scenarios, she then goes on to develop her own utopian vision of how a women's university would look, where for example, education and child care would be central rather than peripheral concerns. Nicholson, on the other hand, after briefly discussing the present context, develops two rather contrasting scenarios as to how the survivor institutions might look in 30 years. Her mega-corporatized university would be called an "advanced learning network," while her "experience camps" would be smaller, more community responsive, and related to service needs.

The chapter by Bussey is both a case study and a preferred vision of the future. Having discussed and critiqued the modern Western university, he argues for the need to recontextualize learning from a spiritual framework. He discusses the seminal ideas of Prabhat Rainjan Sarkar and the traditional idealism of his approach to Tantra. He cites the example of Sarkar's Gurukula university in India, and develops some broader implications and visions for the extension of this model.

Finally, James Grant presents a case study of the Maharishi University of Management, based on the philosophy and efforts of Maharishi Mahesh Yogi. He describes in some detail the scientific evidence for the existence of pure consciousness, the accessing of which being one of the core functions of this university. Grant also develops the implications of the existence of pure consciousness on educational goals and practices, the primary goal being to transform society.

In our concluding section, Inayatullah offers three alternative futures of the university: Mileage Plus-Air Points, where universities are managed by competing mega-structures; Virtual Touch, a scenario in which electronic classrooms are joined with face-to-face pedagogy; and Bliss for All, an ideal scenario wherein multiple ways of knowing and transformative knowledge are at the heart of what the university is about. Gidley summarizes the book, in the light of the dehumanizing effect of the current changes, and offers some clues to a rehumanized future for universities. She examines three roles for faculty: the Broker, the Mentor, and the Meaning-Maker.

DRIVERS AND TRANSFORMATIONS

We now turn to the crucial drivers that are shaping the futures of the university. While there are many, we assert that four are crucial: globalization, multiculturalism, virtualization, and politicization.

- *Globalism*—the freeing of capital and the taming of labor and nation-states, particularly those in the South;
- *Multiculturalism*—an understanding that while reality is socially constructed and we create gender and culture through practice, cultures, civilizations, and women and men know the world differently, and that a good society must authentically reflect this diversity;
- *The Internet*—in all its meanings from the site, the form, the delivery system to the content of the new universities, particularly in the possibility of the creation of the virtual university and decentralized publishing; and
- *Politicization*—in the South this refers to increasing attempts to use the university for repressive measures as well as the university as a site of dissent, and in the North it relates to the university being part of the economic rationalization of society, of the postindustrial problematique.

These general drivers operate at different levels. Globalism and politicization are long-term historical trends and are now fully developed, while multiculturalism and the Internet are more emergent. These drivers, which will impact the dimensions of the University, also include:[1]

- The university as a corporation (which globalism enhances);

- The university as a site of academic leadership (the model of knowledge as philosophy);
- The university as the ideological arm of the nation-state (politicization);
- Polyversities, multiversities, and diversities—the creation of a range of alternative universities, all based on the idea of difference, of finding knowledge niches (multiculturalism);
- The emerging global electronic university, which will overcome the "tyranny of disciplines, replace hierarchy, and through reduced costs and flexible access reach enormous numbers of people"[2] (Internet); and
- The community-based university, whose main function is public service, using the university to help the community thrive, seeing the student as an active participant instead of consumer or rote learner and seeing professors as active and reflective practitioners instead of experts. This last dimension of the university is about the role of the intellectual in society: as beholden to state and capital or serving community/global planetary interests (the expanded public).

Globalism

Certainly if we take the present as a point of departure for understanding the future, there can be no driving force more important than globalism. Academics all over the world have felt the painful pinch of globalism as defined by decreased funding for research, decreased state subsidies, and the calls by deans for academics to be more competitive in not only their own discipline but in the larger national or global economy. This process is structural. Whether one is Marxist, feminist, or postcolonial, the bureaucratic structure forces one into a position wherein the university and the self become corporatized.

Among others, Manicas and Neubauer make the case that the irrevocable forces of capitalism have created a two-tiered university system, and as long as access and convenience are enhanced by the new electronic technologies, issues of quality will continue to fade away. Moreover, faculty have focused on maintaining their jobs and not on the larger debate.

More and more the university is being explicitly tied to the global capitalist system. For instance, California State University is in the process of entering into a long-term partnership with Microsoft, GTE, Fujitsu, and Hughes Electronics. This plan gives the university technology that the state is unable to fund. As Robert Corrigan, the president of San Francisco State says, "If I had my druthers, I think it's something the state should pay for, but as a president who can't get the money either from the students or from the state, I'm driven into working with the corporate sector."[3] But, asks Lawrence Wiseman, once the university becomes just another business, will it lose its "special character, some of its societal privilege,"[4] its moral authority and force—its link with civil society, as a repository of truth and knowledge? Can a university both be a business and fulfill "its potential as an institution of noble and transforming purpose?"[5] Will the university be the axial institution of the postindustrial professional society or, as Dator argues, not needed at all—just a theme park?[6]

Tom Abeles points out that the real transformation that is occurring is the shift from state-centric universities to corporatized/globalized universities—from Oxford to IBM or McDonald's. Abeles sees two levels: grand megaglobal universities and localized highly diversified universities. The mega universities will soon provide core courses through virtual networks while smaller institutions will meet specific local needs. This loosening of the Ivy League Western model with its Greek heritage will certainly lead to enhanced diversity, with alternatives not just coming from corporatist ventures but from civilizational perspectives. Witness the spread of Islamic universities[7] or New Age meditative-type universities (from transpersonal psychology universities to the Maharishi University of Management).

There is also conventional resistance to the globalization of the university. In 1998, students in Germany protested en masse to changes in funding to the university, disputing why they undergo budget cuts while the university is subsidizing corporations, thus serving as the training ground for industrialism.[8]

Irrespective of protests, the long-term trend does appear to be the university as customer-consumer led, where the relationship of the student to the university is not as a member of a community but as a site of transactions—gaining some information and then moving on to the next vendor.

Multiculturalism and Deep Inclusiveness

While market pressures are one force changing the future of the university, another challenge comes from multiculturalism.[9] Indeed, as Anne Hickling-Hudson argues, multiculturalism directly confronts the ideology of globalism. At heart, argues Nandy, multiculturalism is about dissent, about contesting the categories of knowledge that modernity has given us. And, even with multiculturalism often criticized and co-opted by "political correctness" (given the strength of the right, an understandable process), and used strategically to ensure representation, still the future is more and more about an ethics of inclusion instead of a politics of exclusion. Of course, the struggle will be long and hard, and more often than not, instead of new curriculum, there will be just more special departments of the "other." This is a real fear as it narrows the role of the Asian or African or Pacific intellectuals to that of "becoming otherness machines."[10] Or as Kwame Anthony Appiah writes, "Our only distinction in the world of texts to which we are latecomers is that we can mediate it to our fellows"[11] (and then regurgitate it back to the West as the view from the "other"). While Western intellectuals produce general universal knowledge, non-Westerners merely write on what it means to not be part of that enterprise, becoming the official "other."

As "globalism" continues in its varied oppositional forms—as critique of uneven capital accumulation, as authentic encounters with the "other," and even as cultural chic—the multicultural challenge to the future of the university has become more pervasive (moving beyond the catchphrase of "equal opportunity employer") and will not go away.

While the initial trend is multiculturalism in terms of representation and better curriculum, the long-term agenda is a fundamental transformation of the male Western bias of current universities—what Johan Galtung has called the "mama" syndrome (middle-aged male academics). Positively put, this is the vision of the alternative university, whether a women's university, a spiritual university, an indigenous university, or an experiential learning camp.

Multiculturalism, too, however, can become part of official dissent, seen as essentialist instead of an evolutionary practice. Writing from Australia, Patricia Kelly interrogates multiculturalism in the day-to-day practices of universities. She challenges us to go beyond inclusion and to move toward responsiveness—to investigate the points of universalism in relativity, to respond to the changing needs of students, academic and administrative staff, and university management.

In the South, these issues—framed as ethnic minority political representation—are equally relevant, and focus less on epistemological and structural violence and more on direct violence. Pakistani and Indian textbooks write the "other" as violent and themselves as more natural, essential to the future of culture. Textbooks become vehicles for state policy and not for a more neutral transference of ideas of a possible history or future.[12]

Genocide throughout the world shows that unless one incorporates the other—nation, tribe, ethnicity, or religion (as in the cases of South Asia, Rwanda, the former USSR, and the former Yugoslavia) as part of a plurality of selves, of historical cultures that have had episodes of cooperation (living in community) as well as episodes of violence the result will be obvious. Less of all.

Virtualization and the Internet

A third dramatic force, and perhaps the most obvious one, is the impact of the idea of the Internet, which has captured the global imagination. Wildman, for example, believes that it will fundamentally change who is student and who is teacher. It will virtualize the walls of the university, creating "elsewhere" learning. It will allow for new levels of interactivity. It will eliminate the temporal rigidity of office hours or class meeting times. Those who do not jump on the postindustrial knowledge bandwagon will, as Dator warns, become theme parks—places to visit emeritus professors. While the theme in the last decade has been globalize or die, the theme for the future of the universities will be virtualize or disappear. Everyone has joined in, from California Virtual University[13] to the World Bank's African Virtual University.[14] The virtualization of the university will not just be about the delivery of knowledge but also about the skills needed in the future. Multiskilling and other ways of learning will be far more important than the ability to concentrate on one task (of course, anyone having completed a Ph.D. while working, or any mother who must take care of children, run the home economy, and endless other responsibilities know about that as well). Abeles also believes that the Web will allow "bridges between generations where the wisdom from the past can be used to link the future with the present—youth with adults."

However, there are limits to virtuality. Among other revolts, the Belgrade student revolt of 1997 taught us that the university can be a genuine site of dissent. Virtual links can help spread information, telling others of injustice, but it is the physical site that has mythic resonance. It is the marching of fifty to a hundred thousand individuals calling for the resignation of a vice-chancellor or the prime minister that is transformative. Thus, it is not only curriculum that should be seen as dissenting, but the actual physical site of the university that can create an alternative future. Without physicality, virtuality will not be about dissent, but about information-numbed minds. However, while virtuality calls out for responses—and universities attempt to transform—they do so in fetish ways. One university's idea of becoming more interactive through the Net is to require professors to put their lecture notes on the Web. The result: lectures become even more rigid and boring. Instead of using the Net for passing information so that professors can concentrate on the more human needs in pedagogy, that is, encouragement, nurturing, and generation of ideas, as in the mentoring role proposed by Gidley in her concluding chapter, universities transform professors into information automatons. Instead of "sage-on-stage" one gets information-retrieval system on stage. In Inayatullah's concluding chapter, he argues that once the distinction between content designer and professor is made, in the long run, it will be the content designers who will write the software for the new universities, ending domination by academy and capital/state.

Still, the university in the Web/Net vision of the world will dramatically and fundamentally change us. One historical analogy is that of the impact of the Enlightenment on the university. "The rational cosmology—the Enlightenment—undermined the universities as homes of outmoded theoretical knowledge, still based largely on Aristotle and the medieval schoolmen and increasingly out of touch with observed reality."[15] Why go to a university, it was argued, to learn old doctrine of little use outside a career in the church? The university in France of the *ancien regime* was seen with scorn as supporting a dead worldview and state. Certainly the above quote could be applied to the universities of the late 20th century, argue the creators of the Net. If we go further back to 12th through 14th century Bologna, the university was student-run—fines were levied on lecturers if they started or finished their lectures late—"not keeping up with the syllabus, leaving the city without permission."[16]

Politicization: Enter the Violent State

Of course, leaving the city is not the problem, finding time away from quickening of information—of the gaze of the computer screen—is. Thus, while virtuality has its own dangers, particularly technology fetishism (not to mention loss of face-to-face interaction, loss of the wisdom imparted by a truly exceptional teacher, and the gaze of others), another trend (a foundational one) is the continued politicization of universities. At one level this is about loss of political freedom at the national level and the resultant loss of academic freedom,[17] at another level it is, as in Pakistan, taking guns to class and using them as threats for grades but also to ward off the advances of the youth wings of other political parties.[18]

The university is not only a site for finding a future job, for learning philosophy, or for finding a future partner, but also a site of violent state politics—of deciding who will run the nation. In the North, this is often done through admissions and graduations. In the South, it is done through using the administrative apparatus of the state for political benefit, for striking fear in academics—letting them know they must not dissent. The spiral of the decline of knowledge and the university continues due to decreasing funds going toward education. At the same time, with the formal university in the South under sustained criticism (seen as the carrier of national culture—the official culture) a host of business universities have begun to open up. Globalization has created new possibilities—for computer training and for business training, as well as for the endless courses one can take in order to enter an American university.

The challenge in the South is about entering modernity. At one level this is about decolonizing the mind, reforming the colonial heritage that universities grew up in. Similarly, Rahman writes how in India universities grew so as to create lower-level bureaucrats for the British to order around so the British could save on colonial administrative expenses. Part of the decolonization process is about creating universities that are critical of not only the colonial state but the modern independent nation—that is, critical of the postcolonial state and its authoritative power. Universities must become modern—that is, academically independent of the state with fair processes of entry for students—but not necessarily using the modern model of the West. Other models of the modern university are required. These must challenge power in all forms and honor traditional ways of knowing.

The futures of the university are thus not only about revisiting its pasts, discovering what its roots are, and deciding which histories to privilege, it is about recovering the many civilizational approaches to knowledge. Indeed, the future of the university is essentially about rescuing the plurality of knowledge, specifically the plurality of dissent, argues Nandy.[19] As Nandy points out in this volume, the larger problem in understanding the future of the university and creating authentic alternatives is conceptual colonization.

Central to understanding the current predicament of non-Western universities is that they have not evolved naturally from their historical roots—rather the traditional system has gone underground or become exoticized, and is seen as the alternative to the official rational university. As an Indian academic put it in 1917, "The University of Calcutta is a foreign plant imported into this country, belonging to a type that flourished in foreign soil . . . the new system was introduced in entire ignorance and almost in complete defiance of the existing social order regulating the everyday life of an ancient people."[20] This is the cultural violence.

And yet, the colonial university has become universal. However, while the lineage of nonwestern universities is assumed to be nonexistent, Western scholars forget that the modern Western university too must be seen as intimately related to the state and the episteme. Changes in knowledge, as with the Enlightenment, forced dramatic changes to European universities. Nationalism forced universities to reify myths of war and the "other" as enemy. History was rewritten to glorify the state and its functionaries.

While many focus on changes in knowledge, multicultural discourse is also about acknowledging the importance of changes in consciousness. Grant, for example, imagines an age of Enlightenment (not the European nomination but the more classical Vedic concept) that comes about through the use of new technologies developed in the context of meditational practices. These individual practices lead to a cooperative coordinated collective consciousness.

However, alternative visions of the university in themselves—just because they dissent from conventional visions—are not enough to be considered futures that can create a transformative pedagogy. Secularists such as Rahman warn that Islamic universities do not present a local alternative to state-supported universities. Islamic universities disseminate a particular view of Islam and repress other interpretations of what it means to be Muslim. Exclusion instead of tolerance toward others and their ways of knowing, is taught. On the other hand, private universities only teach courses that can lead to immediate wealth. They are not concerned with profound questions of the nature of the good society. Most importantly they are reserved for the wealthy. Thus, for Rahman, it is crucial to modernize Third World universities in accordance with liberal Enlightenment values and not to be overly charmed by indigenous models or pressures from globalism.

Mojab extends this and writes that modernist nominations of the university must be in the context of civic society—of taming the power of state and capital and of autonomous universities that are not physically and epistemologically threatened by the state—whether in its Iranian Islamic guise or its Western secular guise. The state must be civilized. Modernist nominations of the state in the Middle-Eastern context merely expand the state monopoly on education. Attempts to dissent, to create oppositional social movements with different visions of education, are brutally repressed.

It is exactly this vision of the autonomous student-led responsive university that the wise application of the new technologies allow us to create. Unfortunately, the planning and use of these new technologies occur in a context that is currently dominated by economic rationalism, wherein information transfer comes to mean knowledge creation, where the counting of number of e-mails globally is equated with a global conversation of civilizations. In this context, it is difficult to remain optimistic about the institutional ability of current universities to innovate (and why Manicas writes that the great promise of pessimistic futurism is that history is full of surprises). This is why the indigenization of knowledge project—the creation of alternative modernities, such as Milojevic's ideal of the women's university, Grant's vision of a meditative campus, and Bussey's vision of a community of spiritually oriented activist thinkers, writers and artists—carry some transformative potential.

DRAMATIC CHANGES

The traditional university is under challenge/threat from various forces worldwide. Globalization and politicization are the current factors, but the emerging issues of multiculturalism and virtualization will continue the dismantling of the university as it has been imagined and constructed by humanists in the last thousand years—as knowledge for the sake of knowledge.

In the South, the failure has come from within, with low pay and local violence, as well as imitative rote knowledge, making the academic university a place to avoid. However, for the upper middle class, who cannot afford to send their children to America or to send them to private colleges, all that is left is the state-run university. Gaining entrance is a life and death issue—the Third World university will remain the same for decades to come, irrespective of what happens in the West. Modem saturation and regular electricity are still a distant dream, not an everyday normality.

Thus, while the university has deep roots—in its modern form in the Christian 12th century in the West, and in its many different forms (as the formal passing of knowledge) perhaps one to two thousand years earlier in India and China—it does not mean that the university will remain stable.

What the future of the university will be, as with all questions about the future, is unknown. Our intent is both to contour the unknowable as well as provide insights into the alternative futures of the university—to take the various histories, drivers, themes, trends, and emerging issues and weave them together to arrive at alternative futures of the university. While historical forces will dramatically change the current university, there are still choices to be made as to the shape of future universities.

NOTES

1. Ivana Milojevic, "Women's Higher Education in the 21st Century," *Futures* 30, 7 (1998): 699.

2. Ibid.

3. Pamela Burdman and Julia Angwin, "Cal State Forging Partnerships with Four High-Tech Firms Link Upsets Some in Academia," *San Francisco Chronicle* (1 December 1997): A1. Taking a critical note is James Wood. In his essay, "In California, A Dangerous Deal with Technology Companies," *The Chronicle of Higher Education Opinion* (February 20, 1998) (received on the listserve HRCFS-L@hawaii.edu on February 24, 1998), B6. Wood writes that "the proposed partnership would commercialize higher education, allowing profit motives, rather than pedagogical ones, to drive university policies regarding curriculum and employment."

4. Lawrence Wiseman, "The University President: Academic Leadership in an Era of Fund Raising and Legislative Affairs," in *Managing Institutions of Higher Education into the 21st Century*, Ronald Sims and Serbrenia Sims, eds. (Westport, CT: Greenwood, 1991): 5.

5. Ibid.

6. Jim Dator, "The Futures of Universities. Ivied Halls, Virtual Malls or Theme Parks?", Futures 30, 7 (1998).

7. For more on this, see Zia Sardar, "What Makes a University Islamic?," in *How We Know: Ilm and the Revival of Knowledge*, Zia Sardar, ed. (London: Grey Seal, 1991): 69–85. Series editor, Merryl Wyn Davies.

8. See Andreas Hippen, "100,000 Fight Back the Neoliberal Attack on Education in Germany," HRCFS-L@hawaii.edu. December 16, 1997. E-mail of author: sg885hi@unidui.uni-duisburg.de. For more information see: http://fsrinfo.uni-duisbert.de/streik/

9. For an American perspective on this, see Roberto, Haro, "Developing a Campus Climate for Diversity in the 21st Century," in Sims and Sims, Op cit: 49–64. He writes, "Along the Atlantic Seaboard colleges and universities, especially the older, private ones, celebrate these English and European traditions. African-Americans, Asian-Americans, Hispanics, and Native Americans were, for the most part, never involved in the development of these institutions and are, therefore, like 'strangers from different shores'" 51. See R. Takaki, *Strangers from Different Shores* (Boston: Little, Brown, 1989). Haro provides some excellent suggestions for creating a better climate including establishing a non-threatening social environment, changing the curriculum, diversifying the faculty, reaching out to off-campus minority groups, strengthening ties with feeder institutions that have greater minority representation, employing minority leaders in management, and creating a minority commission that meets directly with the university president. However, his suggestions do not touch on the epistemology—the ways of knowing—that constitute knowledge and the university that, too, must be changed before others can feel that they are in the same ocean and are not strangers.

10. Taken from Sara Suleri, *Meatless Days* (Chicago: Chicago University Press, 1989): 105.

11. Kwame Anthony Appiah, *In My Father's House: Africa in the Philosophy of Culture* (Oxford: Oxford University Press, 1992): 157.

12. S. P. Udayakumar, *"Presenting" the past: The Politics of "Hindu" History Writing in India*. Doctoral Dissertation. (University of Hawaii, Department of Political Science, 1995). E-mail: spkumar@tc.umn.edu

13. *Wall Street Journal* (January 7, 1998). The executive director of the virtual-university design team says: "This has got to be one of the largest, if not the largest, investments in on-line education in this country." See: HRCFS-L@hawaii.edu. Organized by University of Hawaii futurist Jim Dator, this listserve focused on emerging technologies and alternative futures.

14. Through satellite-based distance education, the African Virtual University intends to provide Sub-Saharan African countries with "university education in science and engineering, noncredit continuing education programs, and remedial instruction. Http://www.worldbank.org.html/extdr/rmc/guide/africa.htm#2africa. For more information contact: Avu@worldbank.org

15. Harold Perkin, "History of Universities," in *International Higher Education: An Encyclopedia*, Philip Altbach, ed. (Chicago and London: St. James Press, 1991): 182.

16. Ibid.: 174.

17. Shahrukh Khan, "Pakistan" in *Altbach* (1991), op cit.: 533.

18. Ibid.: 535.

19. Ashis Nandy, "The Future of Dissent," *Seminar* 460 (December, 1997): 42–45.

20. Perkin, (1991), op cit.: 194.

Part 1

Western Perspectives on the Futures of the University

2

University Traditions and the Challenge of Global Transformation

Philip Spies

This chapter reviews a few of the implications of social change for universities as educational institutions in the next century. The university, as we know it today, is a product of a number of "genotypical" and "phenotypical" factors. The genotypical factors provided a measure of constancy of practice over the ages. They were shaped by the classical roots and ageless traditions of universities and other centers of advanced learning in society. The phenotypical factors cover the historical conditions that shaped human competencies and society's need for educational services over the ages.

The current transformation toward a postindustrial world order therefore holds important implications for the development and governance of universities. This challenge is systemic in nature, which contrasts sharply with the reductionism of latter day advanced education. Moreover, it seems that the postindustrial world will not just be an adaptation of the industrial world, but something fundamentally different in terms of its mode of wealth creation and in terms of its source of social power. This could affect every facet of the university as an advanced educational institution, that is, its function, structure, processes, and form of governance.

FIVE TRADITIONS OF THE UNIVERSITY

The earliest roots of the university as an educational institution are probably 2,400 years ago in the *paideia* of the classical Greek Sophists, with the Academy of Plato and the Lyceum of Aristotle being the earliest institutional examples of specialized advanced education in philosophy. The Sophists believed that education should develop a person's character for effective participation in *polis* life.

The polis was their concept of an ideal sociopolitical order governed by impersonal uniform laws, rather than by the arbitrary acts of a despot.[1]

The paideia system of education and training was aimed at developing the whole person—physically, emotionally, and intellectually. The 4th century B.C. was the heyday of philosophy. Socrates entered this scene at the height of the tensions between the ancient Olympian tradition and the vitality of the new intellectualism of the Sophists. It was an age of discovery, and of metaphysical and ethical discourse. Athens was too poor to maintain its state medical services, but nevertheless opened private universities that made it the "school of Hellas," the intellectual capital and arbiter of Greece.[2] From this vital Greek tradition sprouted the university as the capstone of a society's educational system.

Being the standard bearer of the education of an age, how can the general state of university education in a specific period be judged? A starting point for developing such a yardstick is to look at the purpose that was attached to the institution of a university over the ages. The following classification expands on the proposition that the earlier development of university education followed the classical Greek tradition of developing the whole person. This implies that a good education should be aimed at

- a search for welfare (the professions and development);
- a search for truth (inquiry and research);
- a search for order and freedom (leadership);
- a search for what is good (ethics and the development of a moral imperative); and
- a search for beauty (the promotion of aesthetics in human enterprise).[3]

A Search for Welfare

The search for welfare suggests that a university should produce competent people who can make useful contributions in terms of their intellectual leadership in the socioeconomic sphere of society. This was, inter alia, the underlying theme of the Greek Sophists, the Chinese civil service examinations of 4,000 years ago and the professional training (medicine, law, accounting) in the Christian and Islam monasteries from medieval times. Today, it is still the leitmotiv of medical schools and of the training of engineers, accountants, and lawyers. The purpose of the university is in this case to provide high-level professional training, which will promote the application of the best knowledge of the times in the designated area of practice. The American "Land Grant" university system was established under such a banner of "science in practice."

A Search for Truth

A search for truth refers to the Socratic tradition of intellectual honesty and integrity and a quest for wisdom[4]—exemplified, inter alia, by ancient Greek educational institutions, such as the Academy of Plato and the Lyceum of Aristotle. Within the modern context it refers to the accepted practice that a university should be a center for research, specifically leading-edge research. The Alexandria

Museum and Library of Egypt, which was established in the 3rd century B.C., was to some extent a forerunner of the modern research university,[5] and the Universities of Bologna and Leiden are two examples of institutions that advanced science studies during the Renaissance. Today, this research tradition is best exemplified by the German Humboldt model.

A Search for Order and Freedom

Universities are expected to develop competent leaders and good managers of human affairs. This is to some extent an "elitist" tradition, which reflects in two ways on the university's role in society. The first is a negative one, where university training is seen as the exclusive privilege of the powerful; one way to maintain control through exclusive knowledge acquisition and life-long "old-boy" networks. The second is a positive one, that is, the university is a crucible—a supreme test of human quality and intellect where only the best of society can make the grade.

Today, educational elitism is a serious problem for many developing societies—sometimes also referred to as the "Effendi-effect." A good university education remains beyond the financial reach of the vast majority of the population in developing countries, which means it is the exclusive realm of an elite. Consequently, the idea of an education for an elite is often rejected in favor of an equalitarian university system which caters for the masses (in the tradition of the Greek philosopher Diogenes)—in some instances with the additional demand that students and workers should run the university (rather than the professors), that education should be free and that all students should be passed if one is passed (exams are seen to be intrinsically unfair).

The "elitist" tradition nevertheless remains one of the oldest and most pervasive traditions of university (or advanced) education—whether it be the ancient Greek, Indian, Chinese, Persian, or modern European systems. The so-called "Ivy League" universities in the United States and the Oxford-Cambridge tripos (PPE) system—where aspiring leaders in business and politics can structure their courses around subjects such as philosophy, political studies, and economic studies—are often-quoted examples of leadership education for the elite. The perception is that by attending such institutions—and by taking these special leadership-oriented courses—one acquires a vastly superior grounding in leadership.

A Search for What Is Good

The fourth tradition directs the primary purpose of education in general, and of university education in particular, toward the preparation of a sound moral-ethical basis for a future society. The dominant role of religion in the establishment and development of educational institutions throughout history is well known. In ancient Egypt the temple schools taught religion, the principles of writing, the sciences, mathematics, and architecture. In ancient India, Buddhist doctrines were taught by priests to, inter alia, Chinese scholars—who in turn spread the teaching of Buddha to the various countries of the Far East. Education in ancient China was also based on the teachings of Confucius and Lao-tze.[6] The Bible, the Torah, the Talmud, and the Quran provided the basis for early educational developments in Europe, the Middle East, and North Africa. The doctrine of Scholasticism which emerged during the Middle Ages applied logic to reconcile Christian theology with the pre-Christian Greek philosophies. The modern practice of the control of education by government can be traced to Luther, Calvin, and other Protestant leaders of the Reformation.

A Search for Beauty

The pursuit of "beauty"—or averting "ugliness"—highlights the importance of aesthetics for the human state of being. The concept was introduced by the German philosopher Alexander Gottlieb Baumgarten in the 18th century,[7] but the discussions of beauty have always been part of the history of philosophy. The debates centered around the objectivity or subjectivity of beauty. Plato, for example, believed that a "reality" (such as beauty) consists of archetypes, which are beyond human sensation, and which are the representations of all things that exist in human experience. This concept is illustrated by Plato's reaction when one of his critics once stated "I see particular horses, but not horseness." Plato answered "That is because you have eyes, but no intelligence."[8]

The aesthetic ideal as a concept of "wholeness" have become a somewhat neglected dimension of Western education. A few survivors are nevertheless still to be found in subjects such as industrial design, gestalt psychology, and social systems theory. The postmodernism debate in philosophy and the associated interest in complexity[9] seem to be opening a renewed interest in connectivity and relational thinking—which form the basis of an aesthetic consciousness. Apart from these, aesthetics as an educational concept seems to be all but lost in the modern discipline-oriented higher educational systems. This should be a cause for great concern to a world that is in dire need of finding creative solutions to a global *problematique*[10] of nonharmonious socioeconomic, political, and natural systems, which is unlikely to be solved by knowing more about a particular issue. There is a need to think creatively, and to be able to understand the general circumstances of life.

SOCIETAL CHANGE AND THE TRANSFORMATION OF UNIVERSITIES

Throughout the history of Western development the university was both the product and coproducer of the age in which it existed. It influenced the way in which a particular age ordered its knowledge base and general development, but was also at times the best exponent of the worst intellectual fallacies of a period. The various sections that cover the history of universities in the ten volumes of William James Durant's "Story of Civilization"[11] paint a picture of transformation following value changes, intellectual renewal, and cultural revolutions.

mined by their research and publication record within a discipline. This means that teaching excellence and the broader "molding of the character" of the student come often a poor second to the challenge of the academic paper chase.

Thus, vested interests are entrenched, and the disciplinary approach to scientific inquiry is sanctified with dogmatic fervor by the "priesthood" of academics. Like the Biblical Tower of Babel the modern builders of the "Tower of Knowledge" are aiming for the heaven of understanding and wisdom through the disciplines, while they are losing their ability to communicate effectively with one another. They are, in effect, solutions looking for problems that can be solved in the light of their specialist knowledge.

Therefore, after years of diligent study and academic excellence, the products of the modern university system may enter life with a serious cognitive disadvantage in that they cannot see the wood for the trees. In the past people were the servants of capital in industrial society, but they are now again facing the prospect of becoming "cogs" in a new "pentagon of power,"[21] namely, the governance of a "nomocratic" world order and the self-organizing complexity of global problems—problems that are the unintended by-products of reductionistic scientific and technological innovations. The inanimate (soulless) information and knowledge systems of Kostoupolos' nomocratic world cannot produce the understanding and wisdom that are needed to manage these growing complexities.

THE NEED FOR A NEW KIND OF INTELLECTUALISM

There is a clarion call for a new kind of intellectualism because (reductionistic) scientific advances and technological innovation are producing ungovernable complexity in the human-made conditions of life. Complexity is a condition that displays nonlinear causality. Consequently, the more we try to solve the problems we are facing, the worse the problematique becomes; the more we try to find solutions for the problems we are facing in our disciplines, the more we discover that at least part of the solution exists outside our disciplines. Problems of complexity flow from human inability to manage the broader systemic consequences of a large number of focused actions. The solution for complex problems lies therefore in quality of thought—not in quantity of information and knowledge.

Quality of thought is contextual in nature. It refers to the ability to "see" something within a broader context, to understand its relational and functional qualities, and to grasp the *meaning* of what is observed within a secular and cosmic (timeless) context. The Greeks referred to the process that produces these qualities in people as "the molding of human character." It implies education and human development in the broadest sense of the word: One that successfully balances the physical, emotional, intellectual, and spiritual development of people along the route of a similarly balanced quest for welfare, for truth, for good governance, for what is good, and for beauty.

It should be the purpose, the mission, of the 21st-century university to educate *human beings* with the ability to choose well in life; providing intellectual lead-

In the following discussion, three fundamental societal transformations of the Second Millennium are briefly touched on, namely:

- The Renaissance and "Age of Enlightenment," which cover a period of approximately 500 years between the late 13th century and the late 18th century
- The "Industrial Age," which covers a period of approximately 200 years between the late 18th century and the late 20th century
- The "Nomocratic Age," which is now being spawned by the information and knowledge revolution[12]

The Renaissance and "Age of Enlightenment"

The modern university system evolved from the profound societal transformations between the late 14th century and late 16th century. During this "Renaissance" (rebirth) the fragmented feudal society of the Middle Ages, with its church-dominated social order, was transformed into a society with central political institutions, an urban commercial economy and lay patronage of education, arts, and music.[13] One invention of this age was the Gutenberg press, which was named after its inventor Johann Gutenberg of Mainz, Germany. The explosion in the printing of books and pamphlets that followed this innovation initiated the first "information revolution"; one which inter alia contributed toward the Reformation and the rapid diffusion of new ideas and scientific theories throughout Europe. This was the catalyst of two centuries of enlightenment that preceded the industrial revolution at the end of the 18th century—a period of explorative intellectualism when scholars such as Galileo Galilei, Johannes Kepler, Nicolaus Copernicus, Francis Bacon, Sir Isaac Newton, and René Descartes, totally transformed the *Weltanschauung*[14] of Western society.

An important shift in educational emphasis followed and directed developments during the Renaissance and its ensuing Age of Enlightenment. The theologically centered Scholasticism of the late Medieval Schools was replaced with Humanism and, especially, a rediscovery of ancient Greek and Roman culture. The sciences, geography, history, mathematics, music, and physical training returned to the curricula of higher education. Overwhelmed by the Renaissance's incessant force of renewal and enlightenment, the Protestant churches (for example, the Academy of Geneva of Calvin) and Catholic church (the Jesuits) had little choice other than to also become involved in the teaching of secular subjects such as the classics, mathematics, and the sciences. This vastly expanded the institutional capacity of higher education from the 16th century—including the scope of institutional control over education. As a consequence, the church institutions educated a number of the leading 17th- and 18th-century intellectuals who paved the way of modern science.

The Industrial Age

Innovations in steam power and the use of coal in iron production during the late 18th century signaled the start of a new era, the so-called "Industrial Age."

In the 70 years following the development of Stephenson's "Rocket" locomotive in the 1820s the world saw a flood of groundbreaking innovations, which cascaded into the 20th century in recurrent economic waves of more or less 50 years in duration.[15] Exponential growth became an accepted norm of performance, with only the rate of growth being in dispute. However, the dark side of this growth process became increasingly apparent during the last few decades of the 20th century. Environmental decay, growing global inequalities, and social decay affect the majority of the world's population. Moreover, the corruption of life by an atomistic "Devil of Self-Interest" (one of the fallouts of reductionism) and the growth of knowledge but not of understanding, produced unmanageable complexities and ethical issues (for example, human cloning). Therefore, while the Industrial Age advanced human ability to create the "Big Picture" by default, the intrinsic reductionism of its processes destroyed the ability of humans to perceive and understand it.[16]

Educational development during the Industrial Age again reflected the evolving perspectives and needs of the times. The institutionalization of mass education systems became the norm. This opened the doors for education to the broader population, whereas before it was only available to a privileged few. The state (national, provincial, or local government) became a dominant player in educational provision, including the financing of educational institutions, educational administration, the determination of educational standards, and the development of the curriculum. The educational development of an individual was programmed through a general (more formative) education during primary schooling, then a slightly greater emphasis on subjects and specialization during secondary schooling, toward (what was perceived as) the pinnacle of education at the tertiary level of education. The organization of schools and educational systems followed the formal hierarchical factory model of the educational age. The learner "raw material" is being fed into this system at the tender age of five years, and after more or less 13 years of cognitive manipulation the final product of this "school factory" is being pushed out on to a job market as finished "parts" for the industrial machine, or as "raw material" for the tertiary educational "machine."

The Nomocratic Age

A number of authors hypothesized that we entered a postindustrial age sometime between the middle of the 1970s and the early 1980s, that is, approximately 200 years after the industrial age emerged. The word "postindustrial" first appeared in print in 1917.[17] The first comprehensive overview of the topic was presented by Daniel Bell,[18] who foresaw an economic transformation from an industrial emphasis toward services. Other related concepts that also appeared in print are "information society," "service society," and "knowledge society."[19]

Kostoupolos described important aspects of the changes that we are likely to face in an emerging "nomocratic society" as a world where knowledge is not the

servant of the people but in fact the master.[20] "Intelligence" is, according to him, the specific "labor force" of a nomocratic world. It incorporates (and integrates) human cognitive qualities, artificial intelligence, stored knowledge and information networks. Kostoupolos argued that knowledge would become the power "axis" of a future (postindustrial) nomocracy, just as agrarian estates represented the "axis" of the preindustrial world, and capital of the industrial world.

THE MODERN UNIVERSITY: AN INTELLECTUAL TOWER OF BABEL?

The shift in the basis of organizational and social power from capital toward "embodied wealth" means that the relevance and effectiveness of education and training will be the key toward the sustainable development of organizations and nations in the next century. Sustainability is only possible if there is a systemic balance in human achievement—a shift from quantity of life aspirations toward quality of life aspirations. The quality of global development in the next century—that is, the capacity of the world to move beyond the Industrial Age's (unbalanced) exponential increases in the "quantity" of life—will depend on the attitudes, values, and quality of thought of people. What is the role of university education in such a world, and can it rally to this challenge?

As was discussed previously, the Greek concept of a good education was to build character—to develop competent citizens. In its educational process it combined gymnastics, grammar, rhetoric, poetry, music, mathematics, geography, natural history, astronomy, and the physical sciences, history of society and ethics, and philosophy. In its ideals it balanced five aspirations, namely, economic aspirations, knowledge aspirations, power relational aspirations, ethical aspirations, and aesthetic aspirations. For them, competence meant having the commitment, knowledge, insight, understanding, and appropriate skills to choose well in life; having the ability to service your own needs while also contributing toward society. It meant living a purposeful life as a human being—that is, not as a dependent being. Competence meant being a leader in a society of leaders (for example, the Athenian concept of democracy).

This contrasts sharply with the educational system of the late 20th century, which stutters when required to provide wisdom for the appropriate application of the new knowledge it was promoting. It has spawned an educational process that emphasizes disciplinary thinking, and that assumes that knowledge of a particular facet of reality is more important than an understanding of the interactions and interdependencies between all the facets of reality. Rather than producing leaders for a society of leaders, students are being molded for functional specialization and line responsibilities.

Not only are universities driven by an inward-oriented disciplinary excellence, but the design of academic achievement also places a high premium on institutionalized self service. The status of academics is today largely deter-

In the following discussion, three fundamental societal transformations of the Second Millennium are briefly touched on, namely:

- The Renaissance and "Age of Enlightenment," which cover a period of approximately 500 years between the late 13th century and the late 18th century
- The "Industrial Age," which covers a period of approximately 200 years between the late 18th century and the late 20th century
- The "Nomocratic Age," which is now being spawned by the information and knowledge revolution[12]

The Renaissance and "Age of Enlightenment"

The modern university system evolved from the profound societal transformations between the late 14th century and late 16th century. During this "Renaissance" (rebirth) the fragmented feudal society of the Middle Ages, with its church-dominated social order, was transformed into a society with central political institutions, an urban commercial economy and lay patronage of education, arts, and music.[13] One invention of this age was the Gutenberg press, which was named after its inventor Johann Gutenberg of Mainz, Germany. The explosion in the printing of books and pamphlets that followed this innovation initiated the first "information revolution"; one which inter alia contributed toward the Reformation and the rapid diffusion of new ideas and scientific theories throughout Europe. This was the catalyst of two centuries of enlightenment that preceded the industrial revolution at the end of the 18th century—a period of explorative intellectualism when scholars such as Galileo Galilei, Johannes Kepler, Nicolaus Copernicus, Francis Bacon, Sir Isaac Newton, and René Descartes, totally transformed the *Weltanschauung*[14] of Western society.

An important shift in educational emphasis followed and directed developments during the Renaissance and its ensuing Age of Enlightenment. The theologically centered Scholasticism of the late Medieval Schools was replaced with Humanism and, especially, a rediscovery of ancient Greek and Roman culture. The sciences, geography, history, mathematics, music, and physical training returned to the curricula of higher education. Overwhelmed by the Renaissance's incessant force of renewal and enlightenment, the Protestant churches (for example, the Academy of Geneva of Calvin) and Catholic church (the Jesuits) had little choice other than to also become involved in the teaching of secular subjects such as the classics, mathematics, and the sciences. This vastly expanded the institutional capacity of higher education from the 16th century—including the scope of institutional control over education. As a consequence, the church institutions educated a number of the leading 17th- and 18th-century intellectuals who paved the way of modern science.

The Industrial Age

Innovations in steam power and the use of coal in iron production during the late 18th century signaled the start of a new era, the so-called "Industrial Age."

In the 70 years following the development of Stephenson's "Rocket" locomotive in the 1820s the world saw a flood of groundbreaking innovations, which cascaded into the 20th century in recurrent economic waves of more or less 50 years in duration.[15] Exponential growth became an accepted norm of performance, with only the rate of growth being in dispute. However, the dark side of this growth process became increasingly apparent during the last few decades of the 20th century. Environmental decay, growing global inequalities, and social decay affect the majority of the world's population. Moreover, the corruption of life by an atomistic "Devil of Self-Interest" (one of the fallouts of reductionism) and the growth of knowledge but not of understanding, produced unmanageable complexities and ethical issues (for example, human cloning). Therefore, while the Industrial Age advanced human ability to create the "Big Picture" by default, the intrinsic reductionism of its processes destroyed the ability of humans to perceive and understand it.[16]

Educational development during the Industrial Age again reflected the evolving perspectives and needs of the times. The institutionalization of mass education systems became the norm. This opened the doors for education to the broader population, whereas before it was only available to a privileged few. The state (national, provincial, or local government) became a dominant player in educational provision, including the financing of educational institutions, educational administration, the determination of educational standards, and the development of the curriculum. The educational development of an individual was programmed through a general (more formative) education during primary schooling, then a slightly greater emphasis on subjects and specialization during secondary schooling, toward (what was perceived as) the pinnacle of education at the tertiary level of education. The organization of schools and educational systems followed the formal hierarchical factory model of the educational age. The learner "raw material" is being fed into this system at the tender age of five years, and after more or less 13 years of cognitive manipulation the final product of this "school factory" is being pushed out on to a job market as finished "parts" for the industrial machine, or as "raw material" for the tertiary educational "machine."

The Nomocratic Age

A number of authors hypothesized that we entered a postindustrial age sometime between the middle of the 1970s and the early 1980s, that is, approximately 200 years after the industrial age emerged. The word "postindustrial" first appeared in print in 1917.[17] The first comprehensive overview of the topic was presented by Daniel Bell,[18] who foresaw an economic transformation from an industrial emphasis toward services. Other related concepts that also appeared in print are "information society," "service society," and "knowledge society."[19]

Kostoupolos described important aspects of the changes that we are likely to face in an emerging "nomocratic society" as a world where knowledge is not the servant of the people but in fact the master.[20] "Intelligence" is, according to him, the specific "labor force" of a nomocratic world. It incorporates (and integrates) human cognitive qualities, artificial intelligence, stored knowledge and information networks. Kostoupolos argued that knowledge would become the power "axis" of a future (postindustrial) nomocracy, just as agrarian estates represented the "axis" of the preindustrial world, and capital of the industrial world.

THE MODERN UNIVERSITY: AN INTELLECTUAL TOWER OF BABEL?

The shift in the basis of organizational and social power from capital toward "embodied wealth" means that the relevance and effectiveness of education and training will be the key toward the sustainable development of organizations and nations in the next century. Sustainability is only possible if there is a systemic balance in human achievement—a shift from quantity of life aspirations toward quality of life aspirations. The quality of global development in the next century—that is, the capacity of the world to move beyond the Industrial Age's (unbalanced) exponential increases in the "quantity" of life—will depend on the attitudes, values, and quality of thought of people. What is the role of university education in such a world, and can it rally to this challenge?

As was discussed previously, the Greek concept of a good education was to build character—to develop competent citizens. In its educational process it combined gymnastics, grammar, rhetoric, poetry, music, mathematics, geography, natural history, astronomy, and the physical sciences, history of society and ethics, and philosophy. In its ideals it balanced five aspirations, namely, economic aspirations, knowledge aspirations, power relational aspirations, ethical aspirations, and aesthetic aspirations. For them, competence meant having the commitment, knowledge, insight, understanding, and appropriate skills to choose well in life; having the ability to service your own needs while also contributing toward society. It meant living a purposeful life as a human being—that is, not as a dependent being. Competence meant being a leader in a society of leaders (for example, the Athenian concept of democracy).

This contrasts sharply with the educational system of the late 20th century, which stutters when required to provide wisdom for the appropriate application of the new knowledge it was promoting. It has spawned an educational process that emphasizes disciplinary thinking, and that assumes that knowledge of a particular facet of reality is more important than an understanding of the interactions and interdependencies between all the facets of reality. Rather than producing leaders for a society of leaders, students are being molded for functional specialization and line responsibilities.

Not only are universities driven by an inward-oriented disciplinary excellence, but the design of academic achievement also places a high premium on institutionalized self service. The status of academics is today largely determined by their research and publication record within a discipline. This means that teaching excellence and the broader "molding of the character" of the student come often a poor second to the challenge of the academic paper chase.

Thus, vested interests are entrenched, and the disciplinary approach to scientific inquiry is sanctified with dogmatic fervor by the "priesthood" of academics. Like the Biblical Tower of Babel the modern builders of the "Tower of Knowledge" are aiming for the heaven of understanding and wisdom through the disciplines, while they are losing their ability to communicate effectively with one another. They are, in effect, solutions looking for problems that can be solved in the light of their specialist knowledge.

Therefore, after years of diligent study and academic excellence, the products of the modern university system may enter life with a serious cognitive disadvantage in that they cannot see the wood for the trees. In the past people were the servants of capital in industrial society, but they are now again facing the prospect of becoming "cogs" in a new "pentagon of power,"[21] namely, the governance of a "nomocratic" world order and the self-organizing complexity of global problems—problems that are the unintended by-products of reductionistic scientific and technological innovations. The inanimate (soulless) information and knowledge systems of Kostoupolos' nomocratic world cannot produce the understanding and wisdom that are needed to manage these growing complexities.

THE NEED FOR A NEW KIND OF INTELLECTUALISM

There is a clarion call for a new kind of intellectualism because (reductionistic) scientific advances and technological innovation are producing ungovernable complexity in the human-made conditions of life. Complexity is a condition that displays nonlinear causality. Consequently, the more we try to solve the problems we are facing, the worse the problematique becomes; the more we try to find solutions for the problems we are facing in our disciplines, the more we discover that at least part of the solution exists outside our disciplines. Problems of complexity flow from human inability to manage the broader systemic consequences of a large number of focused actions. The solution for complex problems lies therefore in quality of thought—not in quantity of information and knowledge.

Quality of thought is contextual in nature. It refers to the ability to "see" something within a broader context, to understand its relational and functional qualities, and to grasp the *meaning* of what is observed within a secular and cosmic (timeless) context. The Greeks referred to the process that produces these qualities in people as "the molding of human character." It implies education and human development in the broadest sense of the word: One that successfully balances the physical, emotional, intellectual, and spiritual development of people along the route of a similarly balanced quest for welfare, for truth, for good governance, for what is good, and for beauty.

It should be the purpose, the mission, of the 21st-century university to educate *human beings* with the ability to choose well in life; providing intellectual leadership in a world of growing complexity. Not only must they educate individuals who are able to control, lead, and manage the knowledge and information systems, but they must also develop the qualities of good insight, understanding, wisdom, and good judgement—qualities that are essential for the management of complex world systems.

The behavior of Kostoupolos' nomocratic society is similar to that of Arthur C. Clarke's mega computer "Hal."[22] The most likely route toward some kind of "Hal" taking control of life in a nomocratic world is obvious, that is, through the continuation (and intensification) of the fragmentation of the learner's reality in disciplinary education, through the continuation of the total domination of reductionistic science, and through the sanctification of (atomistic) self-interest in all aspects of human interactions. A decline in the moral imperative of society—which is one of the by-products of remorseless self-interest—will also contribute to this process because moral insensitivity affects a person's capacity to understand life. Moreover, a neglect of aesthetics will, in all probability, also be an outflow of self-centered reductionism because aesthetic insights are integrative in nature. Reflecting the harmony between apparently contradictory elements of reality, aesthetics is a resonance—it emerges from the interactions of a large number of interrelated conditions and images.

TOWARD AN EFFECTIVE 21ST-CENTURY UNIVERSITY

Whatever the shortcomings of disciplinary studies, they still remain the only way of producing the *depth of knowledge* that is needed for human progress. Therefore, no university worth its name can afford not to provide a good disciplinary grounding for its students; it is a necessary ingredient of advanced studies. However, the student must also develop a *breadth of knowledge*, namely insight and understanding. This requires, firstly, a balance between the intellectual, emotional, and spiritual development of the student. Secondly, this requires a balance between an understanding of the condition (or circumstances) of life, appropriate skills to accomplish practical things in life, and an appropriate balance between personal aspirations and collective aspirations. Lastly, this requires an awareness of the broader context which determines the real value of new knowledge—an awareness that it should be matched with the practical aspiration of human welfare, of promoting order and good governance in human affairs, of finding harmony between all the elements of God's creation (that is, "ethics"), and of a rediscovery of beauty and the aesthetic dimensions of life.

The argument is not that these dimensions of human development are neglected within the broader context of campus life and in the curriculum structure of most universities. However, they tend to be chopped up into separate faculties and academic departments. Learners are expected to become functionally specialized in one or the other "subject," while recognition is given for interdependencies between "subject matter" by the introduction of majors and minors (that is, subjects that supplement the major) in study programs and, later, by problem-oriented multidisciplinary studies and multidisciplinary research programs. The (discipline-based) authority and power that are vested in the institutional structure of a university are thus transferred into these programs.

Multidisciplinary studies are the only practical way of researching complex problems, but participants must then be competent to make an *effective* contribution to the process; that is, they should be more than just specialist knowledge inputs. This requires sound preparation. Falling within the realm of advanced studies (final-year studies or postgraduate studies), multidisciplinary work first of all requires sound interdisciplinary preparation. This means developing the skills and insight of participating specialists by the means of a balanced menu of study subjects, which ought to cover socioeconomic and business issues, the sciences, law and administration, ethics, and aesthetics—in other words, not just a compendium of "relevant" subjects, but a purpose-designed and well-integrated study program. This approach is to some extent evident in medical studies and some business studies—particularly MBA studies.

Secondly, multidisciplinary work requires a sound grounding in transdisciplinary studies. Transdisciplinary studies are not *of* the disciplines but *beyond* the disciplines. It covers the development of appropriate values and thinking skills, and the study of complex systems. The aim is to develop *understanding*, rather than to gain particular kinds of knowledge. Applied studies in philosophy (or "applied philosophy") and systems studies could form the basis of this study program. The current debate on postmodernism and complexity is an example of the type of issue that should be covered in a transdisciplinary study program.

In conclusion, the call is for universities to mold the character of intellectual leaders rather than to train highly qualified functional specialists. Moreover, the need is for them to reconsider the academic focus and institutional structures that developed during the Industrial Age. At least for the next few decades, the basis for university development should center on finding solutions for the complex problems that were produced by two centuries of rampant reductionism in thought and in scientific development. This means that problem- (or task-) focused multidisciplinary schools, rather than disciplinary-focused departments or faculties, should be the main building blocks of university development in the 21st century.

NOTES

1. Richard Tarnas, *The Passion of the Western Mind* (London: Random House, 1991), 19.

2. Will Durant, *The Story of Civilization: Parts 1–10* (New York: Simon & Schuster, 1953), Part 2, 503.

3. This classification and the following discussion benefited primarily from the perspectives of Russell L. Ackoff, *Creating the Corporate Future: Plan or be Planned for* (New York: Wiley, 1981); Jamshid Gharajedaghi, *Towards a Systems Theory of Organization* (Seaside, California: Intersystems, 1984); Clark Kerr, Introduction to the Transaction Edition. In Jose Ortega y Gasset, *Mission of the University* (1992 reprint, New Brunswick, USA, Transaction Publishers, 1944).

4. Tarnas, *The Passion of the Western Mind*, 43–45.

5. Fanie Cloete, "South African Universities: Academic Centers of Excellence or Professional Training Schools?" *Strategy Insights: Political Issues* (Bellville, South Africa, Institute for Futures Research, University of Stellenbosch, Aug. 1997).

6. William W. Brickman, "The History of Education," *Encarta 97* (Microsoft Corporation, 1997).

7. Antony Flew, *Dictionary of Philosophy* (London: Macmillan Books, 1979), 6–7.

8. Tarnas, *The Passion of the Western Mind*, 8.

9. Jean-Francois Lyotard, *The Postmodern Condition: A Report on Knowledge* (Manchester: Manchester University Press, 1984); Paul Cilliers, *Complexity and Postmodernism* (New York, Routledge, 1998).

10. Global *problematique* is a complex, interdependent set of problems, where the existence of a particular problem is systemically bound into (and dependent on) the existence of other problems.

11. Durant, *The Story of Civilization*.

12. *Nomocratic:* A concept derived from the Greek words "nomos," which means "law," and "kratein," which means to rule. This implies that absolute rules ("laws of nature") govern human behavior—that is, there is a disembodiment of social purpose—that human relationships and human purpose are subordinate to their roles and functions in some kind of "Megamachine." In this particular case this "Megamachine" is a self-propagating "Knowledge World."

13. Durant, *The Story of Civilization*, Part 5.

14. *Weltanschauung*: A German concept that broadly implies a "world outlook." It refers to a general view of "reality," and perceptions of the roles and relationships of human beings within this "reality"; that is, how people make practical sense of their world of existence.

15. Robert U. Ayres, "Technological Transformations and Long Waves, Part I," *Technological Forecasting and Social Change* (1990), 37: 1–37, and "Part II," *Technological Forecasting and Social Change* (1990), 37: 111–37; R. J. Van Wyk, "Panoramic Scanning and the Technological Environment," *Technovation* (1984): 2.

16. Kenneth Boulding is quoted to have said the following: "The real name of the devil is suboptimization, finding out the best way of doing something which should not be done at all." Cited in *Beasts, Ballads, and Bouldinghism* (R. P. Beilock, ed. New Brunswick: Transaction Books, 1980), 75.

17. Rubin F. W. Nelson, "Information Society." In *Encyclopedia of the Future*, G. T. Kurian and G. T. T. Molitor, eds. (New York: Simon & Schuster–Macmillan, 1996), 479–81.

18. Daniel Bell, *The Coming Post-industrial Society* (New York: Basic Books, 1973).

19. John Naisbitt, *Megatrends: Ten New Directions Transforming our Lives* (New York: Warner Books, 1984); Peter F. Drucker, *The New Realities* (New York: Harper & Row, 1989).

20. Tryphon Kostopoulos, "The Fall of Capitalism and Socialism," *Systems Research* (1988), 5(3): 189–99.

21. Lewis Mumford, *The Myth of the Machine* (New York: Harcourt, Brace, Jovanovich Inc., 1970).

22. Arthur C. Clarke, *2010: Space Odyssey Two* (New York: Granada, 1982).

3

Higher Education at the Brink

————————————— *Peter Manicas*

It is well to keep in mind that the present system of higher education, which in the United States includes both the research university and two-year community colleges, is of very recent vintage. The research university has its origins only in the last decades of the 19th century; the idea that all capable students should have access to higher education dates only from the end of World War II. We are presently seeing the beginnings of radical change in this system, at least as radical as the development of higher education that began at the turn of the present century. The emergence and development of the modern university system is part and parcel of the 19th-century history of modern industry and the modern nation state. This last radical change can be summarized briefly.

FORCES FROM THE PAST

First, there occurred a symbiosis of science, industry, and the state—in this century an essential attribute of the basic mode of production of a modern economy. Prior to the middle of the 19th century, "science" went on almost completely outside the University. Men like William Cavendish and James Prescott Joule could afford private laboratories and Sir Humphry Davy and Michael Faraday independently pursued their inquiries with help from Count Rumford and funds that they secured from landowners interested in "modern" farming. The establishment in France of the École Polytechnique during the 1790s provided a critical precondition: the breaking down of the barriers that had separated the "classical" mathematical sciences from the Baconian and applied sciences: chemistry, magnetism, and heat. But the Germans—late modernizers—most fully exploited this new opportunity. In marked distinction from the Universities of Britain, Italy, and France, whose roots were medieval, the new University of Berlin (1810) had established the institutional background for a new kind of university in which institutes would provide particular knowledge, as well as general philosophical education.[1]

By the mid-19th century, German science, especially chemistry, mathematics, physics, and physiology, had eclipsed all others. Self-conscious modernizers, the Bismarkian state promoted industrialization and applied science. Some of the discoveries included aniline dyes (1856); cellulose derivatives such as lacquers, photographic plates, and modern plastics (1868); synthetic resins (1909); chemical fertilizers; and poison gas. At the same time, electricity, the self-executed electromagnetic generator, the ring dynamo, and the incandescent lamp, were developed by leading German industrial firms, which were quick to cash in. By the turn of the century, Badishe Anilin, Hochst, AGFA and others had 90 percent of the world market in the new wonders of chemistry. Seimans was a world leader in applied electrical innovation. Not only had science and scientists acquired a kind of authority formerly reserved only for shaman, but its advancement could be secured institutionally: in the new University. In an 1862 address, Herman L. F. von Helmholtz brilliantly summarized the new ideology:

(Since) all nations are interested in the progress of knowledge for the simple reason of self-preservation, men of science form . . . an organized army laboring on behalf of the whole nation, and generally under its direction and at its expense, to augment the stock of knowledge as may serve to promote industrial enterprise, to adorn life, to improve political and social relations, and to further the moral development of individual citizens.[2]

Second, industrialization and urbanization (and in the United States, immigration) created "the social problem." And as suggested by Helmholtz's remarks, it was clear enough to well-placed educational entrepreneurs that "scientific knowledge" could be directed to aiding in its solution. Alongside traditional education in the humanities, a conception of a technocratic social science emerged. The British, the first nation to confront the social problem, responded to the need for social research with institutions that were totally independent of their traditional elitist Universities. Oxford could continue to cultivate gentlemen, while the Manchester Statistical Society whose council "often looked like a subcommittee of a Whig cabinet" would do what it could "to assist in promoting the progress of social improvement."[3]

The Germans, however, were able to integrate new institutes that addressed social issues into the universities. But it was the Americans who, quite literally, invented most of the specialized social science disciplines now taken for granted in every major research university in the world. There were special conditions that made this possible,[4] but critical is the fact that until the founding of Johns Hopkins in 1876, America did not have a university. The existing colleges of the United States, Harvard, Yale, and so on, offered no graduate education and the undergraduate curriculum emphasized the moral sciences, rhetoric, and a smattering of natural philosophy.

Indeed, the modern research university as we know it today derives most directly from the innovations constituted in the new American universities— created and funded by the fortunes of the Carnegies, Rockefellers (Chicago): Hopkinses, Cornells, Stanfords, and Vanderbilts, and then appropriated by the traditional colleges of America, and ultimately, by even the oldest of the world's universities.

Finally, democracy and the accelerating demands for specialized knowledge and a qualified workforce required that the elitism of the older European universities and American colleges give way to the idea that higher education should be more widely available.[5] Charles McClelland reports that in 1870 the student population in Germany stood at 14,000.[6] By 1900 it was 34,000 and by 1914 it had reached 61,000. But in the United States, again for specifically historical reasons, growth far outruns these increases. By 1890 there were 154,300 undergraduate students and 2,400 graduate students; by 1920, 582,000 and 15,600, and by 1930, there were 1,053,500 undergraduates and 47,300 graduate students in the United States. From World War II to the present, growth has been both continuous and remarkable. In 1995, there were some 14,261,781 students enrolled in U.S. colleges and universities. Some 2,954,707 of these are enrolled in four-year private institutions; about half of all those enrolled in public institutions, some 5.5 million, were enrolled in two-year colleges.[7]

FORCES FROM THE FUTURE

Higher education continues to be hostage to political economy and the state.[8] But the conditions that produced the modern research university (and two-year community college) have been profoundly altered. Again, three features are fairly obvious.

First, globalization has undercut the idea that states can underwrite development by fostering the sciences in the universities. This is a consequence of a number of factors: There is worldwide accessibility of scientific information, itself due to new communications technologies; both innovation and the training of qualified technical workers is now globalized, the newer technologies do not generally require massive infrastructure and investment; and most critically, corporations are global, their achievements do not necessarily rebound on the nation where their headquarters are located. With shrinking government budgets and corporations increasingly financing their own research and development, funds for university research, where they are available, are increasingly derived from corporate sources.

Following on this, the social sciences have lost their authority. The findings produced by social science researchers have contributed little or nothing to the solution of social problems, which are also at least part product of global influences not controllable by the state. Symptomatic is the very recent charge of the Chair of the Massachusetts Board of Higher Education, James F. Carlin, who asserted, perhaps generously, that "at least 50 percent of all the non-hard-sciences research on American campuses is a lot of 'foolishness.'"[9] Indeed, if anything, by disavowing the search for underlying causes, most social science research distracts us from real solutions. Small wonder that most citizens get a bit bleary-eyed when they are told that, for example, we do not know what causes crime or poverty or what can be done to prevent environmental disaster! Similarly, currently fashionable postmodern thought in the universities is a symptom of the loss of authority of social science as it was constituted in the university.

Second, higher education is no longer affordable. The Commission on National Investment in Higher Education issued a report entitled "Breaking the Social Contract: The Fiscal Crisis in Higher Education." It reported that higher education will have a $38 billion shortfall by 2015 and that to sustain current spending, tuition would have to double.[10] Tuition in private schools is already astronomical—with the heavy support it already gets, and state budgets have decreasing funds for increasing costs. Thus, with a rapidly diminishing share of state funding, what we once thought of as "state universities" have become "state-assisted universities." Arguably the best system of higher education in the world, the University of California, now gets only about 23 percent of its funds from the state. Indeed, in absolute numbers, California is putting more of its funds into prisons than into its colleges and universities.

To be sure, much of the increase in current costs are for administration and infrastructure. There is deep paradox in this. Although it is easy to be nostalgic, colleges were once collegial institutions where major decisions were at least shared by the faculties. The ideology of professional management insisted that this was not efficient. Preoccupied with their own professional concerns, faculties gladly abrogated government to administrators, and on bread-and-butter issues, to unions. Coupled with a host of demands for ancillary services, the numbers of nonteaching administration and staff has doubled while the numbers of teaching faculty has remained nearly stagnant.

Moreover, while the true costs of higher education were always underestimated, contributing to a distorted view of the current costs, and while there is a sense that quality education in universities remains a bargain, because quality education requires low student/faculty ratios, it is inevitably costly. The main point here, however, is that governments are no longer willing to pay for it.

Finally, computer-mediated technologies, now only beginning to be introduced, provide a highly cost-effective way to increase access and to respond to the demands for new kinds of skills and knowledge.

The aforementioned Commission report called for a radical restructuring of universities. But because the problem is not only fiscal, its suggestions were modest. There is simply no reason not to believe that in the very near future, postsecondary education in the advanced capitalist democracies will be electronically delivered and that propelled by this and other forces, the old system will be dramatically transformed.

THE SURVIVOR INSTITUTIONS

Indeed, one must take very seriously the new taxonomy of higher education offered by the National Center for Postsecondary Improvement, based at Stanford. Instead of the Carnegie schema (with "Research I" institutions, community colleges, and so on) we have "brand name," "mass provider," and "convenience institutions."[11]

"Convenience institutions" are on the cutting edge of both the new technologies and the new markets for education. They are user-friendly, operate fully as businesses (rather than as universities), and serve "job-minded students for whom liberal-arts degrees hold scant appeal." They provide "just about any set of skills and credentials that anybody wants to obtain—at just about any time of the day or night, through just about any medium of instruction." These will be discussed more fully by Neubauer in Chapter 4. By contrast, as Chester Finn writes:

Brand name campuses are selective, high-status places where market power comes from their very status and selectivity. They cater to mostly full-time students from traditional age groups and have a commitment to traditional academic values—a liberal arts core, publication-minded faculty members, governance by the professoriate—and a reputation for high quality.[12]

The dominating group of such "brand name campuses" is, of course, the private, heavily endowed Ivy League Universities, which can attract external funding while at the same time maintaining coherent, resident, high-quality undergraduate programs. Alongside these are a select group of smaller liberal arts colleges, for example, Swarthmore and Williams. These elite traditional residential places of learning will not disappear, but as is very clear, they will be restricted to the very few who are sufficiently well-to-do or, if the attack on affirmative action does not spill over, sufficiently eminent to be awarded scholarship aid to achieve a balanced student body.[13]

The best-known state universities will strive to be in this select group but most will fall into the third category, "mass provider" institutions.[14] Mass provider institutions, beholden to legislators, with obligations to educate as best they can citizens of their states, try to be all things to all people, but they come nowhere near to having the resources, human or financial, necessary to do this. Thus, research and publication is obligatory, but it goes on mostly at the expense of commitment to undergraduate programs, especially since the students are profoundly heterogeneous in terms of background, age, goals, and commitment. The "typical" student today is no longer under 25 and residential. Forty-three percent of the total student population is over 25 and 43 percent are part time. Over 82 percent of all students are enrolled in publicly funded institutions and slightly over 70 percent of those enrolled in for-profit private institutions are getting some financial aid. Many come from poor high schools or have been away from school for years, many have familial responsibilities, most work, and a recent survey confirms what is well known to their teachers: In the fall of 1997, 75 percent of freshmen put "being well off financially" as their goal while 41 percent choose "developing a meaningful philosophy of life." In 1968, these numbers were exactly reversed. Faculty are, accordingly, schizophrenic, faced with students who do not accept their values and driven by criteria that measure their success in terms of shrinking resources for research and publication.

Challenges to Survival for Universities as We Know Them

Most mass provider institutions will also survive, but they will be very different than they were even 10 years ago. The changes have already begun. Under conditions of radically shrinking state budgets, three consequences are immediately evident. First, the drive to cut costs resolves the "schizophrenia" of faculty who find themselves in a three-tract system in which the majority of the teaching is done by part-timers and nontenurable faculty. Thus, the number of part-time teachers has nearly doubled since 1970. Last year they did some 40 percent of all the instruction. These teachers, being produced in droves by Ph.D.-granting institutions—38,000 Ph.D.'s are produced annually—are, of course, paid but a fraction of the salaries of full-time faculty, have no obligations to publish, and no claims on future employment. They are the flexible workforce in our post-Fordist economy. Moreover, tenure is now under threat, both head-on (as in Minnesota) or more imperceptibly—by reducing, through attrition, the relative number of tenurable faculty, now at about 50 percent of the total of full-timers.

Second, in competition with convenience institutions, mass provider institutions will be much more entrepreneurial, both in seeking funds, in experimenting with the new technologies, and in marketing an increasingly diverse set of "products," including, as in Colorado, a plan to offer a two-year degree wholly on the Internet, or as in Arizona, a plan to offer B.A. degrees for vocational programs in, for example, "law-enforcement technology," "fire science," and "chemical dependency counseling." Perhaps they will be forced to adopt something like a Phoenix arrangement with only seminars, tutoring, dance and theater, and laboratory courses given on campus. Perhaps they will need to be allied with one another as the Western Governor's University or perhaps they will form permanent alliances with corporations. As suggested by Gordon Davies (without irony), "an example might be an alliance of the University of California, the Walt Disney Company, and MCI."[15]

Third, there are huge pressures to restrict access to traditional liberal arts institutions. Mass provider institutions have always tried to compete with the brand name institutions and, to their immense credit, to a considerable extent they have succeeded. But these days are now gone. The University of California and The City University of New York lead the way in this respect. As Brent Staples points out, "California's decision to outlaw the use of race in public college admissions has barred most black and Latino students from the elite campuses and raised the specter of a widening professional class in a steadily browning state."[16] Famous for educating the immigrant children of the city of New York, CUNY introduced an open admissions policy in 1970 that guaranteed some place, either in one of the senior colleges, Queens College, Hunter, and so on, or one of the two-year community colleges for every New York City high school graduate. Open admissions was, it is hard to deny, an overwhelming success, providing quality education to perhaps a quarter of a million students who otherwise would not have received it. Increasingly restrictive policies began with NYC's fiscal crisis in

1976, but it was not until just recently that Mayor Guiliani and Governor Pataki succeeded in their wholesale assault on admissions standards and on the tasks of the units. Last May, the Trustees decided that students needing remediation would be barred from the eleven senior colleges, which would no longer provide any remediation. A study by David Lavin and David Hyllegard shows that the new policy will bar 38 percent of whites, 67 percent of African-Americans, 70 percent of Latinos, and 71 percent of Asians. Staples reports that half of these are well-educated immigrants who need schooling in English.

Fallout from the Brink

More generally, these developments toward a radical restructuring of higher education are profoundly exacerbating a widening class bifurcation that is rooted in widening knowledge bifurcation. And, *there are no forces on the horizon to prevent this.* Viewed from a class perspective, most people will accept—as they now do—a highly differentiated system of higher education. The triumph of "neoliberal" ideology, the redefinition of the goals of higher education and the actuality of alternative modes of access and convenience provided by the new technologies, will assuage most people.

However, the idea that the quality of higher education for most people will deteriorate is not a viable response. As noted, very few undergraduates currently accept the idea of "learning for its own sake." In both private and public universities, as in two-year colleges, almost all students are there for the credential. They know that any degree is better than no degree—even if they fail to realize that with increased access, degrees are less meaningful. Moreover, if we put aside the networks established in prestigious private colleges and universities and the benefits in quality of life to be derived from a liberal arts education (now available to but a few), it is wrong to suppose that current graduates of less-prestigious institutions, including Phoenix, are inadequately prepared for a labor market that increasingly demands narrow and clearly defined competencies. Indeed, AT&T has contracted with Phoenix for employee training. We can expect much more of this.

It is also reluctantly acknowledged (when it is acknowledged at all), that higher education, with notable exceptions, is currently of a very poor quality, both because too many students leave our high schools ill-prepared for college *and do not get the support that they need,* and because many of the conditions that define the structuring of higher education are dysfunctional. Because it is easier to blame the victim, this latter reason is too often ignored. Large four-year mass-provider institutions are structured so that faculty and administration have little interest in undergraduate education. Curricula are fragmented and courses become meaningless exercises—filling in squares required by a credential. Students are treated as passive learners and faculty are too often ill-equipped to do what should be required of them: to empower students and stimulate learning. In two-year institutions, faculties are overworked and poorly rewarded. Students are demanding, impatient, independent, and hard to convince. Faculty, meanwhile, have lost confidence in the idea that they know what is good for the student. One solution already mentioned is to raise admission requirements, abrogating responsibility to others. Other more positive responses are possible. In some places, including the present author's current institution, efforts are being made to reform both curricula and teaching in hopes that students will respond to a more meaningful undergraduate experience. Students are rightly turned off by a fragmented disciplinary education, by large lecture sessions taught by disinterested faculty, by passive "learning," and by the alienating environment of a large, unfriendly campus where parking is impossible and public transportation barely exists. We know what needs to be done. The problem is not want of knowledge, but lack of will.

This, of course, contributes to the loss of credibility of higher education and is, accordingly, contributing to its imminent restructuring. On the other hand, if the key agents in higher education, the faculty, were to take control of education, the newer technologies, properly employed, could enhance learning. Instead of being "credential mills," schools might become "learner-center environments where learners actively participate in the act of learning."[17] This is not farfetched and is the thrust of Rooney and Hearn's favored scenario in this volume. Some of the new technologies have remarkable potentials for active learning even if these are now being realized by a very small minority of those who are using them. Indeed, most faculty are not only blithely ignorant of any use of the new technologies, but they also assume, remarkably, that the traditional setting for instruction—itself a fairly modern innovation, is not only effective but the only possible one.

THE RESHAPING POTENTIAL OF THE FACULTY

The foregoing suggests the only possible force to prevent or to shape these outcomes is the faculty. The traditional university is highly labor intensive and thus costly. The new technologies need not be. Currently, except in the convenience institutions, the use of new technologies have tended to supplement rather than replace older modes and thus have added to costs without much gain. As always, technology has both a light side and a dark side. But for reasons already noted, the dark side is likely to be the side that comes to be realized. Thus, instead of improved discussion, equality of discussion among all members, collaborative and active learning, the instructor as expert and facilitator, we are getting taped lectures, canned Web courses, automated correspondence courses, and more generally, the minimizing of high-cost active instruction for low-cost automation.[18] Faculty are clearly sensitive to this, but "downsizing" is already occurring and will, all things being equal, continue to occur. Moreover, faculty unions, like other labor unions, seem perfectly willing to engage in the losing game of trying to preserve jobs—at the expense of highly exploited part-timers, without realizing that they should, instead, be trying to re-secure control over the education of their students.

That is, given the imperatives of the globalized political economy, soaring tuition costs, the problems of maintaining, still less of extending access, the widespread disquiet among the tax-paying public, faculties and students, and the already radically changed character of both students and their motivations, faculty will not be able to resist restructuring. They may, accordingly, capitulate to the worst possible outcomes: a tiered educational system that provides basic and vocational skills to most students. Or they may fully accept the challenges of information technology and put them to the best possible use. If education for the many is not to be reduced to competency, if it is to preserve the older—and already severely compromised—ideal of *Bildung*,[19] then faculty will need to educate themselves to the possibilities of the new technologies. And they will need both clarity of purpose and organization. Present experience suggests that none of this will be forthcoming. But indeed, the great promise of pessimist futurism is the fact that history is full of surprises.

NOTES

1. For a more thorough account of the "new" German university in a comparative context, see *The European and American University Since 1800: History and Sociological Essays,* Sheldon Rothblatt and Bjorn Wittrock, eds. (Cambridge: Cambridge University Press, 1993). For example, while the Humboldtian ideal inspired the new University of Berlin, it was nevertheless the case that it became the vehicle for the specialized research-oriented university, which then became the model for progressive higher education in other advanced countries, especially in the United States.

2. Hermann Helmholtz, *Selected Writings*, Russell Kahn, ed. (Middletown, CT: Wesleyan University Press, 1971), 40.

3. Peter T. Manicas, *A History and Philosophy of the Social Sciences* (Oxford: Basil Blackwell, 1987).

4. Ibid.; and Peter T. Manicas, "The Social Science Disciplines: The American Model," in *Discourses on Society: The Shaping of the Social Science Disciplines*, Peter Wagner, Bjorn Wittrock, and Richard Whitely, eds. (Kluwer: Dordrecht, 1991).

5. Samuel Bowles and Herbert Gintis, *Schooling in Capitalist America* (New York: Basic Books, 1976).

6. Charles McClelland, *State, Society and the University in Germany, 1700–1914* (Cambridge: Cambridge University Press, 1980).

7. *Chronicle of Higher Education*, Almanac Issue, 29 August 1997.

8. See Michael Margolis, "Brave New Universities," www.firstmonday. dk/issues3_5/margolis/index.html.

9. *New York Times*, 5 January 1998.

10. *New York Times*, 18 June 1997.

11. See Chester E. Finn, Jr. "Today's Academic Market Requires a New Taxonomy of Colleges," *Chronicle of Higher Education*, 9 January 1998.

12. Ibid., B4.

13. Small regional colleges are already facing stiff competition not only from "convenience institutions," but from large "brand name" and large "mass provider" institutions, which are beginning to offer highly competitive, in terms of cost and convenience, distance

learning programs. John Wiley, provost and academic vice-chancellor for academic affairs at the University of Wisconsin–Madison "compares the battle between large and small colleges to the competition between neighborhood grocery stores and chair supermarkets." See Jeffrey Selingo, "Small, Private Colleges Brace for Competition from Distance Learning," *Chronicle of Higher Education,* 1 May 1998.

14. Finn seems to hold that the major state universities will fall into the "brand name" category. This is extremely doubtful.

15. See Gordon K. Davies, "Higher-Education Systems as Cartels: The End is Near," *Chronicle of Higher Education,* 3 October 1997.

16. *New York Times,* 26 May 1998.

17. See Jaishree Odin, "ALN Technologies and Higher Education," http://www2.hawaii.edu/aln/alnessay.htm.

18. See Murray Turoff, "Alternative Futures for Distance Learning: The Force and the Darkside," http://eies.njit.edu/~turoff/Papers/darkaln.html.

19. The term *Bildung,* which has no direct equivalent in English, originated in the German Enlightenment and came to refer to an educational process involving the tacit cooperation of the teacher and learner in the learning process, a process that points toward self-fulfillment. One thinks here broadly of a liberal education, that is, an education which is liberating. For discussion, see Sven-Eric Liedman, "General Education in Germany and Sweden," in *The European and American University Since 1800: History and Sociological Essays,* Sheldon Rothblatt and Bjorn Wittrack, eds. (Cambridge: Cambridge University Press, 1993).

4

Will the Future Include Us? Reflections of a Practitioner of Higher Education

─────────────── *Deane Neubauer*

During the past decade we have witnessed events that signal significant changes taking place within higher (tertiary) education. Almost a decade ago the Florida state legislature passed a law mandating the review of the educational output of all publicly funded higher education. Between 1993 and 1996, the Australian Vice-Chancellors' Committee conducted a national quality assurance and audit program for those universities receiving significant funding from the federal government. In the United Kingdom the Committee of Vice Chancellors and Principals has developed an extensive procedure for educational audits. Similar events have taken place throughout other Organization for Economic Cooperation and Development (OECD) states, like Denmark, Sweden, and Finland. In the United States the accreditation association for higher education in the western region (the Western Association of Schools and Colleges Senior Commission) has embarked on a three-year review of accreditation practices aimed at focusing accreditation review on student learning outcomes.[1]

At one level these audits and reviews are manifestly concerned with the broad issue of quality improvement and assessment. At another, they represent the changing role of higher education in the political economy of the postindustrial states, and the increasing role of market dynamics in setting the agenda for the practices and "products" of higher education institutions.

THE SETTING

The macro forces acting on higher education include but are not limited to:

- Budgetary reductions in public higher education resulting from increased pressures on state financial resources.

- The related pressure to offset reductions by increasing user fees and tuition.
- The increased employment of contract faculty.
- Changes in instructional delivery modes resulting from new technologies (especially in distance education).
- Transformations in undergraduate student bodies to older, multiple-entry students.
- An increased emphasis on life-long learning.
- Demands from business to educate students to make them more suitable for the changing demands of business employment.
- Demands that universities be research focused, creating knowledge of direct use to firms operating in national business environments.
- Expectations that universities will become more entrepreneurial in their organization and activities.

Underlying these forces are broad changes taking place within the political economy of the postindustrial nations. From the onset of Reagan-Thatcherism, these have been lumped together as either "economic rationalism" or "neoliberalism." This political program, undergirding the phenomenon we term "globalization," has featured an attack on the welfare state and its organizing assumptions. Neoliberalism emphasizes the privileging of markets; reduction of all taxes, especially income taxes; deregulation; privatization; and overall, a shrinking of the state. When applied to state higher education, this program results in a decrease in overall state support of public higher education, an increase in user fees (experienced as higher tuition costs for students), an emphasis on entrepreneurial activities within universities, and a stated emphasis on focusing higher educational product on meeting "market" demands. Britain's emerging "Third Way" envisions an agenda similar in some respects to neoliberalism while backing away from its categorical oppositions to the welfare state. To one extent or another, the educational reforms and reorganizations that have taken place in the United States, Australia, New Zealand, and Britain have been rationalized in terms of these premises.

THE AGENDA WITHIN THE SETTING

Much higher education reform has been couched in terms of three arguments of economic necessity. The first is an argument about state capacity. The state has insufficient capacity, it is argued, to support higher education at previously accepted levels. To do so drains resources from the society that are better used in the private sector to fuel economic investment. In the United States this move has been accomplished in a shift from notions of "state-supported higher education," to "state-assisted higher education." Many of the Carnegie-designed Research 1 institutions of state higher education now receive as little as 18 or 19 percent of their revenue from state payments, and most are probably in the neighborhood of 22 to 28 percent. The remainder of their revenues comes from student fees and tuition, contracts and grants, income on entrepreneurial activity, and return on gifts and investments. In Australia and New Zealand student fees have been employed to support the growing notion of institutional self-sufficiency. In the United States pressures to reduce taxes result in reduced state revenues and consequent limitations of higher education.

The second argument focuses on the quality of educational product. Higher education is producing a product of insufficient quality to meet the competitive demands of global labor markets. The educational institutions inherited from the welfare state era have not been organized to produce students who possess market-ready skills. This familiar argument has been most commonly applied to lower education; it is increasingly directed at higher education. Reform is required, it is argued, to permit assessment of competency-based student outcomes, which are themselves correlated with the demands of the labor market. This argument, not surprisingly, has come from business elites, translated into policy by sympathetic policy elites.

The third argument focuses on the cost production in higher education and the inefficiencies of its institutions. Traditional higher education institutions are viewed as overpriced labor forces (the professoriate) that operate through inefficient and ineffective systems of management (shared governance) to produce a product (graduates) that costs far more than needed to meet market requirements. These institutions are inflexible, slow to change, and insensitive to market needs. The state has privileged these institutions by subsidizing their market dominance, which has limited the development of effective competition. Educational reform is expected to cure each of these ills, and becomes the program of higher administrators, especially those directly responsible to their political masters (for example, boards of trustees).

NEW ACTORS IN THE HIGHER EDUCATION EQUATION

The reduction of state support is designed to encourage (force) state institutions of higher education to become more competitive. With fewer state resources they must review the relationship of resource expenditures to outcomes. As higher tuition bids up student positions, and as education itself is increasingly framed in market terms, students experience incentives to seek alternative markers of market certification. New firms are brought into the market to meet this forming demand. They do so in part by developing cheaper delivery systems than traditional higher education (for example, distant learning with contract faculty), organized around outcomes defined by the market (for example, competence-based learning), and for enlarged learning cohorts (for example, nontraditional students).[2] These "new students" seek this alternative product and delivery because they are more convenient (they are organized around the time and place constraints of nontraditional learners), less costly (because they create degrees for market requirements, and require fewer "breadth" or general education requirements), and are more parsimonious with respect to student resources (such programs are more likely to supply "credit" to previous experiential learning).

These "Convenience Institutions" enter traditional degree markets with comparative advantage defined by all of the above factors.[3] Traditional institutions are forced to respond to these challenges posed by convenience institutions within their own environments (for example, developing distance education, responding to higher levels of nontraditional students, and employing higher numbers of contract faculty); and by appraising the nature of their emergent demand function. They must also decide which threat is greater, to protect their "own" students from the competitive attraction of the convenience institutions, or to adapt quickly as effective players in the emergent student market comprised of life-long learners, and late-entry or reentry nontraditional students. In short, they must determine whether to view the student market as essentially elastic or inelastic. If the former, then there can be room for both "traditional" student cohorts and the emergent life-long learner; if the latter, then to the extent that traditional institutions become increasingly fee dependent, an inelastic market represents the threat of possibly disastrous revenue declines.

"Convenience Institutions"—A Typology

The three most prevalent forms of convenience institutions suggest different approaches to these student market choices. The three are

- Distance-based "virtual" universities, such as the Western Governor's University or the California Virtual University
- Convenience-based "target" universities, such as the University of Phoenix (now the largest private university in the United States with over 48,000 degree credit students at 57 learning centers in 12 American states)
- Corporate universities.[4]

Other significant, but more "traditional" players, such as the UK Open University, are adopting expansionist strategies that bring them into new markets (the Open University is moving into the U.S. market in 1998).

Some of these players, for example, the Open University and the University of Phoenix, are likely to draw away some students from traditional universities. The corporate universities, focusing for the time being largely on their own internal constituencies, appear to be developing leading-edge capacities to train and educate their own labor forces at levels not commonly available in the broader market. Some estimate the number of corporate universities at 2,000. Their challenge to traditional institutions is twofold: they will supply instruction that might otherwise be outsourced to traditional institutions, and they will redefine the desired educational product in ways that have market cachet, but can only be effectively delivered by the corporate institutions. This strategy appears to be the choice of those universities created by Motorola, Microsoft, and Arthur Anderson Consulting.

A new tertiary industry has organized around the creation of content for distance learning, whether that is delivered by convenience or traditional universities developing on-line delivery systems. The IBM Global Campus, for example, creates sophisticated interrelated tools and services for such environments, employing products from its Lotus division. Some 30 campuses use Global Campus product in a rapidly growing market. Cisco Systems, SCT, Collegis, Microsoft-Simon, and Schuster-Real Education, are all aggressive and deep-pocket players in this arena.[5]

Determining the impact of these emergent institutions is complicated in the United States by the highly pluralistic nature of higher education, which is matched by significant overcapacity for conventional student demand. By the early 1990s, many smaller and relatively expensive private institutions were struggling to maintain enrollment at fiscally viable levels, in some cases hedging admission standards to gain tuition-paying students. These institutions are threatened by the cost dynamics that have led to steadily increasing tuition offsets over the past two decades. Many have responded by increased target marketing, seeking to define their educational niche with greater precision and recruit directly to it, while controlling internal costs.

Larger public institutions, especially those with differentiated mission systems (for example, a set of state colleges headed by a Research 1 campus), have become increasingly cost sensitive as their tuition (especially for out-of-state students) has continued to rise. Some systems have experienced significant overcapacity and reacted with drastic cost-cutting measures. This is especially evident in the paring of "high-end" labor costs. Higher education's version of "corporate downsizing" has reduced the numbers of full-time, tenure-track faculty as a portion of total faculty (nontenure track contract faculty now account for over 50 percent of faculty lines in American higher education) and the reduction of administrative positions through restructuring.

From these observations it appears that the emergent institutions are likely to impact all traditional institutions whose internal practices render them "price sensitive." Those institutions most immune to these pressures are the high-end, brand name institutions whose high prestige permits them to draw students disproportionately from affluent populations. (And globalization phenomena are associated with increased amounts of income inequality: the rich in all four societies to which this chapter makes reference have become richer in relation to other income holders. This is especially true for the top quintile of the population. Indeed, the top 5 percent of the population has as much income in the United States as the bottom 90 percent. Thus, the top end of the traditional higher education food chain has been somewhat price insensitive.)[6] For a more comprehensive view of changes to the professoriate, see chapter 5 by Michael Skolnik.

THE INSTITUTIONAL CHALLENGE

The traditional institutions face three challenges presented by these changing environments. The first is whether they can continue to define an educational

product that can withstand the marketplace challenges of these emergent convenience institutions and state regulatory forces that have contested their autonomy
to define the nature of their educational outcomes. The second is whether they
can sustain parity in the value-added knowledge business with market-based
institutions. The third is whether they can survive at acceptable cost levels given
current market standards. These challenges will be approached differently by
brand name and mass provider institutions, and with different strategies.

With respect to the first challenge, brand name institutions have the considerable advantage of having significantly greater resources to create change if they
choose to. The question is whether they will take that choice. As Barry Munitz,
past Chancellor of the California State University System and current president
and chief executive officer of the J. Paul Getty Trust, suggests, "Ironically, the
greatest challenge [of the convenience institutions] will be to our most respected
institutions, for they are least likely to perceive a threat or to feel any need to challenge their basic assumptions."[7]

The brand name institutions have the ability to couple the perception of quality with restricted access to it, a combination that has allowed them to be almost
price insensitive. Thus, for Ivy League institutions to offer on-line courses in
competition with the University of Phoenixes of the world would be to create an
educational marketplace that may require entirely new symbols to signal the
quality-price association. One wonders how such products could be equally or
comparably priced, given the radically different curriculum generation and delivery structures of the two institutions. Either the Ivy League institution would be
forced to degrade its curricular structure by paying much less for it (entering the
contract labor pool), or provide the product at a competitive price that does not
provide adequate return on investment. Given these choices, many brand name
institutions will probably eschew the game of offering their product in a larger
marketplace to protect against its derogation. If Munitz is correct, and Dator in
Chapter 6 of this volume, then this could prove a costly error.

This dilemma could play out differently for the state university brand name
institutions. The University of California–Berkeley and UCLA, for example,
have had their options shaped by the dynamics of public policy. The decision on
the part of then-California Governor Pete Wilson to create the California Virtual
University (CVU) rather than join the Western Governor's University means that
all the University of California (UC) campuses, the California State University
(CSU) campuses, the community colleges, and all other California-based universities and colleges accredited by the Western Association of Schools and Colleges
are eligible to provide courses within a common frame. This comingles the usually higher status courses of UC and the brand name privates should they choose
to participate with other California accredited institutions. The comparison of UC
and CSU course offerings will be interesting. Within the California masterplan
hierarchy, the top students are eligible to apply for the UC and the vast majority
of students to the mass provider California State University. Placing courses from
both systems within the Virtual University reduces these status differences based
on relative access.

The political strategy that informed the Virtual University is clear. The State of California, the most populous of the states, had invested vast amounts of capital in its public university system. It had little to gain in joining a consortium of the other western states for the purpose of disseminating courses. Further, the high status of the University of California creates a halo effect for the other universities contributing to the CVU, providing a distinctive product in a market to date dominated by recent or lower status entries.[8] One scenario would view many other universities, strapped for resources, discovering relative economies from importing Virtual University course content, thereby shifting the market from individual to institutional consumers. The attraction for institutional consumers would be leveraging their own institutional quality by using the Virtual University courses as templates for quality improvement. However, in the spring of 1999 the University of California, having decided that establishing the California Virtual University as an independent was a mistake, undertook a restructuring of it to bring it back within the structure of the University of California, which in its new form will provide the vast majority of its content. It will reemerge under a new name either in late 1999 or 2000.

The packaged course market permits name brand institutions to create demand based on the presumption of a quality product, for which, presumably, they may also charge a higher price. Mass provider institutions are far more likely to be in a situation in which they are forced to adapt their internal dynamics to meet the threat of market competition, often in ways that force them to price their product at lower levels than the actual costs of production. They will in effect maintain their overall status in the market by subsidizing packaged courses from internal cost allocations. This can succeed as a short-run strategy; it is questionable whether it has long-term staying power.

In this context, market competition will have two meanings. One will be the competition for students, which we have already outlined. The other—potentially far more serious for traditional education—will be the effect of market demand on determining what gets to be labeled and certified as "education," and who does the certification. Currently, convenience institutions can tailor their degree programs essentially for working adults, marketing courses taught by practitioners and organized around content with workplace currency, and they can reduce the overall cost of a degree through certification of prior experience. In theory, when tied to competence-based assessment and evaluation, this model could result in degree certification from competence demonstration divorced in a significant way from formal course work.

While many traditional higher-educational institutions permit challenges to courses by examination, their input-based institutional culture, organized around the Carnegie unit, makes this the rare exception rather than the rule. As institutional culture shifts first to student output assessment, and then to highly individualized distance delivery, students may be much more inclined to test for competence for a fee. When these two elements are combined, the market produces a powerful "product package" that the mass provider institution finds hard to match.

Faculties of traditional institutions have a tendency to dismiss convenience institutions as providing "training" rather than "education." This distinction is one justification for the higher "sunk" costs dedicated to full-time over adjunct faculty in these institutions. The central point is that this may not be a faculty "call," but a distinction drawing substance from market forces. The corporate universities claim a distinction because their content can be more rapidly changed, whereas curricula of traditional institutions change with notorious slowness. And, if employers do not discriminate against the graduates of convenience institutions (on the basis that they are more poorly educated), traditional institutions will have an increasingly difficult time justifying their higher costs. Even more adversely, to the extent that this distinction has continued currency within higher education, it may be based on the class distinctions between elite, brand name institutions— that for the main will continue to provide higher priced "educational experiences"—and mass provider institutions that will be the most vulnerable to the debasing of educational currency in the direction of "training."

The Western Governor's University provides a model for fundamentally revised faculty activities. It extracts economies by "unbundling" all faculty functions—course creation, curriculum, instruction, advising, assessment, and certification—and employing only a minimum of their own full-time faculty to tailor instructional programs for students. Most of the "educational product" of the institution is obtained at contract levels of payment, significantly below prevailing rates for full-time faculty.[9] The University ignores the education/training dichotomy by its competency-based instruction, accepting as a virtue that its curriculum is entirely market driven.

The early stages of convenience institutions have focused on graduate professional programs in part because they can be employment focused and thus more easily denominated for market purposes. (Although WGU's own degree programs start at the two-year technical level.) As the market expands to include undergraduate programs that are not themselves preparatory to graduate professional programs, one can expect to see versions of undergraduate programs that eschew the typical breadth requirements of general education, justified by the argument that the market makes no demand for such unfocused breadth. Mass provider institutions are already experiencing these pressures across the extraordinary range of degree programs that have been developed as undergraduate majors in everything from small-business management, to fashion design, to the management of fast-food establishments. At this margin, the distinction between the convenience institutions and those of mass provision disappears with most of the comparative economic advantages going to the former.

MANAGEMENT DILEMMAS

These market dynamics pose a variety of dilemmas for higher education managers, especially middle managers who are entrusted with the responsibility for accomplishing market-driven changes.

A central issue within much of higher education is convincing faculties and staff that these novel institutional challenges are real and have something to do with the behavior and prospects of their own institutions. Even more difficult is encouraging them to see that more fundamental social drivers may be at the base of these changes, for example, that they may be the early manifestations of how networked informational societies are likely to operate. Intellectually, some faculty and administrative personnel may acknowledge the point that their institutions grew out of an industrial society model and represent its structures and values, but one observes little reflection on how these institutions should change to be aligned with the emergence of an informational society.

Most industrial era higher education institutions performed three primary functions: knowledge creation (embodied in research norms); knowledge transmission (practiced disproportionately as classroom teaching); and knowledge conservation (for which the brick and mortar library was the primary representation). Traditional faculties achieve their continuous identity through their internal norms of publication and achievement defined by disciplinary practices. Convenience institutions challenge this by constructing curricula out of the expressed content demands of workplace situations. This allows them a freedom from the barriers to entry that have been identified as key to the emergence of these institutions. Notes Carol A. Twigg, vice president of Educom:

The traditional campus model requires a large, vertically integrated organization . . . [which creates] huge barriers for those wishing to enter the higher education marketplace. . . . Newer Information Age models, which are distributed and ultimately network-based, eliminate many of the disadvantages of vertical integration, making it easy for many different types of competitors to enter the marketplace rapidly.[10]

Others attribute some of the rapid growth of these institutions to operate in relatively rule-free territory, in an environment not yet regulated.[11] This is no doubt true, but the primary regulators of academic content and requirements of performance have been faculty, not the agents of public authority. The dilemma for those who manage the business of higher education is that they must gain the support of faculty to implement change in the face of these market demands (which the faculty often repudiate) while pursuing institutional alternatives (such as distance- and media-based education) that have the potential for undercutting traditional faculty prerogatives. Thus, the issue is about regulation only to the extent that the effort to "make" faculty responsive to market demands comes from political authority and takes the form of regulation. More specifically, the core issue is about who defines faculty interests and in relation to which values.[12] This key issue is dealt with by Abeles in this volume in more depth.

A staple of policy analysis is the observation that policies tend to change not because of some rational force that impels them to, but because participants become convinced that a crisis of sufficient proportions exists that "makes" policy change imperative. Educational managers are caught in the dilemma of having to promote the notion that crisis is taking place, that it threatens some valuable aspects of their institutions, and that for their organizations to survive on terms attractive to them some kind of change must take place. At the same time, they must be able to fashion change alternatives that are sufficiently attractive that faculty will embrace them. And, just to round things off, in promoting the notion of a crisis, educational leaders must be careful not to oversell it, lest their ostensible supporters (especially governing boards) become "spooked" and believe the existing administration is incapable of dealing with the argued threat.

As one peruses the higher education landscape, one can see institutions developing different responses to these notions of emerging crisis. We can summarize some of these by positing some scenarios that may give substance to higher education in the near future.

SOME ALTERNATIVE FUTURES

Two contradictory predictions about the relationship of higher education to its ostensible markets bump into each other. Jeremy Rifkin, writing about the future of work, has advanced the notion that one aspect of "globalization," the combination of technology replacing manual work and the movement of manual work out of the older industrial nations into newer industrializing nations, will reduce the amount of work available to citizens in these "advanced nations." The "20–80" hypothesis says that in the not-so-distant future, 20 percent of the world's population will be able to do the work currently done by 100 percent; 80 percent will have no work.[13] Most of the world's higher educational institutions are in those nations.

A second prediction drawn from higher education circles foresees a potential market in the next five years of 185,000,000 college students worldwide. These are the teeming millions that have the convenience institutions frothing to capture, and for a substantial profit.

What to make of the juxtaposition of these two macro-level predictions? Each could be correct. One posits the demand created in the shorter run of the still-to-be-completed transition from industrial to postindustrial society wherein new industries arise, transitional worker needs are experienced, and the novelty of the new forms of organization blur our vision of who is doing what work for whom. Coupled with the hard-to-change momentum of higher educational institutions continuing to recruit and educate for jobs that no longer exist, this transitional period produces forecasts for huge student enrollments. Interrogation of the assumptions of those forecasts, many of which are simply demographic projections based on former patterns of economic demand, is an underdeveloped industry.[14]

The 20–80 hypothesis suggests four things: one, as indicated, in aggregate terms a smaller number of workers is able to produce the world's goods; two, to the extent this is also true of services, especially what Robert Reich calls "in place services" remains to be seen[15]; three, the transition itself produces new jobs, especially in the technology industries, management, and finance; and four, demand patterns for employment are expressed through market mechanisms that attenuate their urgency for fulfillment (thereby privileging institutions that can respond most quickly to meeting that demand).

The following implications flow from the above:

- Both a smaller, more selective market, and a burgeoning market-driven flood of education seekers privilege the brand name institutions. The rich will get richer.
- The 20–80 hypothesis will destroy mass provider institutions as we know them should it prove to be correct. Unless, these become institutions of mass socialization and resocialization in a society that no longer is educating for mass work creation. This could become the "re-invention of work."
- Significantly heightened demand will pose particular pressures on institutions, but the market mechanisms for articulating content are relatively incoherent. In such a situation, irrespective of type, ability to adapt to the organizational pressures of numbers will carry the day. This situation would tend to favor convenience institutions.
- And finally, the growing inequality of income may change the way institutions value their products. Those with greater income will use elite institutions to gain superior job preparation and placement, but those with greater income will also employ existing and emergent institutions to gain the central and marginal benefits of the emerging informational society through lifelong education.

I would prefer a future in which Rifkin's 20–80 proposition proves wrong. As Kurt Vonnegut previewed in one of his earliest novels, *Player Piano*, such a world is grim indeed. It would not be a world so much like Hobbes' state of nature where life is "nasty, brutish and short," but it would be one marked by decisive and destructive inequality at every turn where the world is given to the valuing of goods while at the same moment most people are denied these very goods. It would be a world of envy, greed, economic reductionism, and ultimately the need for ever-greater state controls to protect the haves from the have-nots. Some have written about the current stage of globalism as if such a world lies near over the horizon if the dynamics that lead to these profound inequalities cannot be deflected.[16]

I would prefer a solution that explores the "re-invention" of work, a task to which higher education could devote itself were some fundamental assumptions changed about how it is conducted. Rifkin writes in *The End of Work* that the real crisis of the modern world (read postmodern as well) is how to make the work go around sufficiently so that people can find the means of social fulfillment. This is the implied of the previous paragraph. But, one could argue, this is a curiously industrial assumption, the notion that "work" and "job" are production related. And, of course, increasingly they are not. Reich's primary thesis is that "symbolic analysts" are the privileged workers in the world, in part because unlike production workers they are mobile in a globalizing world. To date, symbolic analysts have been elite workers, those who create the means for production capacities (for example, engineers, chemists, biologists), or organize them (for example, lawyers, legislators, bureaucrats public and private), or analyze them for some purpose (for example, accountants, fiscal analysts, university professors). These roles are those close to capital itself and its varied manifestations. The world of work in the emergent postindustrial world, the information society, has closely mimicked that of the industrial world.

One potential future for the postindustrial world would witness the rapid extension of most work as information or knowledge work in the sense that an increasing number of roles are constructed as those organized around and through symbolic content. As these knowledge activities expand, society may move from its current state, wherein we have come to speak of "knowledge" industries, to one of knowledge "post-industries."

The properties of such a world are scarcely visible, but they are immanent in the particular economics and dynamics of software, media, and other information/ knowledge activities wherein the value of something lies in its creative content rather than in the labor associated with its production exploitation.[17] The central feature of such a society is its capacity to undercut many of the dynamics of economic valuation based on an economics of scarcity. Here is a world wherein the notion of 185,000,000 "learners" in the next five years can be shifted from a model in which higher education seeks to educate individuals for the needs of an increasingly concentrated political-economic system to one in which education in the varied modalities of symbolic acquisition, inquiry, and creation can involve enormous numbers of individuals in the formation of new societies and modes of living— what Castells means by a "network society." The challenge for institutions of higher education will be to perceive the promise of such a social opening as an out from the divisive logic of the three-tiered education system described above. In this activity, interestingly, the convenience institutions may—may!—be leaders in their commitment to exploring the form of education as coeval to the substance of that education.

NOTES

1. Many of these dynamics are spelled out in D. D. Dill, W. F. Massy, P. R. Williams, and C. M. Cook, "Accreditation and Academic Quality Assurance: Can We Get There From Here?" *Change* 28 (1996): 16–24.

2. For a general analysis of these phenomena framed in accreditation terms, see Ronald A. Phillips, Jane V. Wellman, and Jamie P. Merisotis, "Assuring Quality in Distance Learning: A Preliminary Review," *Washington D.C., Institute for Higher Education Policy*, April, 1998.

3. This classification derives from the taxonomy created by the National Center for Postsecondary Improvement of: brand name, mass provider, and convenience institutions. Peter Manicas makes excellent use of these categories in his chapter in this volume.

4. The Apollo Group, the parent corporation of Phoenix, recently reported quarterly profits of $12.8 million on sales of $86.5 million. Apollo also owns the College of Financial Planning with 22,000 noncredit students, Western International University (1,000 students) and an Institute for Professional Development that provides contract services for professional development and management at 19 colleges. Apollo's Phoenix divi-

sion now offers computer-mediated distance education programs that enroll 3,750 students (up 53 percent over the previous year). Ted Marchese, "Not so Distant Competitors: How New Providers are Remaking the Postsecondary Marketplace," *American Association of Higher Education Bulletin* 50, 9 (1998): 3–5.

Divining the size of the corporate university market is difficult. The Institute for Higher Education Policy reports that in 1995 over $50 billion was spent on training by employers, and over 1,000 corporate universities exist.

5. Ted Marchese (1998): 2–3.

6. Deane Neubauer, "Globalization and Income Inequality," (in publication).

7. Cited in Ted Marchese (1998): 3–7.

8. www.california.edu. Note the language in the web-site announcement. "CVU is unique because it markets only courses and programs from California campuses that have successfully completed a rigorous academic quality review by the Western Association of Schools and Colleges (WASC). As on-line education expands in the years ahead, this important difference gives CVU a competitive advantage against other providers who may offer courses and programs of low or uneven quality."

9. www.wgu.edu. These activities are accomplished by various councils headed by an administrative faculty employee of WGU and staffed by contract faculty from the member institutions. Thus, one such council vets courses for inclusion in their on-line catalogue, courses that have been created by faculty from any number of institutions. WGU pays the faculty member for classes taken by students, and pockets some increment as profit. Another council assesses students' prior learning, another provides advising, yet another provides assessment of competency. Students in turn pay for these services on a piecework basis. Note the similarity of cost assessment in this model of education delivery to the transition of other institutions, such as telephone companies, which in their "modern, industrial model form" tended to supply a range of services for one price, whereas in their "postmodern, post-Fordist" form tend to charge small amounts for separate services. Consistent with other neoliberal practices, these practices are framed as expanding consumer choice. The net effect of the consumer is often to aggregate a range of individual services, each of relatively low cost, that accumulate to amounts higher than the former packaged services.

10. Cited in Marchese (1998): 9.

11. Cited in Marchese (1998): 9.

12. Note the discussion of regulation and interests in Deborah Stone, *Policy Paradox* (New York: W. W. Norton, 1997).

13. Jeremy Rifkin, *The End of Work* (New York: Putnam, 1995).

14. Currently the U.S. market is said to be short 350,000 programmers, which higher educational institutions are unable to produce. One response is to tailor U.S. immigration policy to make importation of such "critical skill workers" easier. On the momentum side of the coin, just eight years ago, the U.S. health care system was growing at a rate twice that of inflation, and jobs in this sector were among the most targeted. Since then, however, as a result of "reform" efforts in both the public and private sectors, this growth has slowed considerably, but educational institutions have been slow to staunch the flow of new workers, resulting in surpluses throughout the industry, from physicians, to nurses, to allied health care workers.

The California Virtual University is driven in part by its projection that over 500,000 additional new learners will provide demands on the California educational market in the next decade. Drawn from existing demographic patterns, this potential group has been termed the "second tsunami."

15. Robert Reich, *The Work of Nations* (New York: Knopf, 1991).

16. See for example Hans-Peter Martin and Harold Schumann, *The Global Trap: Globalization and the Assault on Democracy and Prosperity* (Australia: Pluto Press, 1997).

17. See Manuel Castells, *The Rise of the Network Society: Vols. 1–3* (Oxford: Blackwell, 1997).

5

The Virtual University and the Professoriate

——————————————— *Michael Skolnik*

A joke that has been making its way around Canadian university campuses involves a former professor who, retired from his position in a large research university in 1998 and out of touch with the university, runs into one of his old colleagues in the year 2003. When the first professor asks, "What's new at the old place?," his colleague says, "Well, the good news is that the minimum salary for tenured professors at our university is now $300,000." He then pauses, and adds, "but the bad news is that there are only 17 tenured professors!"[1]

There are several possible explanations of the trends that might bring about the state of affairs portrayed in this joke. One is the extension to academe of the principle of "winner-take-all" in which the rewards in an enterprise or an industry are disproportionately (some would say obscenely) concentrated in the hands of a few of the highest performers, even if the difference between their performance and that of others is small.[2] A related phenomenon is the alleged general polarization of the workforce in which the trend is toward relatively few high-paying jobs at the top, a large number of low-paying jobs at the bottom, and few jobs in the middle. In a recent review of trends in the professoriate in the United States, Philip Altbach suggests that such polarization is occurring: "The American university is becoming a kind of caste system, with the tenured Brahmins at the top and lower castes occupying subservient positions."[3]

Insofar as these alleged trends are occurring, or will occur—and there is some disagreement about that—a major, if not *the* major factor driving or permitting them is technology. Rapid advances in technology have divided the workforce into various groups: those who can create with it; those who can use it; and those who cannot use it. As for tenure, many in governments, governing boards, and university administration already have wanted to get rid of or significantly curtail it, and doing so has been made more feasible—and more financially rewarding—by recent advances in information technology.

These advances in information technology, when applied to postsecondary education, are often referred to under the rubric of the virtual university. Actually, the term virtual university is not very precise and is used in different ways by different authors. Perhaps the most popular connotation of the term is that of an electronic university, which students access and use through their own computer. Although communications and computer technology is central to the idea of the virtual university, matters of organization, program delivery, and educational philosophy are involved too. For example, a panel of experts at the Joint Educom/IBM Roundtable on the Virtual University defined the virtual university in the following way:

Educators and policy leaders are envisioning new approaches to instruction based on communications and computer technology using learning-on-demand and learner-centered instruction. An immense opportunity exists for institutions to establish new forms of electronic-based collaboration—from the student level to the institutional level—that can bring about major improvements in both access and learning while meeting legitimate public and institutional concerns about cost and quality. There is also an opportunity for new levels of multi-institutional, multistate, and multinational collaboration to provide postsecondary education and training through existing and emerging global networks. . . . This enriched educational environment envisioned by many academic leaders is captured in the phrase *the virtual university*.[4]

Thus far, discussion about the virtual university has concentrated largely on predictions of how it will impact higher education and debates about whether these developments are good or bad. Judgments of good or bad have been offered mainly with respect to learning and student development. What the virtual university might mean for the professoriate has received some attention but mostly in a secondary way. Yet, since professors are in a key position to influence both the speed and manner of implementation of the virtual university, consideration of how it will affect them would seem warranted. The purpose of this essay is to explore what the virtual university might mean for the professoriate. It starts by summarizing some key elements in current visions of the virtual university, and then considers their implications for faculty and relates these implications to motivations for embracing the virtual university. After that, it examines where the support for the virtual university is coming from and particularly the reactions to it thus far among higher education faculty. The concluding section suggests that faculty may soon have to deal with similar forces of automation that have brought radical changes to workers in other industries.

VISIONS OF THE VIRTUAL UNIVERSITY

As suggested in the passage quoted earlier, at the core of the idea of the virtual university is the notion that the full potential of computer and communications technology will be used to enable individual learners to access whatever education they want, whenever and however they want. They may obtain all their education from a single source, or as is more likely, they may choose to combine offerings from different sources, that is, the electronic world is their oyster.

There are many different types of technology that can be employed, but a single word that conveys to most people the enormous potential of technology to affect learning is *Internet*. The Internet removes almost all constraint on time and space—as well as many other legal, financial, physical, and social constraints. It allows individuals to take courses at their own pace, and to choose from all possible courses in the world those which best meet their learning needs. Learning through the Internet can support, complement, or substitute for learning in conventional ways in conventional postsecondary institutions, and the reactions that it arouses vary largely according to which of these types of contributions it is employed to make.

Two fundamental characteristics of the world of the virtual university are that it is intensely consumer driven and highly competitive, features that could have major implications for the security of the individual professor and the institution.

From Campus-centric to Consumer-centric

Regarding the first of these characteristics, George Connick, president of the Education Network of Maine, suggests that the virtual university represents a "shift from a campus-centric to a consumer-centric model."[5] Until now, control over education has been entirely in the hands of the provider, and such functions as admissions, financial aid, and registrarial processes have been "set up for the convenience of the institution, with minimal regard for the needs of the consumer."[6] In the future, it is argued, distance-learning technologies will result in control over education being placed in the hands of the consumer, and providers will have to satisfy consumer demand.

The shift to a consumer-centric model reflects not just a change in the balance of power over the content and processes of education between institutions and their students, but a fundamental change in the idea of education. From earliest times, educators have been guided by an idea of what their students need in designing the learning experience. These ideas have changed over time, and at any point there have been differences of opinion about what was a right, good, or proper education. Nevertheless, the term *student* carries with it connotations of a connection with an institution, and the institution's responsibility for the educational well-being of the student. In contrast, the consumer has no broader or more enduring ties with an institution than those which surround a particular transaction. The institution as vendor has no responsibility other than to provide the product that the consumer requests to purchase.

In the consumer-centric model, the driving force in the design of learning experiences is not a particular educational theory or philosophy, but simply what satisfies the consumer. Of course, some will say that this shift is not a consequence of the virtual university, but something that preceded it and helped pave the way for the virtual university. It could be argued that within the past three decades or so, universities changed from having their own idea of what education should be to simply trying to please their students. Much of the literature of the past two decades on the decline of a meaningful liberal education in North American higher education makes this argument.[7] If critics like Allan Bloom are correct in the view that it is the lack of a central idea of what a university education is that has led to the commoditization of university education,[8] then the shift to consumer-centrism could be even a more fundamental harbinger of the virtual university than the widely heralded advances in information technology, or at least the two need each other.

From Local Protection to Global Competitiveness

In the global "web of learning opportunities"[9] that is spawned by the virtual university, universities and colleges will likely be subjected to more intense competition than they have ever known. In place of protected, or semi-protected, local markets, their competition will become increasingly global. Insofar as this competition forces each institution to concentrate on things in which it has a competitive advantage, there may be a considerable rationalization of postsecondary education. For example, Christopher Lucas asks:

Why hire six different Shakespeare scholars, it is asked rhetorically, when the lectures of one outstanding teacher can be beamed via television to student audiences on scores of campuses? Why should half a dozen or more schools duplicate one another's foreign language offerings when it is possible for students geographically distant from one another to "tune in" on instruction from a single site? Why not let each school specialize in one or two language programs and share its instruction with those enrolled elsewhere?[10]

Marketing and Mergers

The ability to attract customers in this competitive, global market for postsecondary education is likely to depend not just upon the pedagogical quality of the courseware offered, but also upon the way in which learning resources are packaged and delivered, particularly how attractively and effectively they exploit the electronic, technological, and multimedia delivery potential. In this connection, William Plater asks us to "[I]magine what Steven Spielberg's new company could produce for the education market within the decade . . ."[11] Plater suggests that the only thing holding back major competition from private sector media-based companies is the monopoly that colleges and universities have on credentialing. However, this monopoly barrier can be penetrated by partnerships between postsecondary institutions and private sector media and knowledge sector companies, and some observers warn that this very monopoly may be in jeopardy on its own.[12]

In addition to stimulating a rationalization of the postsecondary education sector, the greatly increased competition among colleges and universities which many observers expect, especially if combined with increased competition from other sectors, is likely to result in the failure of many colleges and universities and contribute to a climate of intense financial insecurity and instability for the rest.[13] In the next section I consider what this scenario of institutional change and instability might mean for faculty.

FACULTY JOBS IN THE WORLD OF THE VIRTUAL UNIVERSITY

The competitive pressure, insecurity, and instability that will likely threaten many colleges and universities in the world of the virtual university may lead them to adopt one or more of the following three strategies in dealing with faculty: economizing, controlling, and restructuring.[14]

Economizing

As Plater has noted, faculty time is the most expensive resource used by colleges and universities, and thus, an inevitable response to pressure on them to become more efficient must involve economizing on the use of faculty time. Traditional ways of economizing on the use of expensive labor are to try to substitute capital for labor and to try to substitute less expensive labor for more expensive labor. As for the former, the extent to which the types of technology presently associated with the virtual university facilitate substitution of capital for labor is not yet clear; however, it seems likely that many institutions, especially those which feel themselves to be on the margin of survival, will be attempting to use technology (at least partially) to this end in the near future. Examples of substitution of cheaper for dearer labor are found in the trends toward more part-time relative to full-time faculty, and toward a reduction in tenured and tenure-stream faculty as a proportion of total faculty referred to earlier.

Controlling

Controlling and restructuring are really subcategories of economizing, but are noteworthy in their own right. Over the past decade there has been a strong demand by governments in many jurisdictions for greater accountability for the activities of university professors. At the heart of this demand has been a concern about the amount of time and attention being given to undergraduate teaching. William F. Massy and Robert Zemsky have noted that there has been a "steady increase in faculty discretionary time and [the] decline in the relative importance of undergraduate education" over the last several decades.[15] Faced now with rising costs and complaints about the quality of undergraduate education, university governing bodies and senior administrators are trying to gain more control over faculty time in order to reverse this trend. Tactics employed to achieve greater control include substitution of part-time faculty who are contracted just for teaching for full-time faculty; use of faculty labor on a "just-in-time" basis rather than on a fixed schedule such as the "three-lectures-per-week model";[16] and increased use of contractual arrangements even with tenured faculty. Plater suggests that the "emerging model of faculty time is likely to look more and more contractual," and to involve faculty in setting specific goals with negotiated performance measures.[17] He adds that "there is nothing inherent in the concept of tenure that says faculty can do what they want, when they want."[18]

Redefining Roles

The most pervasive implications of the virtual university for faculty pertain to possible changes in their role. At minimum, there could be a significant shift from transmitter of information toward mentor or facilitator of learning, as a greater amount of codified knowledge is embodied in courseware.[19] However, the changes could be much greater than this; with the many roles that have traditionally been combined within a single faculty member's job being disaggregated and assumed by specialists. Massy suggests rather than having whole faculty jobs in the future, they may specialize in one of the following: "being a combination of content expert, learning-process design expert, and process-implementation manager; [as] presenters of that material; [as] expert assessors of learning and competencies; [as] advisers; or [as] specialists in other evolving roles."[20] Such specialized roles have been emerging in distance education institutions. Movement in this direction is encouraged not only by adoption of technology but also by incorporation of the principles of learner-centered education.[21] It is also accelerated by administrative decisions to purchase commercially available courseware rather than producing it in-house.[22]

The pattern of change in faculty work outlined above—reduction in number of jobs, increased monitoring and control, and the breaking down of traditional roles into specialized, systematically linked jobs—is typical of what workers in many other occupations have experienced when automation has come to their industries. Not surprisingly then, while many observers have heralded the adoption of sophisticated technology and the principles of learner-centered education, which are the hallmarks of the virtual university, others have attacked these developments as representing the extension of automation and modern-day scientific management to higher education.

INITIATORS OF THE VIRTUAL UNIVERSITY

Casual observation suggests that the virtual university did not suddenly appear like "manna from heaven," but is the product of concerted initiative from certain quarters, mainly governments; the computer, electronics, and information technology industries; and university and college administrators. What seems to attract governments to the virtual university, besides the novelty of the idea, is the prospect that it will increase accessibility and lower costs, improve productivity, and increase learning effectiveness.

The revenue-generating potential of the virtual university is certainly one of the attractions that has led many higher education administrators to jump on this bandwagon. In addition to visions of revenue, other things that no doubt attract university administrators to the virtual university are the prospect of reducing costs and gaining greater control over the academic enterprise, and giving their institutions the look of being on the cutting edge of innovation. Also, it is likely that many see in the virtual university a way of making their programs more accessible and being more responsive to student needs.

Besides these three constituencies—government, business, and administration—there are two other constituencies whose attitudes toward the virtual university are vitally important. Neither have yet been major promoters of the virtual university, nor widespread opponents of it; yet how they respond could have a major influence on the development of the virtual university. These are students and faculty.[23]

STUDENT RESPONSES

While students are the main intended beneficiaries of the virtual university, not much is known about their attitudes or receptivity toward it. Looking at the hype about the virtual university, especially all the virtual learning resources—including those that advertise themselves as full virtual universities—available on the Internet, it is easy to get the impression that this is an idea whose time has come.[24] However, from inquiries that I have made, it would appear that the capacity for virtual education already in existence far exceeds the demand.

On the other hand, it is possible that the numbers of students in virtual education is so small only because the phenomenon is so new, and this form of enrollment will take off soon. Those who take this point of view argue that the approaching generation of postsecondary students has grown up with interactive electronic products, use the Internet routinely, and hence, will readily incorporate virtual learning into their lives.

Among the reasons why students might be wary of the virtual classroom are concerns about status and standards. Thus far, the institutions that are most noted for virtual learning are closer to the periphery than the center of the higher education system. So long as that is the case, the diffusion of the virtual university may be impeded by a status barrier and remain in the realm of universal or mass as opposed to elite higher education.[25]

Closely related to status is the notion of standards. Critics of on-line courses, let alone of the full-fledged virtual university, assume that such education must, by definition, be inferior to traditional forms of education. This is an astounding position for any educator to take, given all the concerns that have been expressed about the quality of undergraduate education in traditional institutions over the past two decades. One concern is that on-line courses typically embody not the application of technology in an educational vacuum, but the adoption of a learner-centered paradigm in which there are clearly specified learning goals and systematic strategies for achieving those goals, something that is frequently missing in traditional education. Another concern is that, within the educational philosophy in which on-line courses are situated, there is usually a strong emphasis upon evaluating the extent of achievement of student learning objectives, again something that is frequently absent in traditional education.[26] Thus far, criticisms of the standards in virtual education are based on the assumption that anything new is suspect, rather than upon any evidence.[27]

However, it is possible that once a critical minimum threshold in the number of graduates of virtual education is reached, this barrier might be overcome. The strong support of governments, employers, and higher education administrators should also help greatly to overcome the barrier. However, how virtual education is received by faculty will also matter. It is to that question that I now turn.

FACULTY REACTION AND RECEPTIVITY TO THE VIRTUAL UNIVERSITY

It is difficult to gauge faculty reaction and receptivity to the virtual university, because few faculty have yet had to confront the visions outlined earlier in the paper. To be sure, many faculty have been involved in designing courses for delivery on-line and through the Internet. Some critics of this process dismiss such faculty as "technozealots who simply view computers as the panacea for everything, because they like to play with them."[28] However, the findings of a survey of this subject indicated that by 1995 the use of technology was already "spreading beyond computer enthusiasts to professors in the mainstream" who had come to believe that technology could enhance their teaching.[29]

In searching the literature for faculty reaction to the virtual university, I have been able to find a few examples of strident or vociferous criticism, but relative to the vast amount of welcoming—if not glowing—tribute to the wonders of the virtual university, the amount of criticism thus far is pretty meager.[30] *The Chronicle of Higher Education* has carried a few stories about opposition of faculty at the University of Maine to the idea of the Education Network of Maine seeking independent accreditation as the University of Maine's eighth campus. However, it did not appear that faculty were opposed to multimedia, electronic distance education being offered by the Network, but rather they feared that independent accreditation would lead to "centralizing power and taking influence over degree programs away from academic departments."[31] As a result of this controversy, though, the plan for independent accreditation was shelved. In another case in which the object of criticism was more central to the concept of virtual education, many faculty at Washington State University objected to an initiative involving courses to be delivered solely on the Internet and via e-mail because they "would enable learning without any direct contact with faculty."[32]

In 1996, The American Federation of Teachers released a paper on the use of technology in education in which it encouraged its members to seek curbs on the adoption of technology in teaching. While strongly encouraging faculty members to use new technologies in their teaching, it encouraged affiliates to oppose courses taught on the Internet, through videoconferencing, or with other technologies "unless they meet faculty members' standards of quality," and to bargain for employment contracts that protect the jobs of faculty members who choose not to use the new technologies.[33]

The faculty union in a large Canadian university, York University in Toronto, recently negotiated provisions in its collective agreement along the lines of those urged by the American Federation of Teachers. In what was certainly the first such instance among universities in Canada, and possibly in North America, York faculty obtained "direct and unambiguous control over all decisions relating to the automation of instruction, including veto power."[34]

While incidents of collective opposition to manifestations of the virtual university may attract media attention, there may be many more quiet instances of faculty adaptation to the changes involved that don't attract much attention. A personal account of such an adaptation was by Stan Shapiro, a professor of marketing and former business school dean describing his own "educational epiphany":

Less than two years ago, I attended a workshop for those interested in offering online courses via Virtual U. It took only two hours to realize that I was being exposed not only to a new technology but a new ideology, one that focused on student-centered collaborative learning. . . . The message was clear, although this 60-something professor did not change all that quickly, easily or willingly. But after considerable thought, I eventually bought the whole package. . . . I find that my new emphasis on learning, as opposed to teaching, has given me a "born again" commitment to the classroom.[35]

It is interesting to view the quotation above in the context of a discussion of what the virtual university will mean for traditional universities by Polley A. McClure, vice-president and chief information officer, University of Virginia. In discussing barriers to change, McClure identifies institutional and cultural barriers, including the "faculty learning barrier," as the most difficult to overcome.[36] McClure observes that designing a course to be delivered at a blackboard and designing a course to be delivered collaboratively and interactively across a network are very different things, and that for the latter, professors "have to learn new pedagogical models and ways of interacting with students."[37] It is not known how many faculty have done the kind of learning that McClure refers to, or had a conversion like Professor Shapiro, but those are just as much part of the faculty reaction to the idea of the virtual university as are the collective faculty actions at the University of Maine and York University.

TEACHING DIFFERENTLY IN THE NEXT MILLENNIUM

It is too soon yet to say if faculty unions that take a stance like the York University Faculty Union are behaving more like Paul Revere, Chicken Little, or Ned Ludd. The promoters of the virtual university are quite up front with the prediction that a major transformation of both learning and faculty work is to be expected. That being the case, it would not seem overly alarmist for faculty leaders to warn of significant changes that might be coming, and take steps to prepare for them, even though many past predictions of the way that new technology would revolutionize higher education have not been validated.

If overreaction is not a significant issue or pitfall, Luddism still might be. Certainly there are good reasons for faculty to fear many of the visions and supposed trends from the literature on the virtual university described in this essay. After all, the changes posited here involve a reduction in the number of full-time faculty positions, elimination of job security for faculty, increased monitoring of faculty activity and performance, and most significantly, the breaking down of the traditional role of faculty into various specialized component roles; trends which collectively David Noble calls "the automation of higher education."

Like workers in most other industries who have felt the onslaught of automation, it is to be expected that many education faculty will resist such changes. However, if the experience of other industries is a guide, such resistance might be futile, a point that has been made by numerous higher education leaders already. For example, Goldie Blumenstyk reported that outsiders viewed the policy stance of the American Federation of Teachers to halt the introduction of technology as "a tad naive."[38] She cites the comment of James R. Mingle, executive director of State Higher Education Executive Officers, who has spent some time studying how to adapt public policy in higher education to the changes allowed by new technology: "If students want it, I can guarantee somebody will do it, and somebody else will accredit it." Similarly, Peter McPherson, president of Michigan State University, has remarked that "Every sector of business that has gone through this struggle has always said 'we can't do it.' That's what health care said, that's what the automobile companies said. But the markets do work, and change does come."[39] Not only might higher education faculty ultimately not be any more successful than workers in other industries who have tried to forestall automation, but it is not apparent why they would have any stronger moral justification than did workers in any of the other trades, crafts, and occupations whose work has been drastically changed or eliminated by automation over the past two centuries. The fact that university teaching has been done essentially the same way for most of this millennium is not a good defense against arguments that it be done a different way in the next millennium.

NOTES

1. It is often impossible to identify the source of a joke. However, after reading the first draft of this chapter, Richard Malinski supplied me with a reference to a speech by Oracle

CEO Larry Ellison at the Second International Harvard Conference on Internet and Society in Cambridge, MA. Ellison said that "Educators will make thousands, even millions of dollars teaching courses like Physics 101. That's the good news . . . The bad news is that there will only be about 60 of them who will be doing it . . ." Cited in Mo Krochmal, "Educational Elites Will Deliver Digitally, Says Ellison," *TechWeb News* (May 26, 1998) [Available from: Lexus-Nexus: news; allnws library].

2. R. H. Frank and P. J. Cook, *The Winner-Take-All Society: Why the Few at the Top Get So Much More than the Rest of Us* (New York: Penguin Books, 1995).

3. Philip G. Altbach, "An International Academic Crisis? The American Professoriate in Comparative Perspective," *Daedalus* 126, 4 (1997): 332.

4. Carol A. Twigg and Diana G. Oblinger, *The Virtual University: A Report from a Joint Educom/IBM Roundtable*, Washington, D.C., November 5–6, 1996. [On-line], http://www.educom.edu/nlii/VU.html [December 3, 1997].

5. Twigg and Oblinger, *The Virtual University*, 7.

6. Twigg and Oblinger, *The Virtual University*, 8.

7. Caroline Andrew and Steen B. Esbensen, eds., *Who's Afraid of Liberal Education?* (Ottawa: University of Ottawa Press, 1989).

8. Allan Bloom, *The Closing of the American Mind* (New York: Simon and Schuster, 1987).

9. Twigg and Oblinger, *The Virtual University*, 2.

10. Christopher J. Lucas, *Crisis in the Academy: Rethinking Higher Education in America* (New York: St. Martin's Press, 1996): 222.

11. William M. Plater, "Future Work: Faculty Time in the 21st Century," *Change* (May/June 1995): 25.

12. John Seely Brown and Paul Duguid, "Universities in the Digital Age," *Change* (July/August 1996): 18.

13. M. G. Dolence and D. M. Norris, *Transforming Higher Education: A Vision for Learning in the 21st Century* (Ann Arbor, MI: Society for College and University Planning, 1995): 2.

14. Chris Selby Smith suggests that the climate engendered by these strategies is likely to be one of low trust and that climate may have a major impact on the way that the introduction of new technology is perceived in the academic workplace.

15. William F. Massy and Robert Zemsky, "Faculty Discretionary Time: Departments and the 'Academic Ratchet'," *The Journal of Higher Education* 65, 1 (1994): 2.

16. Twigg and Oblinger, *The Virtual University*, 12.

17. Plater, "Future Work," 32.

18. Plater, "Future Work," 32.

19. Twigg and Oblinger, *The Virtual University*, 12.

20. Massy, cited in Twigg and Oblinger, *The Virtual University*, 12. Glen Jones points out that this list of roles excludes research, and in fact that most of the literature on the virtual university looks only at the university's instruction function.

21. Robert B. Barr and John Tagg, "From Teaching to Learning—A New Paradigm for Undergraduate Education," *Change* (November/December 1995): 13–25.

22. At a conference which I attended recently, an official of a large Midwestern community college in the United States reported that his college had made a policy decision to move substantially toward technologically mediated instruction and to buy rather than develop all of the courseware.

23. In their study of the use of the Internet in Public Administration Programs, Rahm and Reed report that their findings support the view that "much of the perceived pressure to move toward distance learning is not bubbling up from faculty and students but rather is being driven by upper-level university administrators." Dianne Rahm and B. J. Reed, "Going Remote: The Use of Distance Learning, the World Wide Web, and the Internet in Graduate Programs of Public Affairs and Administration," *Public Productivity & Management Review* 20, 4 (1997): 467.

24. There is an enormous amount of information on the virtual university on the Internet, including lists of virtual colleges and universities, discussions of opportunities, problems and issues, and promotional material. A good place for the uninitiated to start a search of these materials is with Carolyn Kotlas's list of learning resources (http://www.iat.unc.edu/guides/irg-38.html) or the virtual university site maintained by John Milam of George Mason University for the Association for Institutional Research (http://apollo.gmu.edu/~jmilam/air95/virtualu.html).

25. Martin Trow, "The Development of Information Technology in American Higher Education," *Daedalus* 126, 4 (1997): 297. The part of the university where virtual education is most likely to penetrate the elite sector is professional education. Students in the new on-line Global Executive M.B.A. Program at Duke University's Fuqua School of Business pay $82,500 for a degree, compared to $50,000 for the regular on-campus M.B.A. Half the students in the former program "commute by e-mail" from outside the United States, as far away as Switzerland and Hong Kong (Gubernick and Ebeling, op. cit.).

26. In view of this consideration it seems particularly ironic for professors in mainstream Canadian universities to be attacking the standards in on-line education as Professor Noble of York University does (Noble, op. cit.). In Canada there is no external assessment or accreditation of undergraduate education, although even the Canadian Association of University Teachers has called for it. Canadian Association of University Teachers, *Governance and Accountability* (Ottawa: CAUT, 1993): 76–77.

27. The movement for nontraditional postsecondary education in the 1970s was bedeviled by the same prejudice. For a discussion of the parallel between nontraditional education of the 1970s and the current movement toward virtual and learner centered education with respect to both the challenge they pose for traditional education and the opportunities which they offer students, see Michael L. Skolnik, "Higher Education in the 21st Century: Perspectives on an Emerging Body of Literature," *Futures* 30, 7 (1998): 635–50.

28. David F. Noble, "Digital Diploma Mills: The Automation of Higher Education." [On-line] List Serve LABOR-L@YORKU.CA. York University [December 3, 1997].

29. Thomas J. DeLoughry, "Reaching a 'Critical Mass': Survey Shows Record Number of Professors Use Technology in Their Teaching," *The Chronicle of Higher Education* (January 26, 1996): A17.

30. Glen Jones suggests that one reason for this lack of reaction by faculty may be that the central focus for many faculty is their research rather than teaching.

31. Goldie Blumenstyk, "Learning from Afar: Students and Professors Have Mixed Reactions to the Education Network of Maine," *The Chronicle of Higher Education* (May 31, 1996): A15.

32. Rahm and Reed, "Going Remote," 459.

33. Goldie Blumenstyk, "Faculty Group Calls for Caution and Curbs on Distance Education," *The Chronicle of Higher Education* (January 26, 1996): A20.

34. Noble, "Digital Diploma Mills."

35. Stan Shapiro, "Let's Get Real About Teaching," *University Affairs* (June/July 1998): 25.

36. Polley A. McClure, "What Will 'Transformation' Mean to Traditional Universities?", Virginia.edu 1(3).http://www.itc.virginia.edu/virginia.edu/fall97/trans/all.html.

37. McClure, "What Will 'Transformation' Mean?"

38. Blumenstyk, "Faculty Group Calls for Caution," A20.

39. Cited in Lisa Gubernick and Ashlea Ebeling, "I Got My Degree Through E-Mail," *Forbes* 59, 12 (June 16, 1997) [On-line edition].

6

The Futures for Higher Education: From Bricks to Bytes to Fare Thee Well!

—————————————————— *Jim Dator*

Hail, fellow revolutionaries and coconspirators in the overthrow of the industrial state, and its handmaiden, publicly funded education! Hail, you servants laboring in the most despised, rejected, and neglected of educational vineyards—the "outreach" colleges of continuing and distance education! Stand up and cease from cowering in the towering shadows of the haughty flagship campuses of the vainglorious land-grant universities, with their addled administrators and preening professors. For too long you have sat and worked, biding your time. Powerpointing here, net surfing there, convening a workshop now, and yet stealthily spinning the wiry web of the virtual university everywhere until, as the crews of the flagships endlessly rearrange their deck chairs, you rise up with righteous fury, engulfing the professors and their stifling administrators, digitizing all libraries, and proclaiming for all who have ears to hear that you, and your colleges of continuing and distance education, are now the proper conduits for learning, just-in-time, for the 21st century.

Even though I am the son of university professors and for much of my own adult life have been a tenured professor at the University of Hawaii, and would like to believe that my university, and all universities, shall continue surging forever forward in their present forms, I just can't assume that. Instead, I am burdened down by the weight of decades of prophecy and false prophecy about the probable death and possible transfiguration of higher (and all) education everywhere.

WHY DID MASS PUBLIC HIGHER EDUCATION ARISE?

While universities are very hoary institutions, tracing their ancestry back several thousand years to the origins of writing, modern systems of mass public education are only about 100 to 150 years old in their origins, and not yet 40 years old since their prime. They were originally created specifically to meet the needs of the early industrial states. Formal education was expected in part to indoctrinate youth into the myths and fables of national tradition (in the North American case, Western Civilization—the dead white guys of story, song, and calumny). Colleges were also allowed to be safe havens where fools like me could attempt to pursue and occasionally stumble upon some novel if often useless truth or other once in a while.

But it is very important to realize that the publicly funded educational system everywhere in the world—the reason hardworking citizens were forced to part with some of their hard-earned cash and give it to the likes of me—had nothing to do either with the myths or the truths. It was only so that we would magically change ordinary people from being peasants and lords into the laborers and bosses (and into the fighters and officers) needed in the factories (and in the battlefields) of the new industrial states, each jostling for dominance over the other emerging industrial states of the world.

At the same time, some among us were also expected to do the scientific research and the technical development necessary to produce the goods and guns of modernity. But no government ever funded a public university primarily to enable academics to "pursue truth." Publicly funded education was established solely to serve the needs of the industrial state, and "truth" has never been one of its needs. This has been the cause of countless conflicts between town (which wants obedient workers and reliable products—and winning athletic teams) and gown (which wants a modicum of intellectual space within their cubicle and adequate parking space near it).

This is all coming to an end as a "post-industrial"—possibly, an "information"—society springs from the rigor mortis of the residual industrial state.

Only a century ago—indeed only several decades ago—few people had any formal education at all. Still fewer had any formal higher education. School-based education was not needed in traditional agricultural and feudal societies. It may or may not be needed in the future. *Learning* will still be prominent in the future, but teaching through *publicly mandated and accredited educational organizations* may be at an end.

It is important to recognize that public institutions of mass education are very new, fragile, and vulnerable.

HOW MIGHT COMMUNICATION TECHNOLOGIES
TRANSFORM HIGHER EDUCATION?

If *schooling* was necessary for industrialization, then so were school *buildings* and *campuses*. Given the technology of the time, there was no choice but to require all students to go to school buildings at the same time; to study and be tested on the same standardized curricula; to change classes when bells rang, and come to an end at a certain time in the afternoon—and then for the campuses to remain vacant most evenings, weekends, and summers.

But what if global communication networks had been in existence in the 19th century? Would we have schools and school buildings and curricula as we have them now? Clearly, our world would be quite different if we had not grown so accustomed to the printing press and to congregating in central locations for everything from education to commerce. So why does the world persist in looking like it does now, and how much longer can it continue to look like this? Indeed why do faculty, administrators, and politicians continue, unnecessarily, to erect even more buildings and to plan even more campuses? It's inertia. It's ignorance. It's greed.

Chris Dede has been tracking the metamorphosis of education for a long time. A few years ago, he very presciently suggested the following:

The National Information Infrastructure (NII) is a vehicle for virtual communities, a conduit for knowledge utilities, and a synthetic environment with new frontiers to explore and experience. During the next decade, these emerging capabilities will leverage more change in education than has occurred over the past two centuries. . . . Interdisciplinary, learning-by-doing experiences in artificial environments made possible by the NII will likely supplement discipline-centered, campus-based teaching-by-telling. . . . At present, most faculty and administrators are coping with its first impact: shifting from foraging for data to filtering a plethora of incoming information. Educational leaders in the next decade must develop a comprehension of how to use this new medium to empower new messages and mission, and how to collaborate with and/or outperform competitors.[1]

Bricks to Bytes

Eli Noam, director of Columbia's University's Institute for Tel-Information, wrote an article on "the dim future of the university" for *Science*, certainly the most widely read and respected journal of the American scientific community. Professor Noam showed that modern systems of higher education share a feature that is very old: the scholars and students out of necessity congregate together physically around collections of books and journals. "This system of higher education remained remarkably stable for over 2500 years. Now, however, it is in the process of breaking down. The reason is not primarily technological; technology simply enables change to occur. The fundamental reason is that today's production and distribution of information are undermining the traditional flow of information and with it the university structure, making it ready to collapse in slow motion once alternatives to its function become possible."[2]

Noam then goes on to show that there indeed are many "functional alternatives" to traditional higher education already well advanced, with more coming. Thus he concludes his essay with a set of questions:

What then is the role of the university? Will it be more than a collection of remaining physical functions, such as the science laboratory and the football team? Will the impact of
electronics on the university be like that of printing on the medieval cathedral, ending its
central role in information transfer? Have we reached the end of the line of a model that
goes back to Nineveh? . . . Can we self-reform the university, or must things get much
worse first?[3]

Later, an editorial in *Science* by Donald Langenberg, once a deputy director of
the prestigious U.S. National Science Foundation and chancellor of the
University of Illinois, and currently the chancellor of the huge University of
Maryland System, stated that:

[M]any universities may die or may change beyond recognition as a result of the IT
[Information Technology] revolution. Barring a catastrophic reduction in the nation's commitment to research, the 100 or so major research universities probably will persist in rec-
ognizable form. . . . Resistance to radical change will probably be substantial within
academe, many of whose members will argue that IT is a threat to the essential traditional
values of real education and that its pervasive use can result only in pervasive mediocrity.
I anticipate that much of higher education's clientele will decide otherwise.[4]

I basically agree with Chancellor Langenberg but I wonder about one assumption of his forecast. One of the major things that is happening is that the nation
has been engaged in a potentially catastrophic reduction of financial commitment
to research—especially basic research. Of course, America never had any
national commitment to research at all unless there was a direct military application for it, and hopefully a commercial spin-off not too far behind.

But the Cold War has tragically come to an end, and despite valiant attempts
to keep the military–welfare state going, federal money for defense-related
research and development is down, while money for purely academic research
and development—especially, but not only, in the humanities and social sciences—is basically lower, in spite of some, almost certainly temporary, areas and
periods of reprieve.[5]

However extraordinarily rich some of their citizens may be, all nations of the
world have decided that they are too poor to continue supporting research at the
levels they did between the Second World War and the end of the Cold War.
Funding for research, as for everything else in the current ideological fantasy, is
now left to private corporations, which generally are only going to support
research that has an immediate and proprietary payoff to themselves. Moreover,
individual corporations don't exist long enough now to be willing to fund anything that might extend further than three months into the future. So who is going
to fund research that will keep any but a handful of the most prestigious research
universities solvent?

So, Chancellor Langenberg's bold prophecy about the future of education may
be rather timid indeed.

So what can we expect of universities and schools in such a privatized and entrepreneurial world? My guess is that while a few elite colleges may indeed remain as they are now—day camps and marriage bazaars for the adult children of the rich and famous—most campuses may become shelters for the homeless— perhaps of the vast number of unemployed teachers and professors—and the unemployed graduates of many academic programs too, whether campus-based, distributed, or virtual.

The "2020World" column in the *Seattle Times* some time ago had a more interesting suggestion:

It's the year 2020. [A] favorite place to vacation is the newest, hottest attraction in Boston: "Harvard, Class of 1925." Just three years ago Bill Gates rescued the shuttered campus from condo developers by turning it into a "re-creation" of a bygone era, a theme park. Now Harvard looks as it had in 1925, with lectures of the period, too: Marxism, physics (Einstein's relativity was the new thing), motion pictures, etc.

If it could happen to Harvard, it could happen to your organization! Which of today's organizations do you think will become theme parks in 2020World? I think the typical liberal arts universities are good candidates; so are retailers and banks. Try this simple test:
1. Is your organization primarily in the information business? (If yes, go to 2.)
2. Does your organization "communicate" existing information to its customers without really adding value? (If yes, go to 3.)
3. Does your organization require a physical location in order to "communicate" the information to its customers? (If yes, a theme park is in your future!)[6]

I have experimented extensively with all forms of delivery systems for years— radio (both "produced" and live talk-back), television (videotaped, live, and interactive), slide shows (once called "multimedia"), PEACESAT, newspapers, "computer conferencing," e-mail listservs, and most recently over the Web.[7] Nothing is growing faster in the educational business than on-line services. Even the "Brand Name" universities are becoming serious "Convenience Store" competitors here.[8] Developments are so fast that it is foolhardy for me to try to imagine what will be available by the time you, dear reader, are perusing these words. The following are some of the URLs for virtual university sites that were operating when I wrote these words on September 19, 1998.[9]

Digital Dreams or Lifetimes of Horror?

In October 1997, and repeatedly thereafter, an article by David Noble was distributed—on-line via many lists—entitled "Digital Diploma Mills: The Automation of Higher Education." This created enormous discussion among defenders and detractors of on-line education. In March 1998, Noble published "Part II" subtitled, "The Coming Battle Over On-line Instruction." His concern in both articles is not only about the technology per se versus classroom teaching, but especially the fact that big business owns, and is pushing, and expects to make big bucks from these new technologies. Given the privatization mania of higher education, most colleges and universities seem either disinclined or incapable of resisting the McDonaldization of higher education, turning all providers into "digital diploma mills."[10]

Several years ago, I became involved in a small way in the development of a major virtual educational venture now called "The Western Governor's University."[11] I believe that, in some ways, what was created and what it will continue to become fulfills many of my lifelong dreams about the future of higher education. But in other ways, it threatens to create a new lifetime of horrors.

First of all, I deeply regret not being able to assume that my best graduate students will be able to enjoy the kind of life in academia that I have had. I have loved every minute of my professional life—except for the charade of assigning grades. I wish I could be sure that the kind of life I had will continue robustly into the future for those who want it for themselves. Indeed, I wish that all teachers at all levels now, as well as in the future—indeed, more importantly, all humans now and for the future—could live in the free, inquiring, and intellectually stimulating community with which the University of Hawaii provided me. I have been truly blessed. All people should be able to live in the kind of environment I have enjoyed, if they wish to.

There is much that will be lost—or at least extremely difficult to maintain—as the global transformation continues. I love to read and to write, which must be obvious since I wrote this message for you (though I must acknowledge that almost every citation in this paper came to me originally from cyberspace, and not from a printed book or journal).

FAREWELL ACADEMIC FREEDOM?

Even though I believe that academic freedom is the most valuable gift higher education in America has given to me, academic freedom has always been fragile and threatened, though comparatively easy to hide and thus to protect.

However, in "Intellectual Freedom in the Virtual University," William Morey, Bart Binning, and Paul Combs observe that:

The walls of the academy that previously sheltered the concepts of intellectual freedom are becoming electronic tentacles that extend into the home and the global workplace. The free exchange of ideas and artistic expressions that have traditionally been acceptable inside the classroom may not be so acceptable when other stakeholders in education can view only portions of the educational process. The messages that are part of the give-and-take of the college classroom processes of synthesis and evaluation may seem different when being delivered over the information highway. The Internet allows educational stakeholders to glimpse classroom 'sound-bites' that may take on entirely different meanings when viewed outside the context of intellectual give-and-take. . . . Liability and copyright laws are of particular concern. How many times has a student made rash and irresponsible statements in a classroom environment that would lead to potential legal liability were the same statements seen in a public television broadcast?[12]

The Telecommunications Act of 1996 contains many provisions that ultimately will have a chilling effect on much of what goes on intellectually in the protective confines of the old Ivory Tower. Moreover, the broader community, in its mad, mad desire to patent, privatize, and profit from everything professors once did modestly and freely for the common weal, seems bent on ending intellectual freedom once and for all. Academic freedom is the only thing about modern public higher education that I believe is truly worth saving. Yet it is something the public doesn't give a damn about because they aren't allowed to have it for themselves in their own places of work, so, they argue, why should we in ours?

WHAT NEEDS TO BE LEARNED?

So far, I have looked entirely at the future delivery systems of higher education, and said nothing at all about what might, or should be, delivered, so I will conclude by merely stating, and not attempting to justify, the following three points:

First, Western culture has dominated most educational systems (including many nonwestern systems) worldwide for the past two hundred years. It is not likely to be the dominant culture of the 21st century and beyond. Instead, Western culture might very well be Number Four behind Confucian, Hindic, and Islamic cultures, and in some parts of the world, such as Hawaii, behind the revitalized indigenous cultures. However, all cultures will themselves be modified and changed by the developments I discussed, and by many I did not. Thus, the future of Confucian—or Hawaiian, or Western—culture is not likely to be a linear extension of its past or present. Curricula of and for the future should recognize this rich cultural diversity more manifestly, and embrace, exhibit, and celebrate it.

Second, the academic disciplines, departments, and schools around which curricula and governance are organized presently arose for historical, ideological, and personal reasons, and not at all because the world is actually and necessarily organized the way academia is. While many things about the current academic disciplines are valuable, and will have a place in the future, these disciplines cannot continue to play the fundamental role they have played to the present.[13]

One of the many reasons is this. Humans, through their various activities past and present, increasingly and fundamentally modify the very "nature" that the various disciplines intend objectively to study. More and more of what was once unblemished "nature" is now "artificial" and thus needs to be conceptualized by scientists as a changing, malleable artifice and not only as a static, objective given.

It is now humanity's challenge to invent, create, and sustain life (if we wish life, especially humans, to evolve into the future), and not merely and passively to "study" it. This is also a profoundly multidisciplinary task, beyond the capabilities of any one discipline now. Thus it is the urgent, and largely unacknowledged, duty of all education from now on to help us learn how to "govern evolution." This is an obligation that may well exceed the capabilities, not only of any future educational system imaginable, but even of humanity itself.

Nonetheless, that is the challenge which lies ahead, whether we are capable of responding to it or not. If universities are to play a positive role in creating an evolvable future for humanity, they must reconceptualize and reorganize themselves accordingly.

And so, thirdly, just as we do not presently have a viable environment for the future neither do we have any viable economic or political systems. Everyone must help us all do the very creative and hard work of envisioning, inventing, creating, and managing a new political economy as well as a new environment and new learning communities during the 21st century if we think humans should exist in the 22nd century.

We have great opportunities and challenges ahead of us, and no one is better prepared to surf these tsunamis of change than the folks presently engaged in distance education. In contrast to the lumbering university flagships floundering about, colleges of continuing, distant, and virtual education are already like so many darting nanospaceships nipping at the buds of time. I expect them to clear the path ahead, if anyone can and will.

NOTES

1. Christopher Dede, "Beyond the Information Superhighway," *Linkages* 2, 2 (Spring/Summer 1994).

2. Eli Noam, "Electronics and the Dim Future of the University," *Science* 270 (October 13, 1995): 247.

3. Noam, "Electronics and the Dim Future of the University," *Science* 249.

4. Donald Langenberg, "Power Plants or Candle Factories," *Science* 272 (June 21, 1996): 1721.

5. Philip Abelson, "Global Technology Competition," *Science* 277 (September 12, 1997): 1587.

6. "Will Colleges and Banks Turn Into Theme Parks?", *2020 World Digest* 1, 28 (Monday, November 7, 1994).

7. The URL for information about this course, Introduction to Political Futures, Polsci 171, is <http://www.hcc.hawaii.edu/hcconline/>.

URLs for some other on-line futures courses include:

http://www.communities.org.uk/events/lmu.html

http://jan.ucc.nau.edu/~rdr/Ant547/

http://ag.arizona.edu/futures/

http://www.csudh.edu/global_options/POL375-Tech.HTML

http://www.eou.edu/ps/webfs.html

8. Stanford University announced in August 1998 that it is offering a degree in engineering entirely on-line, and the following came from the on-line service, Edupage, 17 September 1998:

KAPLAN PLANS ON-LINE LAW SCHOOL

Kaplan Educational Centers, the big standardized-test coaching company, is planning to offer the first online law degree through its newly established Concord University School of Law. Concord has received authorization from the California Bureau of Post-Secondary and Vocational Education to grant degrees, which will allow students to sit for the bar in that state. The school does not yet have accreditation from either the state or the American Bar Association... but the company doesn't plan to apply for accreditation until it can demonstrate its students are learning the same things as traditional students. "We're seeing industry look at the higher-education sector in a way they've never looked before," says Arthur Levine, president of Teachers College at Columbia University. "It's a $225 billion market where there are questions about price and management. It's ripe for private-sector involvement." (*Wall Street Journal* 16 September 1998.)

 Date: Thu, 17 Sep 1998 07:39:00–1000
 From: Edupage Editors <educause@educause.unc.edu>
 To: EDUCAUSE Edupage Mailing List <edupage@educom.unc.edu>
 Subject: Edupage, 17 September 1998
 9. URLs of some major higher education on-line sites or references to on-line sites, active on September 19, 1998:
 http://www.arragon.com/finder.asp
 http://node.on.ca
 http://www2.gdi.net/~hidakota/JOURNAL.HTM
 http://www.aln.org
 http://www2.hawaii.edu/dlit/
 http://fas.sfu.ca:80/0h/css/update/vol6/6.3-harasim.main.html
 http://www.athena.edu/index.html
 http://www.hied.ibm.com/ipc/
 http://www.unisa.ac.za
 http://cuonline.edu/
 http://www.magellan.edu/
 http://www.waldenu.edu/index.html
 http://a2z.lycos.com/Education/College_Home_Pages/Colleges_without_Borders—Remote_Learning/

The best single source for continuing information about the future of higher education in all fads and forms comes from James Morrison, of the University of North Carolina, and his on-line and monthly hardcopy publication, *On the Horizon*. <http://horizon.unc.edu>.

 See also *Journal of Asynchronous Learning Networks* <http://www.aln.org/alnweb/journal/jaln_vol2issue2.htm>

An exceptionally good statement about conventional brick and mortar universities vs. virtual universities is Joseph Pelton, "Cyberlearning vs. the University: An Irresistible Force Meets and Immovable Object," *The Futurist* 30, 6 (November–December 1996): 17–20.

 10. David F. Noble teaches history at York University in Toronto. In April 1998, Noble convened a conference on "Digital Diploma Mills?" at Harvey Mudd College in Claremont, California, where he was a visiting professor. Langdon Winner said that the conference "featured some of the most intense, personally moving discussions I have ever heard in a scholarly setting." It was billed as "a second look at information technology and higher education," for people "concerned about the effects of computer-based learning in our colleges and universities." This is from "Tech Knowledge Review," a column of technology criticism in the on-line newsletter NETFUTURE.

 <http://www.ora.com/staff/stevet/netfuture>

 See also, Michael Margolis, "Brave New Universities," *First Monday, Vol. 3, #5* May 4, 1998. <http://www.firstmonday.dk/issues/issue3_5/margolis/index.html>.

11. The Western Governor's Virtual University offered its first classes in September 1998. For more information, visit the WGU website at <http://www.wgu.edu>.

12. William Morey, Bart Binning, Paul Combs, "Intellectual Freedom in the Virtual University," Bart Binning <binning@aix1.ucok.edu>, presented at the Southwest Business Symposium, April 11, 1996, Oklahoma City, Oklahoma.

13. A valuable argument for multicultural and multidisciplinary higher education is made by Immanuel Wallerstein, et al., *Open the Social Sciences* (Stanford: Stanford University Press, 1996).

7

Why Pay for a College Education?

> It is no longer clear what the place of the University is within society nor what
> the exact nature of that society is, and the changing institutional form of the
> University is something that intellectuals cannot afford to ignore.
> —*Bill Readings[1]*

Spring arrives, the salmon swim upstream to spawn and the plants start to flower.
Fall comes and children go off to school, preschool, grade school, secondary
school and the university. The cycles seem inexorably fixed and compelling.

In a world where acquisition of knowledge is not tied to temporal and spatial
restraints, why are the delivery systems geared to an ancient cycle? In a cyber
world of bits and bytes, where wisdom and knowledge are constantly tested and
testable, where scholars are connected or connectable, regardless of space and
time, what are the functions of bricks and mortar, the campus? In a world where
a person may "earn" the equivalent of several degrees in a lifetime, where disciplines or cross disciplines exist where none existed in the past and where knowledge is generated within a global community and spread almost instantaneously
from the point of creation outward, what is the function of a campus?

In a world where education is historical and common knowledge, what are we
paying for in a postsecondary institution, and why should we consider paying in
units of time and money? In the past, a boy (Alexander the Great) could be studying with Aristotle at age 13 and at age of 16 be conquering the known world, and
yet, today, that same youth would not qualify for a driver's license but could have
access to the world's greatest scholars or their materials in cyberspace, essentially
for nothing. What, then, are the values provided within the academic cloisters?
Why and how do we pay?

While this sounds like a question for consumers, it is actually the core question that must be asked by the Academy. In the private sector inventors often come up with the "better mouse trap" only to find that the consumer has no interest in the new product. Similarly, manufacturers of buggy whips find that even though their products are of the highest quality, the market no longer exists. What is it that an educational institution offers? Is the experience changed over time? Does the fact that those in the Academy believe in their programs make any difference? Does the fact that the Academy has been playing Polonius to public whimsy, with new programs materializing like Topsy, raise questions?

What is it that represents that which is paid for beyond grades K–12? And, with the proliferation of alternative institutions and vehicles for access, where does the traditional four-year institution fit in the global knowledge market?

THE HALF-LIFE OF KNOWLEDGE

"God is Change."
—Octavia Butler[2]

The cost/bit of information is getting cheaper. The cost/useful bit is getting more expensive. Additionally, there is a sense that a large part of the cost is tied to its "age" where some materials are considered quite valuable the more recent they are. Yet, most civilizations talk about wisdom, that information which is eternal, time tested and thus of great value.

If, indeed, there is substantive value to the wisdom of the ages regardless of where it was generated, globally, and it has existed and stood the test of time should it not be readily available at low or no cost through various media, including the World Wide Web? If there is a world community of scholars interested in the study and analysis of these ideas, can they not be tied together seamlessly on the Internet? Does not this make them accessible?

On the other hand, where does knowledge, which has a short half-life, reside? Since such knowledge's value is based on its volatility, can it even exist within the postsecondary educational experience? Some universities have answered in the negative by creating separate research institutes that do not release this time-sensitive information until it has been protected via patents and similar mechanisms. And once released, does it not, then become accessible? And what is its worth and half-life?

It seems that, in tying the human experience together in space, the Web has forced the Academy to look at knowledge in terms of its time value and thus calls into question the value provided by the Academy in a digital age. Knowledge that has endured the test of time becomes ubiquitous and yet may be of most profound importance while readily available. On the other hand, very short half-life knowledge also has great value, immediately, yet even when generated within an academic institution, is not readily accessible to those pursuing traditional undergraduate degrees. Indeed, then, what is being purchased and is it worth the price?

TIME AS A COST

"Is it not a paradox of our civilization that, while we have mastered space, we have become the slaves of time?"

—*Amin Maalouf*

Biological evolution is Darwinian, but knowledge is Lamarckian. Humans can pass on their memetic information to their own generation as well as future generations. Furthermore, knowledge does not reside locked within some limited carrier such as a specific genetic code. At one time, such information was, indeed controlled because storage was limited and volatile, residing in the brain. The printing press and modern science has made information relatively ubiquitous, stable, and increasingly available.

Knowledge has become accessible when and where needed. The electronic Web has mitigated time and space. Since the human biocomputer's ability and interest in accessing such knowledge varies, it seems strange to sequence access over time and in time-based units as currently done in the educational system.

In the past, time was used to control access because both knowledge and the ability and interest in distributing it were limited. Knowledge was dispensed like gasoline, so many units/time. And thus, both the amount and the mastery of that amount could be easily metered.

The expansive nature of the Web has exposed the fact that the size of the knowledge base may be unbounded. Additionally, the interconnectedness provides an incalculable number of pathways to access and combine this information. Thus, the sequential paths for education, particularly at the postsecondary level, creates a time limiting model for accessing information. And, in fact, the model creates a false representation of how such knowledge is accessed outside of the Academy.

Time is a non-leveragable commodity. This means that humans, in gaining access and capitalizing on knowledge, must develop new learning models as this critical commodity expands. What is it that the Academy provides that is essential to effectively coping with this shifting, expanding, dynamic, and wired world and that is worth the current price, not in monetary terms, but in non-leveragable units of time?

Is it possible that the current postsecondary institutions may be contributing to the perpetuation of a model that is raising the time cost of accessing knowledge? This is particularly relevant since the faculty in grades K–12 are trained in the postsecondary institutions. Could it be that the Web's exposure of the time-dependent/time-limited model of knowledge acquisition also exposes a reflexive, self-perpetuating, self-serving system?

Someone once quipped that youth was so wonderful that it was a shame that we wasted it on children. There is a movement now to have children work with older citizens to teach them computer skills. Also, we know that most physicists make their greatest discoveries in their early years. As mentioned earlier, Alexander was conquering the known world at age 16.

In many religions the adulthood occurs at puberty, around the age of 12. Novels like Orson Scott Card's "Ender" series and Neal Stephenson's "Snow Crash"[3] are only recent exemplars of the abilities and capabilities of youth to contribute substantively to their community. Have we deliberately delayed the ability of humans to fully develop at a rate and path that takes into account the entire human potential? Has a Western (Dickensian) vision created and perpetuated a system that may have become self serving? Has time been a discounted or undervalued commodity being usurped by the Academy?

Humans may have four score years on this planet. Modern science may extend this in the developed world or strive to reach this in the lesser developed world. Given the ubiquitousness and increasing accessibility of knowledge, is it a wise decision to measure out our lives in coffee spoons over the first quarter or half of our existence? What religious or cultural ritual is being perpetuated by an "industry" which, up till now has had a market monopoly, the strength of which is only rivaled by religion?

Will the Web browser, nailed to the door of the Academy, have the same consequences that Martin Luther's parchment had on the Catholic Church? The conventional wisdom would believe that the Net levels space and brings peers together. Perhaps, more profoundly, the Net will cross generational lines in a knowledge world. Will youth understand the cost that is being extracted from them to gain entry to the "adult" world? What will be the role of the Academy in a nonlinear, time/generation-sensitive, world?

SPACE AS COST

> "Life is a pattern in space/time."
> —*Doyne Farmer*

A major corporation liquidated its real estate assets and leased needed space. It reasoned that if the business could make the same or more money by owning property that it should be in the property management/development business and not manufacturing. This did not mean that the business did not want a quality environment, but simply that to provide for its own business focus, it was more cost effective to invest in what they did best. Why can't the Academy follow these practices? What is worth the investment in this "sunk" capital? This does not call the question of "Old Main"; rather it asks about effective use of capital assets and the effective use of physical space with the rise of knowledge distribution in virtual space.

At different times, intellectual communities have flourished. The artistic and literary communities in Paris, Greenwich Village in New York, and Haight Ashbury in California serve as examples. On the other hand, we now have cyber communities such as "The Well" and the myriad of listservs, newsgroups, and chat areas on the Internet. Many of these have sensibilities similar to those found in face-to-face relationships on traditional campuses.

It is interesting to note that one university with a distance education program is finding that a large percentage of its on-campus students are also, simultaneously, registering for virtual classes too. When one considers that the cost for living on a campus can equal or exceed the cost of tuition and books, one can ask what is being provided for the differential costs of a campus experience. Similarly, even living "at home" and commuting to a physical space raises the question of why we bring the "many to one."

When the Academy has such a significant investment in these sunk costs, there is a proclivity to want to preserve this value. When a significant portion of the budget and administrative overhead is dedicated to support this infrastructure, the commitment can be even stronger. When the value, like assets in a vault, becomes quotidian, does this not call the raison d'être?

An academic dean at a major research university said that he could not start to build change in his organization until he got the faculty to understand that the institution did not exist for them. Could a visit to a university campus be akin to visiting a historic site complete with actors in costume, a combination between Lewis Carroll's "Mad Hatter's Tea Party" and T. S. Eliot's "J. Alfred Prufrock"?

CERTIFICATION

> "Freedom consists in the impossibility of knowing actions that still lie in the future."
>
> —*Philip Kerr*

Certification provides both a carrot and a stick. In some states in the United States, students in K–12 institutions are required to pass standardized "competency" examinations and demonstrate mastery via preapproved evaluations. In other words, the "State" has determined that external, third party, evaluations are needed because the self-certifying institutions have failed to validate the competencies of their own graduates.

Many distance-learning institutions are also going to third-party testing at the postsecondary level. And, some recognized academic institutions are entering the certification field to provide independent validation of an individual's skills. In essence, with the exception of certain prestige or "medallion" institutions, the Academy has lost a major vehicle of control whether for on-campus or electronic-campus programs. If recognized third-party evaluators exist, for what does one pay the Academy?

Many new providers of postsecondary education have appeared. These are licensed and approved via the same procedures that traditional institutions use for validation. Many of these have adopted novel formats and vehicles that can "deliver" knowledge in a more time- and cost-effective manner. New formats, different learning approaches, and methodologies allow for both increased knowledge building and accelerated certification. While being called into question by conventional wisdom, these same techniques are now being adopted by some members of the established Academy. Additionally, the same faculty, which resides in the Academy, also provide services to the nontraditional institutions. And, the Academy is also starting to look toward independent evaluators.

Where is, or will be, the difference between K–12 and grades 13–16? We are now seeing text and Web-based materials that are usable at either the 9–12 or the 13–16 levels. Does this evoke a nonlinear model for certification where learners, regardless of age and level, move between these artificial barriers seamlessly. Does this raise the same question at the grades 6–8/9–12 interface, opening up the entire system for movement by students based on ability and not seat time? If so, does external certification call the question of both the sequential nature of the education system (the metering of knowledge in time-based units) and the rationing of knowledge?

With the Web, is the physical institution now transparent? With independent certification, is not competence the key rather than a commitment to time and space? With the Web, why pay for a college education? More importantly, with the certification shifts, globally, do we see new intergenerational time bridges rather than the traditional interconnected "spatial weavings." What price has the Academy extracted from the community?

The reincarnation of distance education in its "body electronic" provides the critical vehicle for understanding. For, on the Web, wisdom and knowledge are not sorted by age. "Young" becomes a relevant term and creativity and ability are the levelers. Gender, race, and similar cultural biasing can be effectively masked under pseudonyms. Title, rank, and positions of authority are sapiential and not structural in nature. What distinguishes the University?

Herein we have a seminal issue, particularly in the age-neutral situation. The position held by knowledge or ability is usually short half-life in nature. Computer programming, edge hardware, and technology are usually the purview of youth, Douglas Rushkoff's "screenagers."[4] Or it exists within the domains of specialists.

LONG HALF-LIFE KNOWLEDGE

As Readings cogently shows:

[T]he link between the University and the nation–state no longer holds in an era of globalization. The University thus shifts from being an ideological apparatus of the nation–state to being a relatively independent bureaucratic system. The economics of globalization mean that the University is no longer called upon to train citizen subjects, while the politics of the end of the Cold War mean that the University is no longer called upon to uphold national prestige by producing and legitimating national culture. The University is thus analogous to a number of other institutions that face massive reductions in foreseeable funding from increasingly weakened states, which are no longer the privileged sites of investment of the popular will.[5]

In other words, as the world changed, the Universities, in lock-step reaction, dropped their core or essence and entered the highly competitive "short-term knowledge" marketplace. Admittedly, in the United States the lure of substantive research funding has been and is an attractor at the graduate and research levels. But this shift, globally, left the core of the Academy trying to steer between the Scylla of research and the Charybdis of the "ivy covered" Great Books. Unfortunately, the Academy has struck the rocks, and is now in the undifferentiated free marketplace of ideas.

Requires Wisdom

"I feel wise indeed. When I get used to my brain I shall know everything."
—*The Scarecrow in Frank Baum's Wizard of Oz*

The ability to synthesize these capabilities across disciplines and programs requires long half-life knowledge, usually attained with age and experience. This is the "wisdom" that older generations impart to the younger. This has been the strength of the Academy whether in the ashrams of the East, the monasteries of the West, or the halls of the University. And it is here that the Academy must return to regain its hegemony.

And Critical Thinking

"But I did discover one philosophical author who appeared to me to square the circle between lucid irrelevance and relevant incomprehensibility."
—*D. H. Mellor*

Business, government, and institutions find short half-life knowledge critical in their daily operation. But each individual organization has very specific needs and uses this information in its own manner. This is volatile information. Engineering schools are sensitive to this volatility because it is claimed that the half-life of this technical knowledge is four years. Thus, even at a university, engineering students' knowledge base is eroding at an alarming pace. One might feel much like a cross between Lewis Carroll's Red Queen and the Walt Disney version of Paul Dukas' Sorcerer's Apprentice.

What we find is that the world outside of academia finds ways to maintain its cutting-edge competencies. If it doesn't, then competition will drive the organization out of business or into irrelevance. This holds for government, the science and social sciences, and any cross-discipline where knowledge is growing at a rapid rate.

Earl Shorris, in an article in *Harpers* and his book, *New American Blues*,[6] discusses his work with the socially and economically disenfranchised. His findings and experience are, in many ways counterintuitive. Where "school-to-work" programs emphasize basic job skills, he has concluded that the fundamental need is training in philosophy. People who have the basic skills to analyze, think critically, and articulate their concerns are able to both determine what their basic needs are and to successfully "sit at the table" and negotiate to have those needs met.

The advantage of an appropriate college degree is the skill sets needed to function in a wider community. These are the basics of reading, writing, and mathematics as a foundation and the cross-cultural understanding one obtains from a liberal education, including complex "negotiation" skills. In essence, these are long half-life knowledge skills.

Shorris found what many savvy recruiters have tried to articulate. If a graduate has a strong liberal studies background, the corporation can provide the specialized knowledge. Those with firm skills in these areas move toward management while those with greater technical training usually follow a path closer to the professional practice.

The question has been called. In reality, the question should be expanded to ask, "What is a college education?" or "What is the role of the university in today's world and the world of the future?

What IS a University?

Postsecondary institutions have not struggled with these hard questions. These include, but are not limited to

- What is the relationship between the institution and the faculty? Issues of tenure, unions, research, and teaching are dynamic issues that are changing in the world of today and the world of the future.
- What is the relationship between the student and the institution? This becomes critical when one considers that students have only a short tenure in a space that may have over a century or several centuries of existence and may go on for several more.
- Who has a "say"? Even in private institutions, lines of authority and policy are not clear. And, in publicly funded institutions, the issues are more complex.

Systems mathematicians have labeled their analysis of postsecondary institutions as a "garbage can" model because of its kaleidescoping complexity. What is becoming clear is that the discomfort that is being felt is one associated with emergent change. And there is a sense that this turbulence is not a short rapids from one calm in the river to the next calm. Change is the norm rather than the exception. The safe haven for students and faculty called the academic institution, whether physical or virtual, does not exist.

Joseph Tainter has written succinctly about the collapse of complex societies from an anthropological perspective,[7] while George Land's seminal work, *Grow or Die*,[8] approaches these transformations from a biological metaphor. Both of these writers provide an excellent insight as to the turmoil we are seeing in the Academy today. But the best analysis was carried out by Sir John Daniel, when he used Michael Porter's "theory of competitive advantage."[9] In a sense Porter's characteristics are more retrospective. They are etiological. When a person erupts with the chicken pox, the little poxes are symptoms of a disease that has infected the body for some time previously. Treating the poxes is more palliative than curative.

In the case of the Academy, all the symptoms of the "corruption" are present in Porter's lexicon: the rise of competition from both within and without and even across specific institutional departments, the threat of substitute products and services, the rise of new entrants, and the increased bargaining power of buyers. The future is just a story we tell ourselves about the present. While many at the administrative levels have been aware of this, from the chief financial officer to the admissions office, the faculty seem to have been oblivious. Like Rip Van Winkle, they have awakened, only to find their sinecure threatened. In the history of the rise of the Academy, scholars have gone from a long period where they had to sell their services on the steps of the libraries at Alexandria to an environment where Alma Mater essentially provided "jobs for life." The medieval Castle which protected the citizens, for only a short time, has fallen. This has been further discussed by Skolnik in Chapter 5 in this volume.

The ululation's of the faculty heard outside the walls become a weak marketing program in an increasingly competitive world. The cries heard inside the walls are that of a group that has abrogated their responsibility to participate in the "business" of the institution. A chancellor took unilateral action to restructure a program at a major university. When questioned as to why he essentially violated what was the prerogative of the faculty senate, he calmly replied that when the faculty was ready to take the power, he would give it to them.

In the business world, the struggle of the worker has been to have more participation in decision and directions of the business. We have seen examples of this decision sharing from the open-book management of corporations such as Johnsonville Meats to the joint partnership of union and management as seen with the General Motors' Saturn plant. The Academy, the bastion of liberal and social thought, is the only industry where the workers have essentially given up their power to participate in the operations of the institution.

"Why pay?" is not a question for those who must write checks. Rather it is the critical issue with which the Academy must grapple. The Academy has lost its hegemony with the same surety that the American automobile industry lost its global position. In responding to this challenge, it will be transformed. There will be costs and benefits at many levels and in many directions. The free marketplace of ideas will adjust to the competition in, as yet, uncertain ways. When the Academy, from the chairman of the board to the groundskeeper in physical or cyberspace, can answer the question, the Academy will know the answer.

WHITHER THE ACADEMY

"It is not every truth that sounds as sweet as a bird song, not every discovery that is welcomed among the occult, not every light that is approved from within the shadows."

—Philip Kerr

Information, once diffuse and ephemeral, was captured in libraries that eventually became the core and heart of the University. The wired world has allowed the knowledge to become diffuse again, yet more available. The core dissolves and the scholars can, with greater ease, access this knowledge and engage in collegial exchanges even while physically dispersed.

We have learned that moving of individuals is very expensive in both time and fiscal resources. Information moves before people. Industry has found that it is more efficient to lease rather than own real estate. Interestingly, some academic institutions have found that leasing campuses of bits and bytes can be more beneficial than owning virtual space. What is in its "nature" that makes the overhead burden of the traditional campus worth the cost of ownership?

At the present time, many institutions are providing education in off-campus settings in office parks, corporate offices, and a variety of temporary buildings. Often institutions offer programs across the country in buildings near other major institutions. Why do students and/or faculty want to "go to" a campus?

Those universities that survive the next three decades will be profoundly different. Some will successfully build on their heritage and have campuses which look and feel traditional. Others will choose to sell "Old Main," develop a large portion of their campus for nonacademic purposes and move, in part, to cyberspaces and temporary physical facilities. New uses for the traditional campus will be created.

Simultaneously, some institutions will define their academic programs in a traditional manner. St. John's University in New Mexico and Harvard University in Massachusetts may serve as paradigmatic examples. Others will seek alternative paths including joint ventures with other institutions, creative linkages with corporations, and even local K–12 systems. Many of these are visible even today.

Academia has, traditionally, prided itself on its almost inarticulable culture with a de facto constructive anarchy between the faculty, administration, and student body, when it comes to governance. This dynamic tension will dissolve in all but a select segment of the Academy unless faculty begin to comprehend that to maintain their "academic freedom" they must participate in the changes now occurring. The psychologist Fritz Perls is thought to have said that once a person gives up his/her "No," it is most difficult to get it back.

The largest, unanswered question is whether the faculty have the will and/or the ability to constructively engage with this issue. Many have capitulated to traditional unions while some have chosen course ownership in the distance learning arena as a Maginot Line. Each will suffer the same fate of the original Line in France. We will see a split in faculty into two arenas, research and teaching (with overlap). But within these divisions there will be the equivalent of "super stars" with the majority playing supporting and complementary roles. There will be more faculty with appointments split between public/private sector practices and the Academy.

Eli Noam in a speech before the Educom97 convention predicted the demise of scholarly publications.[10] This complements the trend in faculty rolls where fewer, but larger research groups will come into existence and those faculty who are primarily teaching will not have the pressure to publish for promotion and tenure. Thus, we will be seeing more strategic liaisons among academic institutions at all levels and more creative arrangements between the Academy and the public and private sector institutions, globally. The Global Alliance for Transnational Education is coordinating an effort to establish international standards.

If international standards are, indeed established, this means that academic programs will be universally interchangeable for credit purposes. What this will mean for unique cultural issues in each country is yet uncertain and what it will mean for academics, internationally, who have prided themselves on uniqueness, is unknown also. But more importantly, for those institutions who are funded by governments, particularly in developing countries, one must wonder about courses that impact on both culturally and politically sensitive issues, not just in the humanities and social sciences, but in all disciplines.

As Readings, Richard Lanham,[11] Daniel, and others have cogently pointed out, the Academy, globally, is in many ways rudderless in two dimensions—form and function—within disciplines and across the institution. What it has to offer will determine why one should pay.

A savvy business person said that he reinvented his corporation every month. The board would put up two columns on a piece of paper. On one side they would list what businesses they were in and on the other side, they would list those businesses they were not in. The hardest task was filling in the second column. It is this task, particularly with attention to the second column, that will allow the Academy to find the answer to the opening question.

NOTES

1. Bill Readings, *The University in Ruins* (Cambridge, MA: Harvard University Press, 1996), 2.

2. Octavia Butler, *The Parable of the Sower* (New York: Warner Books, 1995).

3. N. Stephenson, *Snow Crash* (New York: Bantam Books, 1992).

4. Douglas Rushkoff, *Playing the Future* (Harper Collins, New York, 1996), 3.

5. Readings, *The University in Ruins*, 14.

6. Earl Shorris, *New American Blues* (New York: W. W. Norton and Company, 1997), Earl Shorris, "In the Hands of the Restless Poor," *Harpers Magazine* (September 1997): 50–59.

7. Joseph A. Tainter, *The Collapse of Complex Societies* (Cambridge: Cambridge University Press, 1988).

8. George T. Ainsworth-Land, *Grow or Die* (New York: John Wiley and Sons, 1986).

9. John S. Daniel, *Megauniversities and Knowledge Media* (London: Kogan Page, 1996).

10. Eli Noam, *Opening General Session, Educom97* (Minneapolis, MN) (Washington, DC: Educom, Inc., 1997).

11. Richard A. Lanham, *The Electronic Word: Democracy, Technology and the Arts* (Chicago: University of Chicago Press, 1993).

8

Of Minds, Markets, and Machines: How Universities Might Transcend the Ideology of Commodification

——————— *David Rooney and Greg Hearn*

> On a recent business trip a man asked me what I did for a living. I replied that
> I wrote and taught college courses.
> "Oh?" he said. "Where do you teach?"
> A peculiarly honest answer came out of my mouth before I could think:
> "Nowhere," I said.
> For want of a clearer explanation of my career situation, I told the man who
> inquired that I teach in cyberspace. "I'm a virtual professor."
> The man's face remained as blank as a clear summer sky. I couldn't tell
> whether he was silent out of respect or keen confusion. I imagined both to be
> the case, so I settled in to explain what I have to explain frequently these days:
> the decline of the American college campus and the rise of the American edu-
> cational mind—as I see it.[1]

The future of universities can be posited from an analysis of the three most obvious ingredients that appear destined to be in that future—minds, markets, and
machines. The characteristics of each of these suggest certain principles that will
be implicated in any model of university functionality (but of course, whilst the
characteristics of each may be, in theory, quintessential, the understanding of
these characteristics is, in fact, clearly ideological). Our analysis attempts to deal
with essentialist characteristics as well as ideological understandings. In doing
so, we treat the issues in the order of our title, that is, minds, markets, and
machines. We deconstruct the ideology behind the current widespread attempts to
commodify the outputs of universities and argue for alternative futures based on
a more accurate analysis of the essential characteristics of universities.

We argue that markets and technology have privileged a certain ideological view of higher education that is rooted in neoclassical economics and assumptions more suited to the industrial era. A postindustrial economy requires a new view of economics, which places great emphasis on the intellectual capital input into creating value. This necessarily requires challenging the orthodoxy of crude market-forces models in favor of more sophisticated and relevant models of organization for production, and in particular for the production of knowledge.

MINDS

If in a postindustrial society, the intellect has emerged as an increasingly important economic factor, the need to know what is going on in the minds of students and lecturers must also increase. But what do we know about minds and what does this imply for our argument? What conditions lead to the most fruitful deployment of minds? There are three relevant and well substantiated premises we can draw from the discipline of psychology.

- There is substantial variation in the processes by which minds do their work. Note the variation is not just in the information contained in minds but in the way in which they process information. Moreover, the creation of new knowledge is often a product of juxtapositions of different minds.
- A mind's productive capability is highly dependent on the nature of the reinforcement it receives from its environment. The evidence suggests that minds function in different ways, depending on whether they are engaged instrumentally (that is, in activities that are means to ends) or intrinsically (that is, in activities that are ends in themselves). Intrinsic engagement is an essential component of knowledge creation.
- Minds do not exist in isolation from other minds and to at least some extent they are communicatively constructed. Therefore, the notion of individuals, or the compartmentalization of knowledge in individuals, is problematic. That is, knowledge and knowledge creation is inherently a social process.

Recent analyses of "knowledge" emphasize its diverse and socially constructed nature from economic and organizational perspectives.[2] As a result, scholars have been able to examine the conditions that best enable knowledge production and in doing so have been able to determine that the economic characteristics of knowledge are different to the economic characteristics of manufactured goods. Unfortunately, the economic models, which have informed the more recent transformation of higher education in countries like Australia, have been based on the assumption that the old economics of industrial production (manufacturing) apply to the university.

Because of a predominant emphasis on economic orthodoxy in contemporary policy discussions, the university is destined to be poorly understood and mismanaged. This situation arises because of the blindness of orthodox (industrial) economics to knowledge in general and, in particular, to tacit knowledge—wisdom, judgment, beliefs, and the ability to meaningfully process information. The difficulty of dealing with tacit knowledge in arguments based on market-forces models is that they require things to be commodified by being embedded in physical objects (computers, books, blueprints, etc.) to make them easily reproducible, storable, and transmittable, thus making them more readily marketable. However, an ideology of commodification is simply inappropriate in an environment where knowledge, and in particular tacit knowledge, are the hard currencies.

Additionally, the mechanistic models of orthodox economics, which assumes predictable economic trajectories, also betray a fetish for certainty. Yet, uncertainty is a key characteristic of knowledge creation and knowledge itself. The risk attached to knowledge creation is largely because knowledge production and transfer is a human activity and thus a nonlinear process. The risk attached to existing knowledge is that although it may at one moment be a justified belief, at a later moment it may be found to be unjustified. Furthermore, the meaning of any knowledge artifact has to be interpreted and each interpreter will have different characteristics that can lead to different interpretations. This being the case, economic models which rely on certainty, perfect information, perfect knowledge and so on, are intrinsically inappropriate. Furthermore, unless it were possible to remove people from knowledge activities, risk could never be eliminated. Of course, people cannot be removed from these activities because without human agency knowledge could not exist—in fact, knowledge only exists in relation to our ability to interpret or understand its meanings, and to our ability to hold beliefs based on these meanings. In the university there must be students and there must be teachers engaged in activities of uncertain outcomes.

Industrial economics is also based on assumptions about the exchange of goods from one person to another: that is, the process by which possession (or ownership) of goods changes. However, the exchange of knowledge does not require the "vendor" to give up any knowledge. The result is that our inventory of knowledge will not be depleted by giving it away or selling it. Therefore, the stocks of knowledge in the university are not exhausted by the transfer of knowledge to students, regardless of the number of students. This underlines the importance of facilitating exchanges (or conversations), by, for example, making access to the university as wide as possible and removing blockages (knowledge monopolies and oligopolies through, for example, patents) of access to university knowledge. However, although the inventory will not deplete it may depreciate (become obsolete) if new knowledge is not continually added to it.

Fortunately, the exchange of knowledge creates new knowledge. Exchanges between the university, students, and the community are, therefore, essential to the existence of the university. Because the exchange is focused on the student–teacher dialogue some of the cost of creating new knowledge is born by the student without additional monetary expense to the student. These conversations are a cost-effective way for governments to generate knowledge and that means these conversations are of paramount economic and social importance. Furthermore, because the social value of knowledge increases through dissemination the increase in value is also won without additional monetary cost to society. We see here a very good investment for the university, the student and the community because each is earning increasing returns to the use of knowledge. That is, each new "bit" of knowledge costs less to create than the last one. This provides incentives, and implies considerable mutual advantages, for the joint sharing of knowledge between students, the community and the university. In this case, we can say that the cost of producing knowledge is, therefore, independent of the scale on which it is used—an invaluable phenomenon that is lost on orthodox economics. Once again, the need for openness is highlighted, but so too, it gives the scale or level of saturation of learning and knowledge creation importance. As well, scope for growth in student numbers needs to be increased by facilitating lifelong-learning and by the university extending further into the community by breaking its fortress-like institutional restrictions. These are continuous processes, in which the value of knowledge is amplified indefinitely and synergistically by adding new knowledge to existing knowledge, and by diffusing knowledge.

We can infer from this section that the analysis of the mind and the economic dimensions of knowledge should lead us to privilege certain kinds of behavior such as

- Openness about and enthusiasm for the timely disclosure of knowledge
- Cooperative modes of knowledge production and diffusion
- Learning relationships and knowledge investment based on trust
- Diversity of minds
- Democratic values in relation to creating and diffusing knowledge

We have indicated here that there is a mismatch between the economic characteristics of knowledge and the economics of industrial production, but how badly do the behavioral characteristics encouraged by orthodox economics actively discourage the effective operation of the knowledge enterprise?

MARKETS

If we strip away the neoliberal assumptions of neoclassical economics we expose a machinery of power that is hostile to a knowledge economy generally and to the sensible operation of the higher education system. Neoclassical economics tends to focus on achieving things such as

- Individual competitiveness
- Reducing uncertainty
- Efficiency
- Command/control, top/down models of authority
- Adversarial economic relationships

If we quickly examine the behavioral consequences of these characteristics, it will be evident that an alternative and more relevant economic model of higher education is necessary.

Individualism and the economically rational (self-centered) person is a cornerstone of orthodox economics. This starting point can bring little to the concerns we have about knowledge: within neoclassical economics there is little acknowledgment of the place of cooperative behavior, trust, and openness. Reducing uncertainty arises as a prime concern of orthodox economics. This is troubling because it does not account for the inherent unpredictability of people and human systems. It is more concerned with the structures than the actors to whom it denies the freedom of noneconomic rationality (efficiency rather than effectiveness in value creation is emphasized). Doing something for its own sake is incompatible with a narrow cost/benefit focus on linear "input => process =>output => bottom line" models where there is a fixed, predictable proportionality between input and output. The fact that learning is often a circuitous process makes it difficult to deal with under such a scenario. Command/control, top/down authority imposed through a hierarchy, derived from the owners of the means of production cannot envisage partnerships of university, student, and community in an open, democratic, and trusting spirit which mediates the learning process.

Thus, the sterile information flows of market models cannot work when rich, nuanced, mediating conversations between community, student, and university are needed. As well, command/control models take no account of the fact that tacit knowledge cannot be owned by an institutional entity; tacit knowledge resides within people. Adversarial economic relationships, or perfect (utopian) competition through markets similarly deny noneconomic rationality, cooperative behavior, trust, openness, etc.[3] At best, the ideology of commodification betrays a naive, adolescent understanding of control, power, and competition.

But what is the future of a university system subjected to this kind of economics? Survival of the "fittest" means the survival of the few who are selected for not engaging in knowledge-friendly behavior and for supporting the status quo. The continued rise of the multinational university, the demise of the local and regional university, and the contraction of disciplines like philosophy and literature are symptoms of this neo-Darwinism. Furthermore, a scan of the World Wide Web will quickly provide a clutch of M.B.A.s and other fee-based degrees offered by U.S. and British universities, which involve little, if any, face-to-face contact between students and lecturers, and appear to expect very little from students' in terms of research and analytical skills—all the answers are provided in study packs, folios, prepared books of required readings, and so on. This scenario is not simply one of deliberately reduced choice, it is also one that exposes the loss of capacity to change (lost diversity and dissent) and the loss of one of the management holy grails—quality.

Eroding diversity and quality in higher education leads to equity issues as well. However, the emerging oligopoly is also likely to promote rising higher education costs and thus, a further reduction in accessibility. Access, quality, and diversity all appear to be suffering because of the ways that markets operate when imposed on an environment that is unsuited to commodification. By foregoing mutual benefit and obligation for mutual antagonism and exploitation, and misunderstanding the role of cooperation, we hinder the growth and worthwhile use of knowledge.

It is important to note that much of what neoliberals espouse has come to be adopted by managers. This kind of management, or managerialism, is subservient to the same neoliberal ideology. One example of the attempt to translate industrial rationalization to education is the concept of Total Quality Management (TQM), which has been applied extensively over the last decade in Australian universities.[4] TQM is based on the language of commodification. It concerns itself with improving the quality of product as determined by customer satisfaction.[5] However, such an approach may be dangerous when applied to the core business of universities—learning. As we have argued, education depends on students' willingness to participate with teachers, rather than dictate to them.

Furthermore, it is difficult to determine exactly what the product (or service) is, what "quality" means in relation to it, who the real end consumers of education are, and which of their understandings of "satisfaction" is most important. Most importantly for our argument, TQM is about eliminating "error" (variation), yet variation (diversity) should be an objective and a sign of success rather than failure in universities. As well, TQM focuses on measurables rather than qualities, seeks to reduce costs (negative feedback rather than positive feedback), and it is more customer led (market-forces). Such a concept splits research from development with the danger that it will discourage system-wide curiosity, risk taking, and innovation. While it promotes innovation in the production process it tends to be less effective at creating new products. TQM, when applied to knowledge production, is flawed because it conceptualizes a linear process of learning, rather than a dynamic and unpredictable process, which involves learning, unlearning, and relearning. The implications of these tendencies have considerable negative impact on the vision of university managers and make it difficult for them to appreciate a noncommodity view of higher education.

Another manifestation of neoliberal ideology in management is the ever expanding deployment of information technology (IT) in tertiary education. Here machines—often perceived as the embodiment of efficiency, certainty, and rationality—represent the third force shaping the future of the university.

MACHINES

In the last decade technological innovations have emerged as a fundamental ingredient in the future of universities, not the least for their association with the implementation of market-forces strategies. However, the convergence of information technologies and telecommunications have important implications for universities because information and communication are central to the pursuit of knowledge. We seek to isolate the essential roles of IT in learning rather than in markets. These new technologies affect[6]

- Speed, flexibility, and cost of information and materials transfer between university and student.
- Expansion of Internet connectivity due to Network Computers (NCs) and WebTV, and the anticipated increase in access to on-line education.

• Client demand: Number of students who actively seek courses that they can complete via their Web browser, and for whom this is the most attractive mode of study (for example, adult full-time workers updating skills) are likely to increase.

Although there are significant problems with distributed learning at the tertiary level, it is appealing to academics to be able to integrate their own information delivery and student interaction with libraries and access to up-to-the-minute sources of specific and relevant information. Foreign students in a business language course can have a hyperlink to banks or to Stock Exchanges built into their notes. Medical students can access detailed human anatomies unavailable at their own universities. Virtual learning spaces like the IBM Courseroom permit functions previously not possible or much more difficult, such as the ordered recording of all contributions to a discussion in text, audio, and video form simultaneously.

Of course, limitations to the high-tech scenario can also be identified. Perhaps the primary inhibitor to rapid preparation by universities for global, open competition in electronic environments is their 1000-year-old culture, discussed by Spies in Chapter 2. Having changed little during that time, the academics now in the best positions to lead change are in many instances also those most interested in heritage-preservation and avoiding change.[7] The lecture still holds pride of place in universities as a teaching strategy. Of course, the distance education model, which has had a respected place in Australian education because of the tyranny of distance, has also opened a chink in the traditional pedagogy of Australia. Even among academics who accept the need to package education as a product or service, the restriction or elimination of face-to-face and vocal teaching methods that accompanies digital distance classes is a monumental change.

It is tempting to see the technological and cultural drivers identified in this book as unstoppable and coercive forces forging the universities of the future. Clearly, as Neubauer and Skolnik have shown elsewhere in this volume, technological development brings with it the interests of those who invest in its development[8] (that is, the large and powerful companies who are targeting the global education sector for commodification). As well, it is often deployed according to ideological dictates, such as, in this case, the perceived wisdom of commodifying the tertiary sector completely. However, the main lesson from Australian universities is that these macro forces are not unstoppable. Students themselves appear not to be playing out the roles fantasized for them by the architects of the Australian visions. Once again, it is shown that the deployment of technology is often frustrated by users who (according to local social needs or their own cultural understanding) may redefine, subvert, or resist its use altogether.[9]

Clearly then, technology evolves in the context of political, economic, and cultural forces, any of which may predominate to shape a technology's final appropriation.[10] Technological change can, therefore, be a window of opportunity for social change (though not a sole determinant). Technological change disrupts social patterns and perhaps the balance of power, and it is at this point that those who wish to reconstitute the social fabric have their greatest opportunity to do so. But the key question is, how?

The keys here are fourfold, namely, belief, choice, education, and participation. Belief is preeminent because our beliefs about technology and the future will either motivate or discourage us from doing anything about either. For example, the dangers of both the technological determinist and traditionalist views of technologies reside in their single-dimensional approach to the problem. The technological determinist perspective ignores economic, cultural, and political dimensions of new technologies, resulting in failed investments in unused products, as well as perpetuating social inequalities in access to and degradation of innovative and diverse knowledge. On the other hand, traditionalists run the risk of allowing their ideology to prevent the recognition of opportunity. Unless we have an understanding of the socially constructed nature of future technologies we will not take the steps involved in appropriating them to serve rather than coerce.

Choice is the next principle that must be observed. Choice manifests itself in many ways—including the options that are hardwired into new technologies, the way access to these technologies is facilitated, and the choice of software options provided. It also includes the geographical location of the terminals themselves and even what we choose to call them. Without personal choices in relation to these technologies users feel controlled by them rather than vice versa. Budgets for new technologies must include an allocation for education about the technology—not just its use.

Education for the universities of the future should begin in high schools but also should be part of the curricula of universities themselves. Thus, universities should, for example, be engaged in self reflection about their needs for and use of technology. At issue here is the pedagogical case for having technology: how well does it relate to the educational values and strategies of the university, and to the very nature of knowledge itself? Similarly, students need to be challenged to stop learning and reflect on how they are learning. Continuous "data mining," for example, should not be seen as an end in itself. Students, too, must have space for sense-making and to creatively apply their learning.

Finally, all this implies participation in the decisions that are made at all levels regarding new technologies. Participation takes many forms, including, of course, the traditional forums that are well recognized in the democratic process. However, it also must include local participation at the point where technologies enter the lives of people. Having the appropriate processes in place to allow people to reflect on the role and usage of these technologies in their lives is often neglected in their diffusion. Yet the evidence suggests they are critical to effective appropriation.

THREE SCENARIOS FOR THE UNIVERSITY
OF THE FUTURE

Our analysis of minds, markets and machines suggests multiple scenarios for the future of universities. Multiple scenarios imply, of course, that many outcomes are in fact possible. Here we sketch three possible futures of the university, namely: (1) the do-nothing scenario; (2) the commodified university; and (3) the on-line learning community. We then elaborate an argument for the third scenario as our preferred alternative.

The Do-Nothing Scenario

José Ortega y Gasset, the great Spanish philosopher, predicted before World War II the depredation of civilization that would be perpetrated by trained experts, narrowly focused technologists and specialized "new barbarians." The world was soon to see, as he had warned, "how brutal, how stupid, and yet how aggressive is the man learned in one thing and fundamentally ignorant in all else."[11]

Many universities will embrace this scenario and choose to let the momentum of history and the uncertainty of the future determine their strategy. The do-nothing scenario will see either only minimal investment in information and communication technologies or will seek to graft these technologies onto existing modes of operating. That is, the basic forms and structures of the university will not change and the desire will be to force fit the technology into the existing university structure. Technology, therefore, is used to shore up existing structures rather than to bring about change and adaptation. Although in some niche areas this could be a successful strategy, such universities will need to emphasize traditional modes of education to be successful. More likely, they will face enormous pressure from resourcing problems in competing with other universities, who will either embark on a mass on-line selling, as in scenario two, or an on-line community approach, as in scenario three.

The Commodified University

A middle-aged computer programmer was proud of his work. "Do you know all of those middle managers who were laid off during the early 1990s through downsizing?," he asks (and this is my paraphrase of his words from memory). "Well, I did that. Technology that I worked on made it possible for organizations to expand managers' span of control and thus reduce the number of layers in the hierarchy." Those middle managers were redundant, and he was proud to have put them on the street. His next target, he told me, is college professors.

He figures that a suitable cost for four years of college education is something on the order of $60. . . . He was alluding to the economics of the software industry, and of information generally. Nathan Myhrvold says that with personal computers you get $100 million worth of software. Lest this phenomenon seem remarkable, we are already familiar with it at the movies, where we think nothing of, as in the case of "Titanic," getting $200 million worth of movie for $7. A college education in a box, distributed to hundreds of millions of people worldwide, could cost billions to produce and still turn a profit, at the cost of putting the great majority of now-redundant professors on the street.[12]

Under this scenario the university uses the technology that is available to move more toward a commodified model of knowledge distribution. Inflexible packaged programs are developed to be delivered electronically. The technology is used to control and monitor delivery and there is a drive to capitalize on economies of scale in the preparing and delivering of material. Technology is used to routinize learning and economies of scale result in reducing the diversity and quality of knowledge-forms and content. Under this scenario, teaching staff will be laid off or casualized and technology will be used to replace preparation and delivery, and in some cases assessment of learning. Although it will be sold as being vocationally relevant the emphasis will be on codified knowledge, which is easily packaged in an on-line environment. The creation of new knowledge will be stifled because of the risks and costs involved in doing new things, which may upset the customer. Research driven teaching, for example, will become problematic.

The On-line Learning Community

Can people learn without sitting in neat rows in a lecture room listening to the professor—a.k.a. the Sage on the Stage? Yes, absolutely . . . [I] find it hard to imagine teaching anywhere other than in the liberal freedom that is cyberspace.

In cyberspace, I listen, read, comment, and reflect on what my students have to say—each of them in turn. What they know, they must communicate to me in words. They cannot sit passively in the back row twiddling their mental thumbs as the clock ticks away. . . . Thinking and writing: Aren't these the hallmarks of a classically educated mind? The virtual university: Oddly enough, it's just what a classical philosopher like Plato would have practiced—had there been an Internet way back when.[13]

Under this scenario the university invests wisely in technology. The technology is used to connect and increase the diversity of knowledge through networks. The role of the teacher changes to incorporate mentoring activities, and learning itself becomes more self directed. Under this scenario intellectual curiosity and vocational aspirations are developed hand-in-hand. There is a heavier public investment in maintaining the diversity of knowledge by maintaining the diversity of intellectual foci of the university and by blurring the boundary between the university and the community. This also implies that the university loses some of it monopoly status on sanctioning knowledge, insofar as it begins to share the tasks of teaching and learning with a broader community effort. Whilst new technologies are embraced, a heavy emphasis on face-to-face communication is also retained. The form of face-to-face communication is creatively considered to include more emphasis on a variety of individual and group learning contexts. Under this scenario the technology is used to connect, transform, and extend rather than to control.

Implicit in these three scenarios is a recognition of different types of knowledge, namely: know-how (learning based on applied knowledge), know-who (wisdom in knowledge networks), know-what (ability to access bodies of appropriate [mostly codified] knowledge) and know-why (abstract—critical and analytical—skills). In the commodified university model, the emphasis is on know-what knowledge because on-line delivery is biased toward the easy commodification of codified knowledge. However, with the on-line community model, because of the diversity of processes involved attention can be given to stimulating all four forms of knowledge development. In fact, this scenario implicitly recognizes that substantive knowledge is the most rapidly changing form of knowledge and, therefore, the emphasis is on

- Networks of learners to address know-who
- A variety of learning processes to address know-how
- Diversity of knowledge to address know-why thus enabling critical/analytical skills
- Improvement in information systems to distribute codified knowledge to know-what entities

The following table summarizes the three scenarios and how universities might engage each of the four types of knowledge.

Knowledge and Learning Typology

	Scenario 1	*Scenario 2*	*Scenario 3*
Know-how	Depending on tradition, a limited emphasis on practical competencies, and not very future focused.	Unlikely, too labor intensive—cannot be done by machines.	Engendered through variety in pedagogy and learning-by-doing.
Know-why	Possibly strong critical & analytical—depending on the disciplinary base (traditional or vocational).	Unlikely. Requires reflection.	Analysis and critique through traditional forms, mentor relationships, and on-line discussion.
Know-what	Possibly strong descriptive knowledge. Based on focused library searching in relation to a particular problem.	Codified, prepackaged knowledge.	Codified knowledge, transmission and searching for particular problems, and curiosity led.
Know-who	Limited networks and skills developed in know-who. Academics as gatekeepers to knowledge networks.	Limited to proprietary networks. Technology as gatekeeper to knowledge networks.	Emphasis on dynamic networks of learners engenders strong "know-who" competence.

PIPE DREAMS OF IDEOLOGUES

The future of the university can only be planned for if we are in possession of a realistic view of how a knowledge economy works and what kinds of behaviors we need to encourage. First, we need to understand the need for openness about, and disclosure of, knowledge; cooperative modes of knowledge production and diffusion; learning relationships based on trust; knowledge investment based on appropriate acceptance of risk; conversation; diversity; and democratic values in relation to the creation and diffusion of knowledge. Having come upon these understandings, we realize that utopian visions of easy market mechanisms piping commodified packets of information and knowledge through vast networks of computers do not equate with the complex interrelationships and the many other social realities of the environment we inhabit. Indeed, the neoliberal ideology is seen to be anti-knowledge and its tendency to encourage substituting technology for people mitigates against the essentials of a knowledge environment. These are the pipe dreams of ideologues who have not bothered to look out the window and see a changing world.

NOTES

1. Vicky Phillips, "Education in the Ether," *Salon 21st*
http://www.salonmagazine.com/21st/feature/1998/01/20feature.html
2. See for example, W. Brian Arthur, "Increasing Returns and the New World of Business," *Harvard Business Review* (July–August 1996): 100–9; and Robert Babe, *Communication and the Transformation of Economics: Essays in Information, Public Policy, and Political Economy* (Boulder: Westview Press, 1995).
3. David Rooney and Thomas Mandeville, "The Knowing Nation: A Framework For Public Policy in a Post-Industrial Knowledge Economy," *Prometheus* 16, 4 (1998).
4. This section draws on Greg Hearn and David Scott, "Students Staying at Home: Questioning the Wisdom of a Digital Future for Australian Universities," *Futures* 30, 7 (1998). Also see W. Beaver, "Is TQM Appropriate for the Classroom?" *College Teaching* (1994): 111–14; Robert Cornesky, Samuel McCool, Larry Byrnes, and Robert Weber, *Implementing Total Quality Management in Higher Education* (Madison, WI: Magna, 1992); and James L. Fischer, "TQM: A Warning for Higher Education," *Educational Record* (1993): 15–19.
5. See Ricky W. Griffin, *Management* (5th Edition) (Boston: Houghton Mifflin Company, 1996), 637–641; and Lloyd Dobyns and Clare Crawford-Mason, *Thinking about Quality: Progress, Wisdom and the Deming Philosophy* (New York: Times Books, 1994).
6. Hearn and Scott, op cit.
7. Allan Guskin, "Facing the Future: The Change Process in Restructuring Universities," *Change* (Jul/Aug 1996): 18.
8. See discussions in Russell Spears and Martin Lea, "Panacea or panopticon? The Hidden Power in Computer-Mediated Communication," *Communication Research* 21, 4, (Aug. 1994): 427–59; Peter Shields and Rohan Samarajiva, "Competing Frameworks for Research on Information—Communication Technologies and Society: Toward a Synthesis," *Communication Yearbook* 16 (1992); and Rohan Samarajiva and Peter Shields,

"Emergent Institutions of the 'Intelligent Network': Toward a Theoretical Understanding," *Media, Culture & Society* 14 (1992): 397–419.

9. Greg Hearn, Thomas Mandeville, and David Anthony, *The Communication Superhighway: Social and Economic Change in the Digital Age* (St. Leonards: Allen and Unwin, 1998).

10. William J. Kinsella, "Communication and Information Technologies: A Dialectical Model of Technology and Human Agency," *New Jersey Journal of Communication* 1, 1 (1993): 2–18; and Peter Shields and Rohan Samarajiva, "Competing Frameworks for Research on Information—Communication Technologies and Society: Toward a Synthesis," *Communication Yearbook*, op cit.: 349–80.

11. Ken Ashworth, "Virtual Universities Could Only Produce Virtual Learning," http://www.free-press.com/journals/gajal/articles/gajal-article-o40.htm—Ashworth is the Commissioner of the Texas Higher Education Co-ordinating Board.

12. Phil Agre, *The Distances of Education: Defining the Role of Information Technology in the University*. Revised text of a speech at California State University, Fullerton, August, 1998. http://www.egroups.com/list/rre/889.html

13. Vicky Phillips, "Education in the Ether," *Salon21st* http://www.salonmagazine.com/21st/feature/1998/01/20feature.html, 18.

9

At the Edge of Knowledge: Toward Polyphonic Multiversities

Paul Wildman

Why are our "universities floating above the general disorder of mankind like a beautiful sunset over a battlefield?" H. G. Wells asked poignantly as early as the 1930s.[1] Indeed, since World War II our education systems in general, and universities in particular, have done little more than credential the status quo by being primarily knowledge control vehicles for the dominant orthodoxy as it marches into the eco-battlefields of tomorrow. Even worse, the world seems ever more chaotic and less and less organized. In this sense, the idea of polyphonic multiversities seems ideally well suited.

SEVEN KEY EMERGING ISSUES FOR FUTURE UNIVERSITIES

These are key issues that are influencing the course of development of the polyphonic multiversity over the next 30 years.

The Emergent Knowledge Economy

The emergent education pedagogy maintains that once learners have acquired a foundational knowledge architecture, learning is most valued when it is just-in-time, rather than just in case. The new information technologies, with their capacity to support simulations, action learning, and discovery-based problem solving, enable learning to be more highly customized to the individual learner, and to support greater degrees of contextualization than that which characterized traditional lecture/classroom-based learning.

In the knowledge economy, where data and information are the raw material, value-adding will require higher order thinking skills, not only to convert information to knowledge, with all its inherent problems of bounded systems in particular disciplines or institutional frameworks. It will also require capabilities that enable the conversion of "fact and figures" knowledge into "symbolical" knowledge of

- Insight (patterns of interconnected meaning)
- Hindsight (seeing patterns in the past that can point to our future possibilities)
- Foresight (emergent patterns shaping the future)
- Wisdom (holistic awareness, built on the above three, linked to appropriate action)

Thus future competitive advantage may well flow from a capacity to increase our ability to embrace the development of learning from data and information to knowledge, insight, and wisdom—from facts and figures to imagination.

Globalization

The globalization of the economy and the convergence of technologies has placed a premium on learning and knowledge management as the major basis of competitive advantage, whether at the level of the individual, the organization, or the nation. Newly industrializing nations such as Malaysia and China are investing heavily in education, albeit of the facts and figures type, to match the skills advantage that has traditionally been enjoyed by the OECD nations.

Firms are investing in management consultants to help them become learning organizations, while individuals are investing in lifelong learning to keep abreast of new developments in knowledge and technology in their professional fields, or to re-skill to take advantage of new opportunities and avoid technological redundancy in the marketplace.

So the globalization imperative needs to take account of local potentialities and needs as well. This suggests a concept like 'glocal,' that is, simultaneously locally relevant and building from the local to the global while recognizing global emerging issues and experiences elsewhere.

Community Capability

The multiversity is ideally suited to contribute to, and learn from, community efforts toward sustainable development. In this sense "polyversities" can become praxis centers for facilitating innovation on the ground in community economic development and institutional foresight.[2] Presently universities are repositories of thinking rather than doing in the classic dichotomy. Doing is seen as vocational and thinking as real, so praxis tends to get left behind and nowhere more so than in relationships between a university and its community. These relationships tend to be one-way (students to university) rather than a two-way capability building process.

Pedagogy of Alternatives

In all this the university system seems to be lagging far behind not only in the information technology stakes but critically in the pedagogy stakes—chalk and talk dies hard. As an example, in the Byron Bay coastal resort area of Australia at any weekend there are upward of 200 workshops and alternative learning experiences underway all outside the conventional university/government system. Existing political and bureaucratic systems and institutions may be considered irrelevant to many young people today, while initiatives such as 'subversity,' are offering a positive attractor.[3]

The Post-Market Economy—an Emerging North/South Divide

The wholesale substitution of machines for workers is going to compel nations to rethink the role of human beings in social and learning processes. Redefining learning opportunities and responsibilities for millions of people in a "post-job" society largely absent of mass formal employment is likely to be the single most pressing social issue of the coming century. For the whole of the modern era, a person's worth has been measured by the market value of their labor. Now that the commodity value of human labor is becoming increasingly tangential and irrelevant in an ever more automated world, new ways of defining human worth and social relationships will need to be explored.

Referring to this process as the third industrial revolution, Rifkin suggests that without this redefinition, the net effect of the information and communications technologies and global market forces will be the polarization of the world's population into two irreconcilable and potentially warring forces.[4] On one hand, the new cosmopolitan elite of "symbolic analysts" who control the technologies and the forces of production, and on the other, the growing number of permanently displaced workers who have little hope and even fewer prospects for meaningful employment in the new high-tech global economy.

This process can, in part, trigger the rising levels of crime, violence, and imprisonment, for instance, in the United States. While displaced poor whites have retreated to armed vigilantism combined with a growing hostility to their government, poor blacks find themselves trapped in inner city ghettos and criminal subcultures. The third world is no longer "over there." For instance, in Washington, the capital city of the richest and most technologically powerful nation on Earth, 40 percent of the black men are either in prison, in court, or on the run.[5]

Fragmented Futures

What has become frightening in my futures research is the "broken-openness" and fragmented nature of the world today, especially for our youth, as many of yesterday's "certainties" are now "shards." Today, the world is more like a holographic reproduction of a broken vase than the original. When working in this environment, one never really knows when one is working with a holographic piece of the whole that will "fall/holo off" in your hand. Indeed much media representation is via the ubiquitous broken off 30-second sensational "video bite," with any serious ongoing review of the issues glossed over.

Field research into futures perceptions of street kids has supported this sense of gut-wrenching angst and meaninglessness.[6] The future is seen as alien, unknowable, and unknown. In a horrifying sense, educational systems seem unable even to recognize this issue. All predicate and legitimate their pedagogy on the empirical epistem of science. Such a view generates a tacit way of knowing that seems to betray all "within system" attempts to find alternative education and learning systems.

So many of us find ourselves inhabiting interstice futurescapes as intersections of multiple, contradictory, overlapping futures not reducible to "one" particular paradigm. Perhaps it is these shards that lead to the "cracks" in the world that Leonard Cohen sees in his song, The Future, as a necessity for the paradigm to shift.

New Renaissance

Universities have, in my opinion, become part of the "new barbarism" of narrowing of rational inquiry to evidential empirical ways of knowing. Clearly we see the results in the world around us today from social to environmental system warping. Ken Wilber clearly establishes that intuition, theatre, dreams, introspection, imagination (symbolic logic), even passion were all part of broader rationality that existed at the beginning of the Enlightenment in the early 1700s. Little of this grand panorama now exists—only detritus.[7] The western world needs a "new renaissance" to cycle back to the original understanding of rationality and then cycle forward to our children's learning and education—our future generations.

TOWARD A FUTURES ACTIVE LEARNING SYSTEM

In this section we try to get a picture of what a "futures active learning system" may look like. The emergence of such systems is in many ways blocked by present academic debris and hubris. Clearly if future universities are to reach beyond this reactionary inertia they will have to actively contribute to ways society can envision itself 30 to 50 years in the future. Critically, almost all of our energies today are directed toward discovering our ancestors rather than seeking to proactively involve our forecestors in foresighting their and our futures. Business, government, community, and learning systems seem incapable of reaching beyond the present. Intriguingly some business and spiritual systems seem more able to do this than universities. Richard Slaughter calls for Institutions of Foresight (IOFs) to be formed to redress this lack of futures focus.[8] In addition, other "futures active" ways of making meaning include web learning, subversive or system challenging options, and some corporate alternatives.

Web Learning

Through the WWW, learning for foresight will become more a process of student exploration, and the university's role as one of brokering knowledge will emerge. Brokering is used in a broad sense to include:

- Brokering courses from several sources and packaging them for a specific student's needs
- Codeveloping student learning projects and contracts
- Helping students navigate their chosen learning path
- Acting as a critical/creactive friend and providing peer and net support
- Engaging in co-generative learning and joint publishing
- Establishing strategic alliances between learning institutions, industry, and community organizations
- Piloting innovations such as sustainable communities, information networks, industry innovations, and so on, that action the creactive edge of the IOF
- Establishing Future Watch (or watching briefs), as systems of helping society keep track of emerging issues some 20, 30, and 50 years on, while strategic planning takes us only 10 years into the future.

In Australia the now moribund Commission for the Future could have provided this role. Presently there are essentially no such institutions, and futures studies remain the province of the enthusiastic few. Such an IOF role seems crucial if this thing called University is to have any significant social change meaning in Australia post 2000.

Subversity

A group in rural Australia, of which I am a member, is seeking to develop an "off-grid" futureversity, realizing that many people today see the "off-grid" nature of much of our future. We see our market as backpackers and youth growing up in and then moving away from alternative communities. There are around 200 such intentional communities in the region (Northern New South Wales) with an estimated 20,000 people and 6,500 youth. Today, most youth leave the communities in their late teens, seeking an "alternative to the alternative," yet often not being suited to "fitting into" mainstream society either.

The concept being developed is called a *subversity*, recognizing that most cutting-edge research is now done outside universities that have tended to degenerate to "credentialing the status quo." Accreditation is deliberately not being sought, and in addition, the concept will provide an alternative to "sage on stage" lecturing on the one hand, and Web-based nonpersonal "hyper learning" on the other. Learning processes will combine workshops using theatre and bush settings sprinkled with Socratic dialogue in an attempt to embrace the original Enlightenment vision of rationality. Subversity will combine a living-learning experience with several key issues: activism to change the system, inner knowledge and cultural empowerment all bound together with a "Global Citizens Charter," which in turn is embedded in "planetary consciousness," even spirituality.

These options really are at the edge and require people who are not only dreamers but also have resources and a methodical ability to implement such options.

Corporate Options

Another option is to look for learning structures that are already international. Some corporate universities offer practical examples of such structures. Generally, though, they tend to remain within the system and see their role (uncritically) as riding the wave of globalization.

An example of the corporate option is the International Management Center (IMC) now recognized worldwide through various accreditations. Now, in some 16 countries worldwide, the IMC originally derived from the United Kingdom and specializes in management education using action learning. Starting in the early 1960s as a reaction to established management learning processes that were essentially classroom based and separated thinking from doing, IMC today is recognized as a global specialist in management education using action learning. It is supported by MCB University press, a large academic publisher with a strong Web presence. Presently IMC is piloting environmental and futures courses.

Additional Pointers from the Periphery of Knowledge

A futures active (and sensitive) learning system will also seek to

- Be holistic in that it embraces math and myth, data and dreams, dissection and dance, that is, a broader understanding of "rational," including and beyond empiricism.[9]
- Be transdisciplinary and include gnosis and relatio as well as techne, scientia, and praxis.[10]
- Develop ways of brokering learning, such as strategic alliances between industry and other universities, navigating the Web, student-oriented degree structures and so on. For example, through interactive CD-ROMs that take the classroom to the student, students can speak with other students and lecturers anywhere in the world.[11]
- Articulate to a post-job economy and a social system undergoing rapid change— shards.[12]
- Help universities become action learning institutions themselves and to deal with the end of the metanarrative and increasing fragmentation.
- Help learners learn the ability to think and act creatively (even creactively) in ways that help generate their own futures narrative and reduce feelings of meaninglessness.
- Move universities toward becoming Institutions of Foresight that undertake actions to demonstrate this commitment and in particular relate this to their local communities.
- Incorporate indigenous and multicivilizational perspectives.
- Give voice to future generations.[14]
- Incorporate an esoteric component in learning.

RECONSTRUCTING TRUTH

This article has argued that the current university system is not able to cope in many ways with the changes even now upon it. So much of its energy is absorbed within its bureaucracy and bricks and mortar. Consequently the transition to polyphonic multiversities must not be seen as an inevitable, or final, step. The argument was advanced that we need to look beyond the status quo to the periphery, for innovative and effective ways of knowing that can work toward resolving these dilemmas. This will mean reconstructing truth and its constituent facts and figures toward seeing the "math/myth" balance as crucial to meaning making. It is such an approach to knowledge that recognizes the "edge" (or knowledge periphery) as crucial to the learning process, that can help us move from monophonic universities to embrace the idea of polyphonic multiversities.

NOTES

1. H. G. Wells, *"World Brain" H. G. Wells on the Future of World Education* (first published in 1938), (London: Adamantine Press, 1994).

2. Jennifer Gidley and Paul Wildman, eds., "Community Economic Development," *New Renaissance* 7, 4 (1994).

3. Paul Wildman and Sohail Inayatullah, "Ways of Knowing, Culture, Communication and the Pedagogies of the Future," *Futures* 28, 8 (1996): 723–40.

4. Jeremy Rifkin, *The End of Work: The Decline of the Global Labor Force and the Dawn of the Post-Market Era* (New York: Tarcher/Putnam, 1995).

5. Barbara Lepani, "Designing Education and City Futures for the 21st Century," in *LETA Conference*, 29th September–4th October (Adelaide: 1996).

6. Jennifer Gidley and Paul Wildman, "What Are We Missing?—A Review of the Educational and Vocational Interests of Marginalized Rural Youth," *Education in Rural Australia Journal* 6, 2 (1996): 9–19.

7. Ken Wilber, *Sex, Ecology, Spirituality: The Spirit of Evolution* (Boston: Shambhala, 1995).

8. Richard Slaughter, "The Foresight Principle," *Futures* (October 1990): 801–19; Richard Slaughter, "Toward an Agenda for Institutions of Foresight," *Futures* 27, 1 (1995): 91–95.

9. Jennifer Gidley, "Prospective Youth Visions through Imaginative Education," *Futures* 30, 5 (1998).

10. Wildman and Inayatullah, "Ways of Knowing . . ."

11. Sohail Inayatullah and Paul Wildman, *Futures Studies: Methods, Emerging Issues and Civilizational Visions* (Brisbane: Prosperity Press, 1998).

12. Paul Wildman "From the Monophonic University to Polyphonic Multiversities," *Futures* 30, 7 (1998).

13. Allen Tough, "What Future Generations Need from Us," *Futures* (December 1993): 1041–49.

Part 2

Nonwestern Perspectives on the Futures of the University

10

Recovery of Indigenous Knowledge and Dissenting Futures of the University

——————————————— *Ashis Nandy*

DEFINE OR BE DEFINED

The old, clichéd saying, "knowledge is power," has acquired a new potency in recent years. For nearly a century it was fashionable to study how interests and material forces of history shaped knowledge. The world that has come into being in the aftermath of World War II seems to have reversed the relationship. It has forced us to recognize that dominance is now exercised less and less through familiar organized interests, such as class relations, colonialism, military-industrial complexes, multinational corporations, and the nation–states. Dominance is now exercised mainly through categories, embedded in systems of knowledge.

Categories now break old worlds and build new ones, and they are doing so with increasing ease. Today, television, videocassettes, movies, electronic mail, and newspapers can bring down the most formidable of regimes or sustain the most unsustainable movements by vending categories and, in the process, entire ways of life and worldviews. The war cry of our times is now: "define or be defined." Definitions have in the last few decades turned at least two billion human beings to seeing themselves as underdeveloped, not merely economically, but also culturally and educationally. And all around us the battle of categories is turning neighbors into strangers or feared monsters and strangers into uneasy next-door neighbors—so that characters in Hollywood potboilers and television soap operas can enter households in Shanghai and Bombay as familiar guests. It has sometimes made children dedicated enemies of all that their parents have stood for throughout life; it has converted communities that have lived with each other for centuries into sworn enemies whose lives, religions, rituals, and marriages are not complete without each other. In Bosnia, 30 percent of Bosnian

Muslim families are said to have Serb relatives through marriage. That has not ensured them any protection against ethnic hatred; they and their "enemies" are both armed to the teeth with categories that have wiped out their pasts.

Universities have come to share this new power, for they specialize in handling categories. In many societies, they have even begun to hegemonize the politics of categories, depending upon the accord between the intellectual and the academic. The intellectual and the academic never fully overlap, but they are never fully orthogonal either. In the 1950s and 1960s, French intellectual life was dominated by a few highly creative intellectuals who did not teach in universities but were only taught there. In the United States these days, the situation is just the reverse. It is difficult to find an influential intellectual who does not bear the imprint of a university. In such conditions, universities may even come to dominate a society's self-reflexivity.

In much of Asia and Africa, on the other hand, the concept of "public intellectuals" until now is a trivialization of the role played by thinkers from outside the academe, who have not merely influenced public opinion, but led religious and social reform movements, initiated political campaigns including anti-imperialist struggles, and fought for the oppressed and the marginalized within their societies. These intellectuals have often included persons who have emerged from the interstices of the society, steeped in traditional knowledge and sensitivities. They have linked the cultural resources of their society, especially the heritage of vernacular knowledge, to contemporary politics and social needs. That tradition of intellectual life has not allowed the Western-style universities to dominate intellectual life. Writers, artists, traditional scholars, and religious leaders have a different kind of role in at least the older Asian and African societies. That role is now shrinking; the intellectuals are increasingly being redefined as academics and looked upon as specialists and troubleshooters. This has further consolidated the power of universities as producers and depositories of specialists, experts, or professionals.

Not that universities were ever strangers to power. As institutions of higher learning, they could not but have a special relationship with the state and the élite. Their new power, however, is of a different kind. It directly influences economic decisions, security policies, and even what we eat, how we bring up our children, or behave in bed. It is taking over every area of life, paradoxically, often by denying the autonomy of the individual in societies fanatically committed to individualism. The recent triumph of global capitalism has encouraged us to think of the universities as another variety of corporate structure with a distinctive style of self-management and research and development. Many universities, too, have tried to redefine themselves to conform to this popular image. As more and more areas of life are "scientized" and taken out of the reach of participatory politics to be handed over to experts, the universities as the final depository of expertise have become a major global political actor of our times. In addition to their other tasks, they legitimize the "expertization" of public affairs and the reign of the professionals.

This dual role of the universities only confirms that, contrary to the fears of conservative politicians, skepticism is not natural to universities. It is imposed on them, usually by the outside world, but often by that part of the intellectual community that refuses to accept the self-declared pace-setting role of the academe. A number of examples can be given. Up until the 1970s, many North American and European universities had investment portfolios that reflected South African interests and corporations having strong South African connections. They did not seem particularly embarrassed about them, until public opinion began to change. British and French universities took almost one hundred years to take a position on imperialism, and many American universities only a little less to become serious critics of slavery, racist biology, and social evolutionism. I am not mentioning the record of the universities in the Third Reich only because it is all too well known.

This is not always a product of political timidity and naiveté, or of the various romantic versions of radicalism and conservatism that periodically invade the citadels of learning. For the record of universities is often no better in areas that politics and public policy enter only indirectly. Nearly all influential basic criticisms of the urban-industrial vision during the last one hundred and fifty years have come from outside the universities.[1] The first serious critiques of modern medicines also came from outside the universities in the nineteenth century; in this century, the critiques have been led by the likes of Ivan Illich.[2] The universities have mainly reacted to these critiques and, only then, slowly began to move toward a more serious, nuanced response. Likewise, the philosophy and practice of ecology as a discipline has been predominantly a "non-academic" one.[3] Recent attempts to convert environmentalism into a proper university discipline can even be read as an attempt to tame environmentalism from the point of view of the established political centers of knowledge. In this sense, the universities have not always been even good, alert mouthpieces of the establishment, anticipating major developments in the politics of knowledge. Some aspects of university-based socialist thought, offering radical criticisms of the capitalist worldview and political economy, may look like an exception, but that is probably because such socialism never included a frontal attack on urban-industrialism and Baconian science.

TAMING TRADITIONAL KNOWLEDGE SYSTEMS

Yet universities are a fact of life, even in the backwaters of Asia, Africa, and Latin America. A large proportion of nonwestern intellectuals have been educated in universities and their children and grandchildren, too, are likely to be educated the same way. They will have to cope with Western-style universities as an unavoidable intellectual and political presence that shapes human futures. The most they can hope for is that the universities will shape their futures in dialogue with other traditions of knowledge they have trivialized or helped marginalize.

Fortunately, while universities themselves willingly take on certain roles given their social location, other roles are thrust on them. Their changing profile of students, for instance, can dramatically alter their intellectual and moral concerns. Sometimes universities, even if unwittingly, may be forced to be self-reflexive on behalf of society. At such times, they begin to act not as mere depositories of knowledge and expertise acceptable to the ultimate centers of contemporary scholarship—the famous universities in the Western world—as valid, universal or true; they begin to act as sources of skepticism toward the victorious systems of knowledge, and as the means of recovering and transmitting knowledge that has been cornered, marginalized, or even defeated. They even occasionally come to admit that, in a world in which dominance is exercised through categories, knowledge systems can sometimes be defeated not because they are false or useless, but because their carriers have been defeated or lost cultural self-confidence.

But even when forced to take on such a role, the colonial legacy handicaps the nonwestern universities. Not only in the matter of the indigenous, the vernacular or the local, but even insofar as their own versions of the modern, the exogenous, and the universal go. Their self-hatred is reminiscent of Mark Twain's much-used aphorism—that he did not want to join an organization that would be low-brow enough to admit him. Few Asian universities will like to belong to a new order of knowledge that takes them seriously.[4] In many cases, they have already begun to interpret the growing sensitivity to the dying little cultures of the world as a passing fad and begin to use subterfuges that would allow them to project a politically correct image, while allowing them to do business as usual.

Three of the more popular and, at the same time, sophisticated subterfuges are

- Openness to traditional systems of knowledge, combined with a cost-benefit analysis that decontextualizes the systems entirely and fits them into the existing institutionalized structure of commonsense on pragmatic grounds;
- Acceptance of a cultural relativism that sees every culture as having its ethnic versions of knowledge (ethnoscience, ethnomedicine, ethnomusicology), while at the same time holding the modern systems to be universal and transcultural, so that the former can be partly neutralized as an object of scholarly inquiry and expertise of the latter;
- Emphasis on equitable, just distribution of "universal" epistemic and technical knowledge in the expectation that such redistributive justice will redeem the alienating, oppressive aspects of some systems of modern knowledge and to divert the criticisms of the contents of these systems to their contexts, specifically to the control exercised over them by organized vested interests.

Today, each of these three technologies is both a developed science and a popular art.

As a result, the last thing that academic self-definition will take into account is that universities could be, in the words of Alistair Pennycook, "a key site of struggle, where local knowledge meets global knowledge in a battle to represent different worlds in different ways," because "how we view universities around the world, and their relationships with each other, clearly depends fundamentally on how we understand culture, knowledge, education, and international relations."[5] The very openness of nonwestern universities to Western disciplines and Western classification of knowledge, therefore, has a double meaning. There may not be barriers in receiving disciplines across cultures but, for that very reason, philosophies of knowledge travel less well across cultures.[6]

PROTECTING LOCAL KNOWLEDGE

In the middle of the 1990s, we no longer have to make a case for traditional or indigenous systems of knowledge. For example, no one assumes, a priori, that traditional Chinese and Indian medicines are worthless. Even the multinational pharmaceutical companies seem to be in a desperate hurry these days to study, reorder, or reclassify traditional medical systems for their own purposes and to draw some alkaloids here or active principles there from the medicinal herbs and other constituents of local medical systems of the world—presumably to patent them and make them a part and parcel of the modern pharmacopoeia. This recovery of traditions does not grant them any intrinsic dignity; it is motivated by greed and guided by the principles of instrumentalism. Yet, in the context of the growing crisis of confidence in the dominant system of modern medicine, it has made a large number of people aware that the diagnoses and cures their grandparents swore by were perhaps not the comic superstitions and atavism they were made out to be. Likewise, the environmental movement in the 1970s and 1980s has reestablished links, sometimes spectacularly, with traditional agronomy, water management, forestry, and even, indigenous technologies of protest.[7]

However, it is doubtful if universities in the nonwestern world would take up the responsibility of protecting knowledge that has become unfashionable, politically weak, and seemingly of no immediate practical significance. I cannot share the optimism of Hassan Gardezi in this respect.[8] Yet, I do recognize that things could have been otherwise in the tropics. Universities here, established in the nineteenth century and mostly modeled on the European universities, do not carry the cultural baggage of their models. There are exceptions like Alhajar, but in most cases Asian and African universities have not grown out of indigenous traditions of university; they have emerged as a consequence of colonial intrusion and then, self-consciously and sometimes defensively, established links with some of the older traditions of higher learning. Nalanda and Takshashila (Taxila) might have been thriving universities until the decline of Buddhism in India in an early medieval period, but for the modern Indians comfortable with modern universities, they are primarily rediscovered symbols of cultural nationalism, forged in the 1920s and 1930s.[9] Their relevance even as symbols of anti-imperialism has naturally declined after independence.

Nonetheless, theoretically and even practically, it should be possible for nonwestern universities to break with their colonial past and renegotiate their self-definition. Surely it must not be that difficult—for those claiming to study the real world—to acknowledge that things have changed in one important respect. At one time, traditional systems of knowledge looked safe, at least in the peripheries of the world; they had the allegiance of a majority of the people, if not of the westernizing élite. (Even today, according to some estimates, more than two-thirds of all South Asians go to traditional healers; I do not think the figure is lower in China.) However, though they are still being used by a minority, the modern systems of knowledge are now triumphant. They have won the battle of categories decisively. No five-year development plan in China or India cares to spend more than a page or two on nonmodern systems of knowledge, and that too, they do more as a compromise with nationalist sentiments or as a ritual that cannot be avoided, than as a serious enterprise. The situation is no different in countries said to be proudly Islamic. Even in predominantly traditional societies, few hydrologists are interested in what the natives think about their grand irrigation projects and mega-dams; health planners depend almost entirely on modern medicine; and agricultural innovations are not introduced in consultation with farmers. Certainly no state in the Third World sheds a drop of tear that the politics of knowledge have broken the back of the traditional systems of knowledge.

Under these new circumstances, Southern universities that seek to set pace in higher learning may be persuaded to perform a dual role. No one can stop them from continuing to transmit in a capsuled or packaged form what they believe to be universal modern knowledge, which has grown up with almost total contempt for its non-modern cultures of knowledge, and thus caters to the demand of the westernizing élite and the state. However, they may begin to transmit this knowledge with a certain critical awareness and skepticism. Perhaps more even than criticism and skepticism, the future universities may be forced to cultivate a sense of limit.

The sense of omnipotence and omniscience that Western-style universities have acquired in the nonwestern world is not a product of the secularization of knowledge in the West (which has led citizens to associate the omnipotence and omniscience once imputed to a divinity, with science laboratories and factories). Whatever omnipotence and omniscience one sees in the nonwestern universities is a direct product of their concept of modern knowledge, especially modern science, as a new marker of traditional social status and, hence, partly magical. It is painful for those who have shared the modern university's concept of the post-Enlightenment, time-and-space-and-time-free, universal knowledge that, like all other forms of human knowledge, it is neither free from human greed nor uncontaminated by sectional interests. It is not much of a space within which indigenous knowledge can flourish but, then, such knowledge has adjusted during the last one hundred years or so to such humiliating existence and its practitioners have learned to survive at the margins of our consciousness.

Now that the back of the traditional systems have been broken, the universities in the South may have to develop a new openness, generosity, and protectiveness toward nonmodern, local systems of knowledge. These systems are obviously the ones that need protection now.

RECOVERY AND AFFIRMATION

Finally, three simple propositions seem to be in order: First, if the recovery of indigenous knowledge involves the affirmation of one's cultural self, that affirmation is no longer easy. The natural is no longer available naturally. It has to be recovered. Such self-conscious recovery of the self may not be alien to universities, but will the universities make that effort when modern knowledge is available to them in a ready-made, capsuled form? On the other hand, the tense, reactive self-affirmation that is entering the public sphere in many societies— a belated reaction to the humiliation and self-abnegation of the last hundred years of searching pathologically, and sometimes pathetically, for the culturally pure and uncontaminated—is threatening to dismantle the very freedoms and cultural self-confidence that protected dissenting xueyvans and traditional universities like Nalanda. The question is: can such self-consciousness ever be truly creative?

A decade ago, some welfare agencies in India took out advertisements in Indian newspapers to declare that human mother's milk was best for human babies. As in other parts of the world, in the Indian middle classes, too, breastfeeding was going out of fashion. Now, I did not expect to see the day when Indians would have to be told this profound truth. But obviously, times have changed; the obvious has to be sold today like any other trendy commodity. High-pitched advertisements, the pseudosciences of many multinational corporations (we have all heard of how Nestle, for instance, used to dress their salespersons as nurses when selling baby food in Africa and Asia, and stopped doing so only when activists through law courts interceded), and mega-consumerism has already, in many cases, done its job. And in generating that global climate of dependency on the manmade and the professionally sanctioned, the universities have contributed handsomely. At least some universities may now like to own up to their record and share the responsibility of undoing the damage.

Second, in owning up to their colonial legacy, universities in the Southern world will also have to acknowledge that their imperial presence in Southern societies is not the same as the élitism and commitment to "high culture" of many older, First World universities. That imperiousness comes from a different stratarchy of cultures—from an institutionalized ideology which values the universal, Western knowledge systems as definitionally superior to other forms of knowledge and which believes that the Enlightenment vision of a desirable society and reliable, valid knowledge must have priority over all alternative formulations. They have attributed to this borrowed vision magical qualities previously associated with shamans, astrologers, Brahmins, Fa shuens. Unfortunately for them, that dream of the purveyors of modern knowledge systems in nonmodern societies has remained unfulfilled, though it has come tantalizingly close to fulfillment. The cussedness of the ordinary citizens stands in their way. This only sharpens the imperiousness and hostility toward the recalcitrant multitudes who "unthinkingly" continue to go to traditional healers, architects, and astrologers.

As a consequence, universities in the Third World usually better the Western universities in their fear of any philosophy of knowledge that speaks of cultural uniqueness and basic cultural differences in the goals and modes of acquiring knowledge. Many university-based scholars nervously remember that, despite their closeness to the state and the ruling élite, modern universities established in many Asian and African countries in the 19th century were forced to enter (during the anti-imperial struggle) a dialogue—however distorted or partial—between the knowledge acquired over centuries and over generations by a community and the more elegantly packaged, apparently universal, now increasingly experimental, laboratory-based knowledge.[10] True, in this dialogue, the former were often the object of inquiry of the latter and almost always set up to lose. When modern Asians and Africans talk of syncretism, or of a synthesis of the best in the East and the West, it is this predictable form of dialogue between two unequal participants they have in mind. But some communication was there. In some nonwestern societies, this communication was considered politically prudent; it was seen as a technique of survival in an environment hostile to a modern university. Even that partial dialogue has now broken down. Reestablishment of even that flawed dialogue requires a confidence in the ordinary citizens who have been carriers of, and have often kept alive, local knowledge, defying the contempt of their university-educated compatriots.

Third, there is a need for a new consensus that it is not the job or responsibility of a center for higher learning to produce a "New Man" at the behest of a state, a party, or on behalf of economic planners and development experts. It is already obvious that much human misery during the last 150 years has come from attempts to engineer human nature. (I have in mind not merely the engineered industrial man the socialist utopias vended but also the retooled Indians and Chinese a majority of social reformers and thinkers pined for in place of the messy, disorganized, and embarrassingly unpredictable masses of Indians and Chinese.) The universities in the Southern world have sometimes joined politicians, policymakers, and ideologues in this enterprise. Did the modernization of indigenous cultures and the dependence of their universities on nineteenth-century European utopias steal these cultures' concepts of their own futures during the war of categories that took place in colonial times?

PLURALIZING KNOWLEDGE

The main responsibility of a university is to pluralize the future by pluralizing knowledge in the present. This they can do only by producing a better, more honest, and wider range of options—material, ideational, and normative—for human beings and societies to choose from.

If this occurs, then universities in the future will come back to offer such a range of choices for future generations of indigenous people and, for that matter, the rest of the world—for no strain of vernacular knowledge is entirely local. Every scrap of local knowledge is not only a global heritage; it is an alternative form of universal knowledge seeking recognition and, if I may add, justice from the world of knowledge. Above all, it is seeking justice from the very communities that have disowned it in the first place. The entire world will have much to gain from universities that draw from the uniqueness of indigenous cultures, as reflected in the rich diversity of their culturally embedded knowledge systems.

NOTES

1. For example, Martin Green, *Prophets of a New Age: The Politics of Hope From the Eighteenth Through the Twenty-First Centuries* (New York: Charles Scribner, 1992).

2. See, for instance, Frédérique Apffel Marglin, "Smallpox in Two Systems of Knowledge," and Ashis Nandy and Shiv Visvanathan, "Modern Medicine and its Non-modern Critics," in *Dominating Knowledge: Development, Culture and Resistance*, Frédérique Apffel Marglin and Stephen A. Marglin, eds., (Oxford: Clarendon Press, 1990): 102–44, 145–84.

3. For instance, Andrew Dobson, *Green Political Thought: An Introduction* (London: Unwin Hyman, 1990).

4. Crudely speaking, in West Europe and North America, more than half of all people die of cardiovascular diseases, about one-third from various kinds of cancer, and between 5 to 7 percent from accidents. If you add them up, you will see that less than 5 percent die of other causes in those countries. In South Asia, more than four-fifths die of waterborne diseases, which are classified as "other causes," in the West. Yet, a South Asian who graduates from a Western university, having almost no experience in treating the kind of patients he confronts in his home country, is often more respected in South Asia than a doctor trained in South Asia. I am sure that the situation is not dramatically different in East and South-East Asia, Africa, and South America.

5. Alistair Pennycook, "English, Universities and Struggles over Culture and Knowledge," in Ruth Hayhoe and Julia Pan, *East-West Dialogue in Knowledge and Higher Education* (New York: M. E. Sharpe, 1996): 64–82.

6. Cf. Ian Winchester, "Cultural Differences and the Reception of University Disciplines," Hayhoe and Pan, *East-West Dialogue* . . . : 17–25.

7. Some random examples are Seyyed Hossein Nasr, *Western Science and Asian Culture* (New Delhi: Indian Council for Cultural Relations, 1976); Vandana Shiva, *Staying Alive: Women, Ecology and Development* (New Delhi: Kali for Women, 1988); Lokayan Bulletin, Special Issue on the Naramda Dam, 1991, 9, 3/4; Vandana Shiva, ed., *Biodiversity Conservation: Whose Resource? Whose Knowledge?* (New Delhi: Indian National Trust for Art and Cultural Heritage, 1994); Frédérique Apffel Marglin, ed., *Who Will Save the Forests*, forthcoming; Wolfgang Sachs, ed., *Global Ecology: A New Arena of Political Conflict* (London: Zed Books, 1993); Ziauddin Sardar, ed., *The Touch of Midas: Science, Values and Environment in Islam and the West* (Selangor, Malaysia, Pelanduk, 1988).

8. Hassan Gardezi, "ŒSufi Cosmology: An Indigenous Oral Tradition," Hayhoe and Julia Pan, *East-West Dialogue* . . .

9. For a clue to this process of rediscovery of the traditional university in India, see Patrick Geddes, *The Life and Works of Sir Jagadish C. Bose* (London: Longmans, 1920). Also, Ashis Nandy, *Alternative Sciences: Creativity and Authenticity in Two Indian Scientists* (New Delhi: Oxford University Press, 1995), 2nd ed.

10. Experiments such as Rabindranath Tagore's Vishwabharati, which the poet tried to institutionalize as an alternative university in colonial India, and M. K. Gandhi's "buniyadi talim" or basic education, which Gandhi saw as an alternative to the university system, are examples that show that certain possibilities can at least be explored.

11

Pakistani Universities: Past, Present, and Future

———————————————— Tariq Rahman

While the 21st century is only months ahead; the Pakistani universities still exist in the middle of the 19th century—almost when they were first established in 1858 (the University of Calcutta) by the British rulers of India. Is that too harsh a judgment? That is up to the reader to decide after going through this chapter. There are two aspects of the question: first, what were the characteristics of the colonial university in British India? and second, do Pakistani universities share most of these characteristics? These questions are answered in the sections on the past and the present. The last section, that about the future, is entirely subjective. It proposes reforms in the universities, which are presented here not as definitive answers but as the basis of further questioning.

THE PAST

In the Dispatch of 1854, the Court of Directors of the East India Company, which effectively ruled India by this time, conveyed the order that universities be established in India.[1] They were not to be academically prestigious. Hence, it was specified that the examination for common degrees was not to be "as difficult as that for the senior Government scholarships" and "the standard required should be such as to command respect without discouraging the efforts of deserving students."[2] Among the reasons for establishing universities was that many British officers felt that the cost of running the administration would decrease if the lower jobs were given to Indians. Moreover, as James Sullivan testified before a Parliamentary Committee in 1832, the Indians were alienated from British rule by the fact that they were excluded "from all offices of trust and emolument, and from that position in the administration of the country, civil and military, which they occupied under their own princes."[3] Such a large number of respondents agreed that, for various reasons, Indians should be educated—educated to be Westernized—and employed under British superiors, that in a letter of 29 September 1830 to Bengal, the Directors of the Company expressed their "earnest wish and hope" to "see them qualified for situations of higher importance and trust" and, for this purpose, to "rely chiefly on their becoming, through a familiarity with European literature and science, imbued with the ideas and feeling of civilized Europe."[4] Thus, even before Thomas Babington Macaulay had put it in his well-known Minute in 1835, British policy was to Westernize the Indian elite.

Yet, already in England, the most prestigious universities, Oxford and Cambridge, were autonomous institutions. They had been established by the Church, in itself a very powerful institution in medieval England, and derived their autonomy and prestige from it. Even in the 19th century, the universities were highly elitist and not subordinate to the bureaucracy of the state. Indeed, Sheldon Rothblatt tells us that Cambridge dons did not appeal to the state for funds even if they wanted them for fear of losing their independence. It was not, however, true that they always used their independence for the good of society in general or even of the elite.[5]

In India, a conquered country, such independence could not be given. Hence, the universities were not to be governed by academics nor were they completely free of the administrative control, or at least influence, of the higher bureaucracy. Thus, the Act establishing the University of Calcutta declared that the Governor-General would be the chancellor and the chief justice of the Supreme Court the vice chancellor of the University. Its fellows would include the lieutenant governors of Bengal and the North West Provinces, the Bishop of Calcutta, and members of the Supreme Council of India.[6]

As if this were not enough guarantee to keep the universities entirely under the government's thumb, they also lacked both students and faculty in the beginning. They were merely affiliating bodies on the model of the University of London. This meant that they only took examinations while the actual teaching took place in affiliated colleges. The college faculty was part of the civil service with all the disadvantages of that status but few of the advantages. As Irene Gilbert and Edward Shils have pointed out, Indian academics have few traditions of autonomy, creating a mentality of subordination.[7]

Whether intended or not, the effect of creating state-controlled affiliating universities was that academics never got the confidence to challenge the government. Being subordinate members of the elitist bureaucracy they mentally accepted its authority; its moral claim to legitimate exercise of power even in academic matters. In any case, as Shils shows, governors kept warning academics to eschew politics.[8] In short, the colonial state had produced a colonial university—one which did not have the psychological, economic, social, or legal potential to confront the powers that be.

In addition, because of the deep spiritual heritage of India/Pakistan, the academic feels, or professes to feel, that he is a moral mentor—something of the Sufi pir (mystic mentor) or a guru. Being, as it were, in a "sacred" profession he professes to despise wealth and power. Thus many Pakistani academics, and other Pakistanis as well, say that academics should not seek the kind of privileges or consumer goods that other members of the elite can legitimately seek. Moreover, the academic profession was unable to attract able young people.

Another characteristic of the colonial university was that it was supposed to teach and not to conduct research. The faculty was seen, and saw itself, as teachers. Indeed, the term academic was never in use, nor is it still in common use, in South Asia. The major reason for this seems to be that in the 19th century, English universities were teaching, rather than research, oriented institutions. Only German universities, as discussed by Manicas, emphasized research. James Morgan Hart, a visitor from America to Germany, commented thus on the German professor:

The professor is not a teacher, in the English sense of the term; he is a specialist. He is not responsible for the success of his hearers. He is responsible only for the quality of his instruction. His duty begins and ends with himself.[9]

But the Oxbridge professor was a teacher and not necessarily a scholar in 1874 when this was written. In India the professorial title was further devalued, more than it ever was in England, because college lecturers appropriated it. This degradation of the professoriate also had political implications. Such a professoriate, not comprising scholars of widespread fame, did not have the intellectual prestige to stand up to the raj's bureaucracy whereas scholars could. Thus, whether it was planned or not, the result of filling colleges and universities with teachers rather than prestigious scholars was that the raj had little to fear from the Indian academia.

Higher education, then, was a depressed sector of the society—a sector that had never been allowed to take off. Did it take off then when British rule ended in 1947 and Pakistan, a country carved out of British India with a majority of Muslims, emerged on the map of the world? Let us turn to the next section for the answer.

THE PRESENT

First, let us sum up a few facts about Pakistani universities. Pakistan started with just one university, the Punjab University, at its creation in 1947 and now there are 26 in the public sector and 10 in the private one. For the purposes of this article I will only focus attention on the public-sector universities. The private ones (or colleges) are very much as colleges were in India: substandard, bureaucratic, government controlled, poor, and inefficient. The universities are sometimes better than colleges but do not compare well with good Western universities.

Government Control

As in colonial times, the chancellor is still a high state functionary. For the provincial universities, he is the governor of the province; for the three federal ones, the president of Pakistan. The vice chancellor is always his nominee which, in practice, means that the bureaucrats of the ministries of education have a major say in deciding who he or she will be. While the provincial, or federal, governments exercise administrative control over university affairs, financial control is exercised through the center, which provides funds through the University Grants Commission that was established in 1974. In short, governmental influence has increased since British times because at that time, the only controlling body was the provincial government. Now three separate sets of bureaucrats are involved: the provincial bureaucracy; the federal bureaucracy and the University Grants Commission's bureaucracy. While control has become more diversified and red-tapism has multiplied, responsibility has become diffused. In the words of a World Bank report of 1990 that are still valid today:

This divorce of administrative from financial responsibility means that neither federal, nor provincial, nor university authorities can be held to account for the overall management of the university system. Especially in an environment where tough decisions are required, nothing significant can be accomplished to improve the universities until this duality of management control is ended.[10]

In addition, the universities are still ruled by the syndicate. In British times, as we have noted earlier, the senate and the syndicate were dominated by high government officials. This has not changed today. The only academics are those elected from among assistant professors, lecturers, or associate professors, as the case may be. Members nominated by the chancellor (who is always the governor or the president of the country) can hardly be expected not to tow the official line.

Poverty

The colonial universities were poor, though much richer than colonial schools and colleges, as are the Pakistani ones. The public expenditure on education now is only 2.25 percent of the GNP[11] while the military expenditure on the other hand, is around 5.2 percent of the GNP.[12] The apparent increase in the development budgets of the universities between 1985 and 1997 was uneven and did not cover inflation in the 1990s. However, in real terms, the budget decreased. The campuses are often large, with plenty of space per student, as the World Bank Report referred to in the notes brings out,[13] but only because the faculties have not expanded.

Quality of Academics

As in British times, Pakistani universities are staffed by people who are not among the best and the brightest to begin with. A number of high achievers among students, especially middle class ones, are still attracted to the civil service because it gives one the power to manipulate the system for personal gains. Among the gains are illegal ways of obtaining money, favors, and hidden benefits from the state. In a society where even legitimate rights and routine services cannot be obtained without using one's connections (that is, somebody's influence) or bribing somebody, it is understandable that young people would be attracted to the civil bureaucracy. As for upper class students, or those who are lucky enough to get scholarships, they go to study abroad and generally settle down there because the affluent lifestyles they are used to cannot be supported by the salaries the universities offer. To make matters worse, no incentives are offered for improvement. For all practical purposes, once one is hired one is not removed—at least for academic incompetence. The World Bank sums up the situation as follows:

Remuneration based on performance, a central motivating factor in most national systems of higher education and research, is an unknown concept in Pakistani higher education. Similarly, for practical purposes, promotions are based entirely on seniority, although in the universities there are also stated minimum requirements for articles published during the requisite period before promotion can be given.[14]

The number of required articles is abysmally low and although they are required to be published in "reputable journals" no criterion of the journal is laid down. In practice, then, papers published in newspapers, magazines, and substandard journals are accepted.

Other Problems

Other problems which plague the universities are

- The system of evaluation is stereotyped, memory-based, corruptible, and stagnant;
- The universities are often closed because of student unrest;
- Student unions are highly politicized and violent; and
- Graduates of universities lack the necessary skills for employment.

All of these problems have been addressed by researchers. The problems of the examination system have been recognized since its inception. In India many reports, beginning with the Report of the University Education Commission (1948), have reiterated that it needs major changes.[15] The World Bank Report (1990) and a recent report of the UGC in Pakistan also address the problems of the system of examinations.[16] One hopes all systems would work well in the hands of really competent academics.

As for violence on the campus and the closure of the universities as a consequence, Hafiz Pasha and Ashraf Wasti calculate that it is unacceptably costly.[17] The World Bank Report takes a view which, though counterintuitive at first sight, seems to be nearer truth than the view that if student unions were banned, all would be well. This view is

campus unrest is probably first and foremost attributable to raging student frustration with the deeply unsatisfactory nature of the educational experience and with the often dubious prospects of suitable employment thereafter. The intrusion of partisan politics into academic life is only an exacerbating factor.[18]

In short, if the universities were better and the job market more just, there would have been no (or less) unrest. This brings us back to where we started from—the universities are inadequate. They are fossils from the age of British colonialism. And day by day they become less and less fit to serve the needs of an ever-expanding population trying to enter the 21st century. The question, then, is whether anything, and if so what, can be done to improve them?

THE FUTURE

There are at least three alternative directions for Pakistani universities in the future. They can move toward

- creating more private universities (privatization) rather than state-sponsored ones;
- creating new Islamic universities (Islamization), presumably with the help of Saudi Arabia on the model of the International Islamic University in Islamabad;
- improving and modernizing the state-sponsored universities of Pakistan.

Let me briefly touch upon the first two alternatives before giving more detailed treatment to the third one.

Privatization of the Universities

The Agha Khan University was established on 16 March 1983 in Karachi as the first private university in Pakistan. It comprises a medical college and a school of nursing, which are considered to be of a high standard. Another well known private university, this time for business administration, is the Lahore University of Management Sciences (LUMS). For engineering and technological subjects, there is the Ghulam Ishaque Khan Institute of Engineering and Technology (GIKI) at Topi. The whole discourse of the private university, at least in Pakistan, and indeed globally, revolves around marketability. David Fraser's words from a paper he read at the international seminar on Higher Education in November 1996 illustrates this tendency. He said

By fostering a market in higher education, one may also try to ensure quality, but creating an efficient market is not easy, given the importance of informing a consumer about the quality of the product.[19]

Education is a commodity to be bought at these institutions. Moreover, it is bought not because it is an end in itself, but because it is the means to an end— the securing of a good job. That is why private universities offer technical education—medical, engineering, and business administration, rather than a generalized liberal education. In short, there is a narrowing of focus as far as the attainment of knowledge is concerned in the process of privatization of higher education.

In addition, private universities charge higher tuition fees and are, therefore, for the elite of the wealthy. A few scholarships and loans to students—and it is not always the poor ones who get them—do not alter the fact that they are for people who can afford to pay much more for education than other Pakistanis can. In short, there is a narrowing of the clientele involved in the process of privatization.

Islamization

The same kind of narrowing is in evidence when powerful lobbies create ideologically motivated universities. The International Islamic University at Islamabad is one such institution. It is financially supported by Saudi Arabia and is meant to disseminate the ideology of the Sunni Wahabis who rule that country. The university imposes a dress code on women and does not accommodate academics whose interpretation of religion is openly or significantly different from that of the decisionmakers. The Jamat-i-Islami, a Muslim revivalist party of Pakistan, has a strong voice in this university. The Jamat, and other groups in the Islamic lobby, were demanding that women should be segregated from men.

If Pakistan moves further toward Islamic rule, either because of the myopic and corrupt policies of its rulers or because of confrontation with the West, such Islamization of higher education could be our future. However, the Islamic university could prevent freedom of academic enquiry because its decisionmakers would have the power to decide which ideas are Islamic and which are not.

Another kind of narrowing of both clientele and subjects of study is the result of the Pakistani military's creation of the National University of Science and Technology (NUST) in Rawalpindi. Although this university does enroll fee-paying civilian students, it is primarily meant for free military employees. It too concentrates on technical, skill-enhancing, utilitarian subjects—hence its popularity among civilian students—and is directly controlled by the army. The idea that the military, perhaps the most reactionary force in any state, should control a university goes against all liberal ideas of what a university should be. However, since such institutions cannot multiply, they need not be considered a possible future for the university in Pakistan.

So far, then, we have seen that privatization and Islamization (as well as militarisation) of higher education in Pakistan cannot create universities of the liberal kind, that is, institutions which should enable research scholars to produce knowledge in all fields, of all kinds, with any ideological implication without fear or favor. These alternatives will tend to narrow down either the fields to be investigated or the kind of people who can enter the university (by excluding the poor or the ideologically suspect). But if art and culture are excluded, if philosophy disappears, if history, sociology, and political science are not studied either because they do not help make money or because they are ideologically undermining, then learning as a whole will suffer. Pakistan will never have a philosopher and all our ideas about the world, about human societies, about what makes life worth living will either come from outside or tend to be dictated by people in authority.

Proposals for the Modernization of the State Universities

The proponents of the private universities, in common with other informed people, seem to have given up on the possibility of reform altogether. Nisar A. Memon, Country Director of a business organization, said in the Agha Khan University seminar in November 1996 that the government had failed in creating good universities. As such, he proposed

Shall we not spend our efforts to diverting whatever the government is spending today on education or higher education to the private sector universities, and allow the private sector universities to evolve their own mechanism for supplementing the required resources.[20]

If the state does anything of the kind it would wash its hands of higher education which, in my view, would narrow education to a few technical skills and a few (rich) people. Instead, I would propose an agenda of reforms along the following lines:

* Creation of apex bodies for giving and implementing overall policies.
* Removing the universities from direct provincial and central control by making them independent institutions under a Board of Trustees.
* Removal of subsidies to students' residential accommodation and increase in tuition fees between 35 to 45 percent of the present ratio.[21]

Obstacles to reform

Admittedly there are obstacles to the modernization process. The present power structure is an impediment for the development of the universities in many ways, such as:

* The powerful bureaucracy does not want to reduce its power. Thus, despite all the reports the public has paid for, the hold of the government remains as strong as it was before.
* The level of spending on the armed forces and the bureaucracy would have to be curtailed and the savings diverted to the universities if they are to be brought up to internationally acceptable standards. This, neither the armed forces nor the mandarins of the bureaucracy are prepared to accept.
* The very red tapism, unresponsiveness, and corruption of the system makes it necessary to possess power or know people who do so. This is the major attraction of the

bureaucracy and the military. If the system becomes just, transparent, and imper-sonal—as Western bureaucracies are in most public dealings—there would be little incentive for bright people to join the bureaucracy. These people would then be avail-able to universities.

However, they would still be attracted to big business, which pays more than universities all over the world. This is a problem in Western countries too, but uni-versities do attract people who want enough time to pursue their own agendas of research; enjoy lecturing and interaction with informed peers and students, and enjoy the security (after getting tenure) of university professorships. Besides, the universities are prestigious and being part of the faculty of a good university is a badge of distinction. So, for psychological reasons too (that is, for recognition), distinguished scholars and intellectually inclined young people are attracted to universities. These, then, are the factors that should operate in Pakistan too. But bringing about changes in the political system is a tall order. No powerful group can be expected to relinquish its own power. Thus, if changes are to take place, they must come from the pressure of public opinion—in this case, the informed opinion of educated Pakistanis. That better institutions, even in the public sector, can be created is suggested by the fact that the Indian Institutes of Technology are much better than other Indian institutions of higher learning. In these institutions financial investment is high; the faculty is research-oriented; government repre-sentation on decision-making bodies is minimal and there is a sense of pride in the institution.[22]

This does not mean that entirely new institutions should be created. Indeed, one reason for the deterioration of universities is that too many of them have been opened in response to political expediencies. Some such substandard universities might, indeed, be curtailed but the remaining must be improved by massive investment and restructuring. Among specific proposals, the following are offered.

Academics should be among the best paid people in the country. At the moment, university professors do not get either the perquisites, privileges, or even the salaries of either the higher bureaucrats or the senior-most armed forces officers. However, such highly paid faculty must be well-published too. Indeed, the faculty members' promotion and emoluments should be dependent upon peer review of faculty publications, student evaluation, and "income-earning scholarly activities" in fields in which contract research is possible. Here one agrees with Pervez Hoodbhoy who, in a paper on improving the public sector universities, recommends that the "present system of lifelong tenure for every university teacher" must be terminated.[23] It should be, but only after the universities are equipped with libraries and laboratories comparable to their Western equivalents where research is possible.

Universities should be governed by Boards of Governors, which should include nobody from the bureaucracy or the military. However, a representative of the legislature and the higher judiciary may be included. The rest of the gov-ernors must be intellectuals, scholars, businessmen, and eminent journalists.

The governors should elect the chancellor who must not be a state functionary. The professors of the university should elect the vice chancellor, from people with recognized academic standing, who should hold office for a specific term. This would be a considerable departure from current practices but such a departure was made by the Sarkar Committee (1946) when it set up the Indian Institutes of Technology in 1946. In the IITs of India, contrary to ordinary practice in Indian universities, the board of governors and senate do not have any government official or politician. However, the president of India has powers as a visitor of each institute.[24]

The universities must charge higher fees, produce their own resources, undertake contract research, and generate resources in other ways. However, the state should invest heavily in them in a way which does not compromise their autonomy. If some scheme of granting loans as practiced in many countries of the world[25] is put in practice, the tuition fees can be increased. Scholarships, paid by the state, could also be given to poor students as in the case of European welfare states. Other resources must come from business, ownership of property, and endowments.

A NEW WORLD OF INDIVIDUALISM AND FREEDOM

The future prospects of Pakistani universities are tied up with the present and the past. The colonial past has left behind a legacy of the overdeveloped state with the power-wielding modern institutions—the higher bureaucracy and the officer corps of the military—controlling all other institutions and consuming most of the resources. This has had both tangible and intangible consequences. The tangible ones have been catalogued in this article: poor universities; incompetent faculty; substandard teaching and very little original research; subordination to the bureaucracy; and outmoded curricula. The intangible ones are not easy to list. The most significant of them seems to be a closing of the mind among both academics and other opinion molders.

There is great dissatisfaction with the present state of affairs, but there is a vague feeling that this is because academics are basically incompetent and unable to reform themselves. Academics might blame each other or politicians for patronizing "black sheep," but the idea of reform is seen in moral terms—as if it were a matter of voluntary moral change.

What this article argues is that the central issue is one of governance. Short-term changes—such as changes in the fee structure, recruitment of competent faculty members, and so on—are related to comparatively minor changes in governance. Long-term changes—such as making universities more attractive than other state services, reducing the number of people who come to them by giving jobs after school, and offering job-specific training—entail radical reforms in governance. The higher budgetary allocations for universities proposed here entail a reduction in expenditure on the elite of power while alterations in the pattern of recruitment to elitist services (such as the civil service and the army) means a major reduction in their prestige and attraction.

The biggest changes—those of creating an impersonal bureaucracy, establishing the rule of law, making people respect academic achievement rather than power or saintliness—is not only a change in governance but the completion of the transition to modernity that is taking place. South Asia has been making this transition from the pre-modern, feudal/colonial order to the modern/democratic one since colonial days. When this is completed, a new world view will be born. This world view, contingent as it will be upon individualism and freedom, will support democracy in the domain of politics and rationalism in that of ideas. The universities will help to create this world view as they will be products of it. By establishing new and more competent universities, Pakistan will hasten its transition to modernity—a transition that started more than a century ago, but lags far behind its East Asian neighbors.

NOTES

1. J. A. Richey, ed., *Selections from Educational Records. Part II: 1840–1959* (Calcutta: Superintendent of Government Printing, 1922), 371.

2. Richey, ibid., 372.

3. James Sullivan, "Evidence Before the Parliamentary Committee on the Affairs of the East India Company," in *Indian Education in Parliamentary Papers: Part 1,* A. N. Basu, ed. (Bombay: Asia Publishing House, 1952), 274.

4. Basu, ibid., 303.

5. Sheldon Rothblatt, *The Revolution of the Dons: Cambridge and Society in Victorian England* (London: Faber & Faber, 1968).

6. Act No. II of 1875 in Richey, op cit.: 410–11.

7. Irere Gilbert, "The Indian Academic Profession: the Origins of a Tradition of Subordination," *Minerva* 10 (July 1972), 384–411. Also see Edward Shils, "The Academic Profession in India," in *Elites in South Asia*, Edmund Leach & S. N. Mukherjee, eds. (Cambridge: Cambridge University Press, 1970), 172–200.

8. Shils, ibid., 194–96.

9. James Morgan Hart, "German Universities: A Narrative of Present Experience," in *The Origins of Literary Studies in America: A Documentary Anthology*, Gerald Graf and Michael Warner, eds. (New York: Routledge, Chapman & Hall, 1989), 22.

10. World Bank, *Higher Education and Scientific Research for Development in Pakistan Vols. 1 & 2* (Confidential Report NO. 8231-Pak) [Henceforth abbreviated as World Bank 1 & 2].

11. *Economic Survey of Pakistan 1997–1998* (Islamabad: Government of Pakistan, Ministry of Finance, 1998), 122.

12. Mahbub ul Haq and Khadija Haq, *Human Development in South Asia 1998* (Karachi: Oxford University Press, 1998), 184.

13. World Bank, Vol. 2, 199–220.

14. World Bank, Vol. 1, 16.

15. Matthew Zacharia, "Examination Reform in Traditional Universities," in *Higher Education Reform in India*, Sama Chitnis and Philip G. Altbach, eds. (New Delhi: Sage Publications, 1993), 155–206.

16. "Reforms in Affiliation and Examination System in the General Universities of Pakistan," Cyclostyled Report, UGC, Islamabad, 25 July 1997.

17. Hafiz Pasha and S. Ashraf Wasti, "Social Costs of University Closures," Cyclostyled Conference Paper, 9th Annual General Meeting, Pakistan Institute of Development Economics, Islamabad (1993): 17.

18. World Bank, Vol. 1, 3.

19. David Fraser, "The Role of Private Universities in Higher Education," in *Higher Education: A Pathway to Development*, J. Talati et. al, eds. (Karachi: The Agha Khan University and Oxford University Press, 1998), 222.

20. Nisar A. Memon, "The Role of a University vis a vis Business and Industry," in J. Talati, ibid., 238.

21. World Bank, Vol. 1, 46–65.

22. P. V. Indiresan and N. C. Nigam, "The Indian Institutes of Technology: Excellence in Peril" in *Chitnis and Altbach*, op cit.: 334–84.

23. Pervez Hoodbhoy, "Pakistani Universities: Which Way Out?", in *Education and the State: Fifty Years of Pakistan*, P. Hoodbhoy, ed. (Karachi: Oxford University Press, 1998), 278–79.

24. Indiresan and Nigam, op cit.: 335.

25. George Psacharopoulos and Maureen Woodhall, *Education for Development: An Analysis of Investment Choices* (New York: Oxford University Press for the World Bank, 1985): 153–59.

12

Civilizing the State: The University in the Middle East

Shahrzad Mojab

> The universities should be completely freed from CIA and from Pentagon con-
> trol, through grants of money and otherwise. Faculties and students should
> have the basic controls so that the university will be a revolutionary force that
> helps shape the restructuring of society. A university should not be an adjunct
> of business, nor of the military, nor of government. Its curriculum should teach
> change, not the status quo.
>
> —*William O. Douglas (1969)*[1]

On the thirtieth anniversary of the May 1968 movement of France, students in
Indonesia went on the offensive and overthrew General Suharto, one of the
world's unbending dictators who enjoyed full support from Western powers.
However, these two May movements were neither unique nor accidents of history.
From the democratic revolutions of 1848 in Europe to the anti-colonial and revolutionary movements of Africa, Asia, and Latin America, students have left their
mark on the politics of their country and the world.[2] Still, the student "factor" in
political change or even in university reform remains, at least theoretically,
underrated. Students are generally treated as "objects" of university operations.

That students are not visible as "subjects" of the history of higher education is
not surprising. They are recruited to be "trained" and to graduate as bearers of a
knowledge that is indispensable for the functioning of the economy and the reproduction of the state and the nation. In Western democracies, even when students
are allowed to engage in student government and be represented in the academic
and administrative organs of decisionmaking, they are dwarfed by the power of
the faculty and the administration. There is no student representation in two centers of power—the state and the market—which directly or indirectly shape
higher education.

The unequal distribution of power on campus is most visible in the developing world. Student participation in decisionmaking is either denied or remains on paper. The state is omnipresent to ensure that the university loyally serves its purposes. Any call for changing the status quo, on or off campus, leads to state violence against the students, faculty, and staff. Reports of widespread violence against the academy are regularly documented by Amnesty International, Human Rights Watch, professional associations (the Middle Eastern Studies Association, as an example), and other human rights organizations.

The presence of students in the past and present of the university is felt usually when they show serious "unrest" and engage in "disturbance." Here, they join the peasants, workers, women, and other social forces that are noticed only when they disrupt the status quo. Their everyday, small-scale resistances do not make history. The absence of students from the history of higher education makes it difficult, if not impossible, to predict their presence in the future. Yet, I try in this chapter to contemplate the future of the Middle Eastern university by focusing on the potentially most powerful human element in that institution.

DIVERSITY IN THE LAND OF "ARABS, OIL, AND DESERTS"

The Middle East is imagined, worldwide, as the land of Arabs, oil, Islam, submissive women, and deserts. The cost of this Eurocentric construction has been an imagined homogeneity. In fact, the Middle East is remarkably diverse. Many faiths are practiced and there is racial and linguistic diversity. In spite of the universal rule of patriarchy, gender relations, too, are heterogeneous. Women and men in urban, rural, and tribal areas enter into diverse patterns of gender relations.

While there is remarkable heterogeneity, parts of the region share much in common. Politically, the conflict between despotism and democracy is ubiquitous. Civil society is either nonexistent or stifled by the state. There is an unending struggle over the separation of religion and politics. Educationally, in spite of the diversity of traditions (for example, sexual segregation and Islamization in Iran, Gulf States, and so on; ban on women's education in Afghanistan; coeducation in some countries), the state dominates the nontraditional modern system. Some of the shared practices in higher education include the centrality of the teacher and the text, focus on teaching rather than research, absence of academic freedom, state control of the institutions, and the exclusion of students from decision-making processes.

The Risk of Predicting the Future

We usually imagine the future and the past on the basis of our knowledge of the present. One limitation in predicting the future is the fragmentary and uncertain state of our understanding of both the past and present. Another constraint is imposed by the reality that we hope to predict. Even if we were in a position to adequately understand past and present processes of change, nothing can guarantee their smooth and uninterrupted continuity into the future. The dynamics of change are riddled with unpredictable ruptures and discontinuities.[3]

The university combines diverse factors or forces that enter into often unpredictable relations of conflict and coexistence: the concentration of a usually large number of young students; the running of the institution by a smaller group of staff and faculty who occupy the higher ranks of the hierarchy of power; the dominance of intellectual and analytical work; the relative ease of assembly; access to information and means of communication and mobilization; diversity of political and ideological positions; the presence of diverse forms of authority including the power of the state. At least two sources of power—the state and the university administration—are most interested in maintaining the continuity and smooth functioning of the institution.

Students in many universities in the Middle East have revolted against both the administrative hierarchy and the state. The antistate struggle has, however, often overshadowed the revolt against the institution itself. The rulers, both colonial and postcolonial, have consistently looked at education in general and higher education in particular as sources of sedition.

The Sedition of the University

The political systems of the Middle East, theocratic or secular, are predominantly étatist. Sovereignty is, in practice, vested in the state, rather than the people. Civil society, even if it exists, is subdued by the state. In fact, a growing body of research on civil society in the Middle East emphasizes the prevalence of antagonistic relationships between the two formations. It is no secret that, as the reviewer of a major work on the topic notes, "[I]n the Middle East, speaking of the state means talk of despotism, dictatorship, political exclusion, corruption, bureaucratic authoritarianism, repression, or simply milder forms of control over, and restrictions on, social, economic, and political activities."[4] The formation of "a vital and autonomous civil society" is viewed, in this literature, as "a necessary condition of democracy (though not a sufficient one)."[5]

It is not surprising, therefore, that state–university relations are often antagonistic. The kings, emirs, sultans, presidents, and prime ministers have traditionally looked at education, in general, and higher education, in particular, as sources of dissent and even sedition. As recently as the 1970s, the Sultan of the then British colony of Oman banned reading, writing, and owning any written material. By 1970, there were only three primary schools set up to serve the male members of the ruling sultan. He closed the three primary schools because they had become "centers of communism." The Sultan told a British advisor: "This is why you lost India, because you educated the people."[6] By contrast, the national liberation movement led by the Popular Front for the Liberation of Oman from the 1960s until 1975 introduced extensive education for males and females in the "liberated areas." Although the movement was suppressed in 1975 through the military intervention of Iran supported by Western powers, it nevertheless led to a palace coup, which replaced the Sultan by his son. As a result, primary and secondary schools were gradually opened.[7]

DESPOTISM AND DEMOCRACY: THE UNIVERSITY IN IRAN

Among the many forces that shape the present and future of the university in the region, I focus on the conflict between despotism and democracy, which continues to draw the contours of educational, cultural, political, and religious life. An active participant in this conflict, the university changes the balance of forces and is at the same time changed by it. The case of Iran, in spite of its specificities, highlights some of the persistent trends in the development of higher education in the region.

The formation of a modern university system under Reza Shah Pahlavi (1925–1941) in Iran was clearly related to his projects for building a Western-type, modern, secular (though not democratic) nation–state. One aim was to discredit the traditional Islamic educational system. The universities turned, however, into hotbeds of leftist and nationalist struggles against the monarchy. By the mid-1970s, the second Shah's project of building a "Great Civilization" (the transformation of Iran into a military base for the United States under Nixon) required the rapid spread of higher education. However, the expanded universities played a fundamental role in the overthrow of the monarchy in 1978–1979. The faculty and staff joined the students in the showdown, which cost many lives. The secular university had already been dignified as sangar-e azadi, that is, "Bastion of freedom."

The liberated, radical, secular, and left-leaning university was powerful enough to resist Khomeini's "Islamization" project. A situation of "dual power" in which students/faculty overran the power of the state, prevailed until April 1980, when Khomeini mobilized coercive forces in order to integrate the institutions into the Islamic regime. Once the leftist and secular students were driven out of the campus, the offensive was labeled " the Islamic Cultural Revolution," and the universities were closed down for two years. The Islamic leaders decided to tame the university once and for all. Two years of planning included, among other things, the extensive purge of students, faculty, and staff; the Islamization of the curriculum; the formation of Islamic student associations in order to spy on students and faculty; the admission of pro-regime students on a quota basis; the founding of a special university to train loyal Islamic faculty members; and total repression of academic freedom.[8]

A rigid system of screening was designed to ensure the rejection of any student who could be potentially disloyal to Islam. This included passing centrally administered entrance exams that included ideological tests, "local investigation" of the applicants in their neighborhood and in the secondary schools where they graduated, and security checks by the "Revolutionary Guards," intelligence organization, and the local mosque. Some of the brightest applicants who had passed all the tests were not admitted only because security checks could not or did not confirm their loyalty to the state or because a close relative of the applicant had opposed the Islamic state. Post-admission controls were equally repressive. The result was a reign of terror on the campus to the extent that the architects of terror complained about the depoliticization of the students and their reluctance to participate in pro-regime activities.[9]

The Islamic Cultural Revolution failed, however. Resistance to Islamization came from faculty and students over issues as diverse as the closure of numerous fields of specialization to female students and the question of student housing. Although the only political activism allowed was supporting the regime and its policies and practices, students participated, by the mid-1990s, in the factional conflicts between "fundamentalists" and the "moderates." At the time of this writing (October 1998), students at Tehran University, the major institution of the country, had protested, in a rally, the violation of freedom of the press, and called for the release of political prisoners. Joined by nonstudents, they also stressed the need for a functioning civil society, and even called for reforming the Council of Experts (which oversees parliamentary legislation) so that its members were elected rather than appointed. Students in Baheshti University protested the admission of pro-fundamentalist students through the quota system. They noted that "these individuals are sent to the universities not to study, but to suppress student movements." In turn, the leader of the Islamic Republic, Ayatollah Khomeini, sent a message to the congress of pro-fundamentalist students and called on them to "identify and neutralize sedition and seditionists especially in student environments."[10] Although the student movement was to a considerable extent confined within the framework of factional conflicts, it was clear that given a modest degree of freedom they would go on the offensive against the regime. The politicization of the depoliticized students of the Islamic Cultural Revolution confirms the failure of one of the most ambitious projects of taming the university. It would not be unrealistic, therefore, to claim that students, as well as the faculty, will continue to be major actors in the struggle for the democratization of Middle Eastern political systems.

In spite of the concerns of the state about the adversarial role of the universities, higher education is expanding. The dynamics of expansion is complex and different in each case. Generally, the spread of secondary schools results in more demand for college education. By the early 1990s, universities were established even in Oman, and were expanding in the Persian Gulf states and throughout the region. Even countries with a strong tradition of state monopoly of education such as Iran have allowed the formation of private institutions of higher education. There is in fact an unprecedented spread of colleges and universities in this country. Almost every city and town has a branch of the Islamic Free University or other "distance education" institutions. However, privatization in a society that is hungry for university degrees has helped the inflation of higher education without contributing to the growth of the economy. The non-trained or under-trained are in a better position to find jobs that degree-holders are reluctant or unable to take. Although privatization has not alleviated state control, it will contribute to the formation of a student body that is less dependent, financially and politically, on the state, and more critical of the educational institution. One important consequence will be the increase in the number of women in higher education, which will in turn pose a challenge to the status quo, especially in countries where the state pursues a policy of sexual apartheid (for example, Saudi Arabia, the Gulf states, and Iran).

Adversarial relations between the state and the university are inscribed most visibly in the official, and sometimes constitutional, denial of academic freedom. While in many countries the universities are closely guarded by security and intelligence organs, a system of "thought control" is also in place. The denial of academic freedom is often justified on grounds of national interest, patriotism, territorial integrity, religion, peace, or law and order. Thought control is, in some states, virtually unrestrained. In Syria, access to fax machines was not allowed until 1993; by 1997, access to the Internet was granted to only 150 subscribers from state institutions and ministries.[11] In Turkey, which is promoted by some specialists as "the only Muslim democracy," the army generals, who conducted a military coup d'etat in 1980 in order to "save Turkish democracy," purged some 2,000 faculty members, and imprisoned many others.[12] In the Constitution of the country, scripted by the generals, academic freedom is granted only to "universities, members of the teaching staff, and their assistants" provided that "this shall not include the liberty to engage in activities directed against the existence and independence of the State, and against the integrity and indivisibility of the nation and country" (Article 130).

Alternatives: The Kurdistan University

Since the conflict between democracy and despotism is far from resolved, the university will most probably continue to be engaged in the struggle for democratization on and off campus. Within the institutions, students and faculty will demand academic freedom and university autonomy. Indeed, alternatives to a state-run institution have already been tried, for instance, in Iran. The history of university reform in Iran shows that radical reform of the university is achieved in the absence of state power. State power, both monarchical and Islamic, has been an obstacle to the democratization of the university. For example, in the period of "dual power" on the campus during 1979–1980, the majority of students/faculty were running the institutions from below. In spite of innumerable obstacles created by the Islamic state, students and faculty were able to democratize the institutions and run them as arenas of radical reconstruction between 1978 and 1980.

In the absence of effective state control over Kurdistan in western Iran, dozens of faculty members from all over the country, helped by the Kuris themselves, were able to set up a university with an entirely new mandate and structure. The aim of Kurdistan University was to serve the needs of the region (one of the most underdeveloped in the country), to avoid unnecessary investment in buildings and huge bureaucracy, to admit students mostly from the region, and to train them to deal with local problems thereby combining theory and practice in a balanced and creative manner.

The first draft of the plan for Kurdistan University was discussed at a meeting in Mahabad, one of the major towns in the Kurdish areas of Western Iran. Representatives from all Kurdish towns and one of the prominent figures of the National Organization of Iranian Academics participated in the event. The university was to provide training in medicine and public health, agriculture and animal husbandry, industry and technology, and social sciences, and Kurdish language and culture. By mid-summer 1979, the final plan was drawn up and locations were determined. People from all walks of life donated money, land, buildings, and other resources. A considerable number of faculty members from all over Iran volunteered to teach at the University with subsistence salary only. A meeting was scheduled for August 29, 1979, to announce the admission of students for the coming academic year beginning in September 1979. However, Khomeini ordered the armed forces to attack Kurdistan on August 19, 1979, and to wipe out the Kurdish autonomist movement. The newborn university was eliminated.[13]

Civil Society and the University

The world has visibly changed since the late 1970s. The Soviet empire has evaporated. China has openly embraced capitalist economy. The formation of new nation–states has changed the political geography of the world. Theocratic states in Iran and Afghanistan have assumed power and religious forces are struggling for statehood.

In the wake of the disintegration of the Soviet bloc, political and intellectual elites expressed much optimism about the spread of democracy throughout the world. We are told that the State, as the site of absolute sovereignty within its borders, is withering away. Sovereignty is "leaking away" from the State, both "upward to supranational institutions and downward to subnational ones." The erosion of State power opens the political space for non-state actors. These spaces, lying between the State and the market, are the sites of civil society where new social movements act as agents of change. Eva Egron-Polak, however, warns us that "we must not fail to underline that the rules and the functioning of civil society are laid down by the State. Any analysis of the role of the civil society must therefore take into consideration both the role of the State and the wider context of interdependent global relationships."[14]

Without endorsing the optimistic declaration of a borderless and stateless world, we educators can avoid the pessimistic view of the world as a single space closed by the powers of the State or the market, or a combination of them. The question should be about the scale of openness and the ways we can contribute to opening intellectual closures. The largely forgotten concept of "civil society" was revived after the fall of East European "communist" or, rather, "state-capitalist" experiment. The domination of the State over civil society in Eastern Europe as well as the Middle East makes the concept a very attractive explanatory tool.

There are many differences between the Middle East and the West, however, and I refer to two features here. First, the State rather than the market, is the main locus of power in the Middle East. Kothari argues that:

the modern state, particularly in the Third World, has not only grown substantially, but remains considerably outside the control or accountability of its citizens. In each of our societies, States have acted coercively to oppress and contain sections of civil society. Societies also continue to witness the pressing power of both traditional feudal and upper-class networks, as well as of predatory and polluting industrial and economic elites.[15]

Second, formal education continues to be a state monopoly. The gradual privatization of educational institutions does not replace the rule of the State by the power of the market. The Turkish constitution, for instance, decides which languages can be used in education, and does not allow teaching in the non-Turkish languages of the country. Thus, the Kurdish citizens, who number about 12 million, do not enjoy the right to learn their written language, let alone be taught in it.[16] Some teachers who secretly taught the language were assassinated.

In spite of the commitment of the State to compulsory education, this has not fully materialized yet. Neither has mass literacy been achieved. Tens of millions of women and adult men, especially in rural areas, continue to be illiterate. If we put aside the national minorities and the illiterate population, education is also used primarily to integrate the population into the nation–state. Thus, in Turkey the primary goal of education is to turn the population of Turkey into citizens that are loyal to the official ideology of Kemalism, which is Turkish ethnonationalism.[17] In Iran, Saudi Arabia, Kuwait, and other Gulf States, education is a tool of Islamization of society. In Iraq and Syria, education is used primarily to turn the people of these countries into loyal members of the ruling national socialist Ba'th parties.

If the civil society paradigm advocates the non–state sector as the panacea for democratic development, the "modernization paradigm" has promoted the modern state as the engine of economic transformation of the Middle East. For decades, the modern state was celebrated as the principal agent of change in an ocean of "traditional" and "backward" people. It is true that many states assign a good proportion of the budget to education. However, the peoples of the region demanded education even before the modernizing states came to power during this century. The Iraqi state, created by Britain in 1918 and under British Mandate until 1932, provides a relevant example. Popular demand for education was so extensive in Iraq that the British mandatory power openly resented it and called it "dangerous," and rejected the demand for establishing more schools for girls or even a teacher training college for the Kurds.[18]

In the Middle East where a civil society similar to the West has not emerged, in part because of state despotism, the principal means of control are the coercive forces. The modern universities in the region have acted as public spheres where issues such as the nature of the state, democracy, socialism, feminism, and other political topics are debated especially by students and, quite often, outside the classroom. The campuses were, from the beginning, among the most powerful sites of resistance against colonialism and dictatorship. Since the State suppressed the press and monopolized broadcasting, the universities remained the only outlet that was not easy to silence. The suppression of the universities is often bloody. Thousands of students and faculty have perished in countries such as Iran, Iraq, Syria, Egypt, and Turkey.

CHALLENGES FOR THE FUTURE

In spite of the rapid changes taking place on a daily basis in the Middle East, I would argue that many traditional structures of power—economic, political, and social—are still in place. The future of the university in the region will be shaped by the conflicts resulting from the struggle over the unequal distribution and exercise of power.

The desire to change the status quo is strong among the peoples of the Middle East. Contrary to the claims of some Western observers and consultants, the main source of "underdevelopment" must be sought, not in the attitudes of the people, but rather in the institution of the State. The autocratic state is still a major obstacle to the unfolding of democracy. Kothari argues, "it must still be acknowledged that it is the failure of the state to democratize itself, to make itself into a neutral arbiter in civilian affairs, to intervene in favor of the underprivileged, and to contain predatory economic interest, that has impelled a wide range of popular movements seeking democratic control over their resources and their lives."[19] It is clear, however, that in the absence of powerful social movements, the Middle Eastern state cannot be expected to "democratize itself." Many social scientists argue that the state can be harnessed through the promotion of civil society. This is a model based on the experience of democratization of Western societies in the post-Renaissance period.

Without emphasizing the uniqueness of this experience, one must admit that the rise of bourgeois democracy in the West was not as simple as it seems now. In France, for example, democratization entailed three major revolutions—in 1789, 1848, and 1871. Many democratic movements in the Middle East have been and continue to be suppressed with the assistance of Western powers. Between 1984 and 1997, Turkey destroyed no less than 3,000 villages in the Kurdish provinces and has forced more than two million rural people into the city slums.[20] We are witnessing, according to a British peace journal, the "crushing of Kurdish civil society."[21] Turkey ranks first among the countries where journalists and writers are jailed and murdered. The United States and European powers generously support the Turkish state's suppression of the Kurdish nationalist movement. Looking at the relationships between the West and the Middle East, it is difficult to agree with those who theorize a postcolonial world free of (neo)colonial forms of dominance. While in the West, the enhancement or re-creation of civil society may lead to further democratization, the process in the Middle East requires first and foremost the civilizing of the state.[22] Once the state is transformed, civil society will flourish. In some countries, civil society is on the brink of explosion. The State in Saudi Arabia, Kuwait, Oman and other dictatorial regimes suppresses those women who demand freedom, equality, and suffrage rights.

Toward an Autonomous University

If the university is to play a constructive role in democratizing Middle Eastern societies, it should be allowed to enjoy autonomy. However, a legalistic view of autonomy will not be effective. There is demand for independence in all kinds of decisionmaking, from admission of students to hiring faculty to curriculum planning. Non-state initiatives, as in the case of the failed Kurdistan University, should be allowed, and even encouraged, to establish institutions of higher learning. Politically, full academic freedom should be granted to the faculty and students.

No state in the Middle East is, however, willing to tolerate an autonomous university enjoying full academic freedom. Indeed, Turkey, the "only Muslim democracy," did not tolerate even a democratically elected prime minister, Mr. Necmettin Erbekan of the Refah Party.[23] A moderate Islamic leader, he served a year (1997) in a coalitionary government when the military forced him out of power and the justice system tried him on charges of overthrowing the democratic Turkish state. The Algerian state did not do better when democratically elected Muslims were denied access to power.

Under such conditions, there seems to be little room for a peaceful resolution of the conflict between the dictatorial state and the university. Higher education in the Middle East will remain a highly political institution. It continues to engage in revolutionary struggles to change the status quo. This is not surprising if we look back at the recent history of the region. The earliest democratic and anti-colonial revolutions in the Middle East—one in Iran (1906–1911) and the other in Ottoman Turkey (1908)—failed to achieve their goals of independence and democratization of politics and society. These revolutions have continued in a succession of minor and major struggles, usually suppressed by the state and its Western allies.

The expansion of the university in the Middle East is generating an extensive intelligentsia, including both women and men, urban and rural. It has all the ingredients for explosion—political despotism, growing poverty in the midst of rich natural and human resources, continued neocolonial domination, war and brutality, and gross violations of the rights and dignity of human beings.

NOTES

1. William O. Douglas, *Points of Rebellion* (New York: Vantage Books, 1970), 94.

2. See Susan Morrissey, *Heralds of Revolution: Russian Students and the Mythologies of Radicalism* (New York: Oxford University Press, 1998); *UNESCO, The Role of African Student Movements in the Political and Social Evolution of Africa from 1900 to 1975* (Paris: UNESCO Publishing, 1994); Ahmed Abdalla, *The Student Movement and National Politics in Egypt* (London: Al Saqi Books, 1985); Philip Altbach, ed., *The Student Revolution: A Global Analysis* (Bombay: Lalvani Publishing House, 1970).

3. V. Gordon Childe, *What is History?* (New York: Henry Schuman, 1953). For the controversy between Marxist and postmodernist views on historical change, see Steven Best, *The Politics of Historical Vision: Marx, Foucault, Habermas* (New York: The Guilford Press, 1995).

4. Denis Sullivan, review of A. R. Norton, ed., "Civil Society in the Middle East, Vol. 1," in *International Journal of Middle East Studies* 29, 1, (1997): 124.

5. Ibid., 125. See also Ghassan Salame, "Al-mujtama' wa al-dawla fi al-Mashreq al-'Arabi," Beirut, Center for Arab Unity Studies, 1987, cited in B. G. Massialas and Samir Ahmad Jarra, *Arab Education in Transition: A Source Book* (New York: Garland Publishing, Inc., 1991), 237.

6. See Fred Halliday, *Arabia Without Sultans* (Middlesex, UK, Penguin Books, 1974): 275–76, 373–76.

7. Report by His Britannic Majesty's Government on the Administration of Iraq for the Period April 1923–December 1924 (London: His Majesty's Stationery Office, 1925, Colonial No. 13), 214–15.

8. For an account of the violation of academic freedom in Iran, see Shahrzad Mojab, "Education and Human Rights: Iran," in *Academic Freedom 3: Education and Human Rights*, John Daniel et al., eds. (World University Service, London: Zed Books, 1995).

9. Shahrzad Mojab, "The State and University: The 'Islamic Cultural Revolution,'" in *Institutions of Higher Education of Iran, 1980–87*. (Unpublished Ph.D. dissertation, University of Illinois at Urbana–Champaign, 1991.)

10. See reports in the Persian weekly *Shahrvand*, Vol. 8, No. 377, October 9, 1998.

11. *Walls of Silence: Media and Censorship in Syria* (London, Article 19 Publication, 1998), 33.

12. Steve Niva, "Academic Freedom in the Middle East: Institutional Legacies and Contemporary Predicaments," in *Academic Freedom 4: Education and Human Rights*, Y. Erazo, M. Kirkwood, and F. de Vlaming, eds. (London; Zed Books and World University Press, 1996), 207.

13. Iranian daily newspaper *yandeg n*, Khurdad 23, 1358 (1979 June 13): 8.

14. Eva Egron-Polak, "Civil Society, Development and Universities," *Policy Options* 15, 4 (1994): 21–23.

15. Smitu Kothari, "Rising From the Margins: The Awakening of Civil Society in the Third World." *Development* 3, (1996): 19.

16. Amir Hassanpour, Tove Skutnabb-Kangas, and Michael Chyet, "The Non-education of Kuris: A Kurdish Perspective," *International Review of Education* 42, 4 (1996): 367–79.

17. Mark Muller, "Nationalism and the Rule of Law in Turkey: The Elimination of Kurdish Representation During the 1990s," in *The Kurdish Nationalist Movement in the 1990s: Its Impact on Turkey and the Middle East*, Robert Olson, ed. (Lexington, Kentucky: The University Press of Kentucky, 1996), 173–99.

18. Report by His Majesty's Government in the United Kingdom of Great Britain and Northern Ireland to the Council of the League of Nations on the Administration of Iraq for the Year 1929. London, His Majesty's Stationery Office, 1930, Colonial No. 62, 139–49.

19. Halliday, *Arabia Without Sultans*, 276.

20. James Ciment, *The Kuris: State and Minority in Turkey, Iraq and Iran* (New York, Fact on File, Inc., 1996).

21. "The Crushing of Kurdish Civil Society," in *War Report*, No. 47 (November-December 1997): 22–54.

22. Smitu Kothari suggests that an "egalitarian order" is a "prerequisite of a 'successful' civil society."

23. Bernard Lewis, "Why Turkey is the only Muslim democracy?," in *Middle East Quarterly* (March 1994): 41–49; Andrew Mango, *Turkey: The Challenge of a New Role* (Westport, CT: Praeger, 1994), 53.

13

Scholar-Activism for a New World: The Future of the Caribbean University

──────────────── *Anne Hickling-Hudson*

In this chapter I argue that the "soul" of the Caribbean university is the tradition of scholar activism, which puts itself at the service of changing the conditions of the poor and dispossessed. The university's main imperative is outlined as being its contribution to sustainable socioeconomic development and to increasing the human development index. While there are a range of alternative futures ahead for universities, I put forward the scenario of scholars working together to put their research and advocacy at the service of Caribbean development, thus helping to build a sustainable future. Their role would be to reinvigorate the Caribbean mission of the university and restructure it to better meet community and regional needs, so that it is not overwhelmed by those negative trends within globalization that work against equity and suppress or co-opt cultural diversity within the frame of corporate capitalism.

THE SOUL OF THE UNIVERSITY

The universities of the English-speaking Caribbean operate in societies that are "democratic in form but oligarchic in nature."[1] Graduates are the elites of these societies, a one or two percent minority, the other side of the coin of their impoverished fellow citizens. They fill professional and managerial positions in government ministries, social services such as hospitals and the high-status schools, consultancies, and private-sector enterprises. The universities are seen as the source of national research, strategic advice on development, and as intermediaries that will modify scientific and technical knowledge developed elsewhere for Caribbean requirements. They have also been valued for providing independent advice on social and political issues, and for recording and helping to maintain and develop Caribbean cultural traditions. They are expected to make a major contribution to the solution of the economic, technological and cultural crises of the present era.[2]

Caribbean societies recognize the value of this higher education role, yet, in keeping with the oligarchic nature of the ownership and social control patterns, which have a vested interest in keeping the majority of the population at the margins of power, the tertiary college and university sector has been kept extremely small. The universities in the region are the federated University of the West Indies (UWI), which serves sixteen countries, the University of Technology, Jamaica (UTech), and the University of Guyana. These small institutions, with only about 24,000 students between them, are far from being adequate to serve the higher education needs of a region of some five million.[3] The situation is exacerbated by the heavy loss of skilled graduates who migrate to wealthier countries.[4] It is not only the quantitative needs that are not being met. The universities themselves, in spite of having produced pockets of excellent intellectual work, have not sufficiently contributed to the decolonization of the societies in terms of systematically leading the exploration and tackling of development problems. The failure of political will, which has neglected to develop an adequate education system, or to sufficiently utilize graduates at home and abroad, has been unable to lead the societies out of the constrictions of neocolonial development.[5]

The University of the West Indies marked its 50th anniversary in 1998. In the tradition of 50th birthdays, it engaged in celebration, retrospection, and attempts to chart the future. One of the celebratory events was a symposium of papers presented by academics from UWI campuses and centers all over the region. A symposium paper by Dr. Brian Meeks, a senior academic in the Faculty of Social Sciences, made important points that have the potential to influence future research and academic activity. Entitling his paper "Saving the Soul of the University,"[6] Meeks saw UWI's "soul" as having to do with its rootedness in Caribbean soil and the deep concern of its intellectuals with the task of understanding and changing the Caribbean condition, putting their scholarship to serve Caribbean people, especially those impoverished and marginalized. Musing particularly on the Faculty of Social Sciences, which had played a leading role in intellectual activism in the 1960s and 1970s, he argued that this activist role was now in retreat.

Meeks saw the university's development in the following three phases:

- The first was characterized by the tremendous optimism of West Indian nationalism in the 1950s and early 1960s. This ended with the disappointment of the aborted West Indian Federation. It became clear that the newly independent societies were failing to make meaningful changes in the impoverishment, racial stratification, and political underdevelopment of the colonial heritage.
- "Counter-hegemonic praxis," which challenged neocolonialism, marked the second phase of UWI's development from the late 1960s to the early 1980s. The signature fea-

ture of this phase was the radicalization of scholarship. Intellectuals who blended a socialist and a Caribbeanist orientation, such as George Beckford, Walter Rodney, and many others, challenged the continuing impoverishment of the majority and the economic subordination of the region in the international economy. Their writings and activities addressed the concerns of the poor and of cultural nationalists. The counterhegemonic movement influenced the growth of cultural self-confidence, yet was not strong enough to change deep-seated stratification.

- Conservatism won out in the third period, from the early 1980s to the end of the 20th century, a period that Meeks describes as "Thermidor," borrowing the term used for the time of the defeat of the French Revolution.

The project of the Caribbean intellectual as activist, and the left-wing movement that emerged around this, collapsed in a two-fold process. First was the defeat of the left-leaning Manley government in Jamaica in 1980, then came the self-destruction of the Grenada Revolution and the invasion of Grenada by the United States in 1983. What followed, for most academics, was a vacuum—a state of ennui and self-censorship as far as radical scholarship was concerned, a turning to individualist pursuits such as that of private consultancies—all framed by a timid acquiescence to the status quo.

Meeks argues that Guyanese historian, Walter Rodney, author of the pathbreaking study "How Europe Underdeveloped Africa," embodied the best of UWI's scholar-activist tradition, by living out and consolidating the notion that the intellectual's role was to serve the people. Rodney worked in the 1960s and 1970s to overthrow "the hegemonies of the plantation and its Western institutions, and (for) the emergence of an alternative consciousness,"[7] not only as a university lecturer, but also in his educational work with dispossessed Rastafarian communities in the urban slums of Kingston, for which he was deported from Jamaica by the then government. He served the people in his home country Guyana by his collaborative leadership of the Working People's Alliance, a multiracial party that challenged the mono-racial government of the day. Rodney carried furthest the debate on the philosophical foundations for a Caribbean radicalism. Assassinated in Guyana in 1984, he paid with his life for his inspiring leadership, but the Working People's Alliance has continued his political education and organization at the grass roots.

Of course, radical scholarship is not the only kind of scholarship, and is never the only concern of a university. Caribbean university development in the 1980s and 1990s has kept pace with worldwide trends. For example, a polytechnic college in Jamaica earned an upgrade into a University of Technology, and UWI has undergone important internal change. Starting from the mid 1980s, it improved its ability to raise a part of its own finance, changed aspects of governance, increased the numbers of students and became more accountable to them, established staff development programs and an information systems unit, expanded distance education capacity, and established a thriving university press that is publishing a continuing flow of research.[8] Yet it is worth taking seriously Meek's view that in the conservative political contexts of the late 20th century, there is no longer a "critical mass" of staff and students whose primary focus is to engage in issues of social transformation. It is hard to see how equitable progress will take place without this radical leadership role coming out of tertiary and higher education. The region has to develop new economic and cultural activities, improve and modernize existing ones, and find a way of transcending the inequities and divisions of the past. Higher education has a key role to play in helping to generate the innovative knowledge needed as the foundation for developing and implementing this vision.[9] The sections that follow paint scenarios for the future, exploring the role of Caribbean universities in the next 50 years. Since this role is unlikely to change without prior political change, the focus is on the process of collective striving, which will underlie the transition to greater social justice. This gets underway in the first two decades of the new millennium, and scholar-activists play an important role in helping to forge the new vision. The emphasis is on agency. Next, the scenario sketches the new structures of university education developed by the year 2050. These point to increased access, a wider and more global range of academic options, and the systematic application of research to improving the economy and society.

SCHOLAR-ACTIVISM AS A LEVER OF CHANGE: A SCENARIO FOR THE DECADE AHEAD

In the new century, the important task is to strengthen those aspects of Caribbean political culture that will empower people to push their governments to bring about change. One aspect of change will be a new pattern in which high-quality tertiary education will move from being the preserve of a miniscule five percent elite to becoming accessible to a much larger proportion of the society. My scenario envisages the region's universities as playing an important role in helping to bring this about.

In the first decade of the 21st century, more academics will reorient their work toward social and political activism in a way that builds on the tradition of Walter Rodney and other radical scholars. This change is led by a group of academics calling themselves the New World Group Mark II, after the New World group that had contributed to the radicalization of Caribbean scholarship in Jamaica in the late 1960s and 1970s. The Mark II group commits itself to developing this tradition of scholar-activism, putting intellectual work not only at the service of students and regional development, but also at the service of poorer communities not connected with the university. It articulates affirmative critical thought to discover and utilize culturally relevant ways of empowering people at all levels of society—in the homes, in the schools, at the workplace, in the Church, and in the various political organizations. Critical thought means putting forward creative solutions to the present impasse hindering the progress of Caribbean societies. All of this resonates with the spirit of points made by Meeks in 1998 about the urgent role of radical academics in response to current crises:

Someone has to rethink the broad models of development, question their assertion as to what is "normal," with boldly proposed alternatives. Someone has to pose the issues as to what standards of behavior are acceptable in public as in private life. Someone has to face governments and openly raise issues of corruption where those may be appropriate. . . . Someone has to speak out for small, defenseless states in a world dominated by large, unimaginably powerful mega-blocs. Someone has to speak truth to power.[10]

By 2004 the New World Group Mark II has members not only from UWI, as its earlier New World counterpart had, but also from the other Caribbean universities and colleges, and from community group leaders such as the "Sistren" theatre collective[11] in Jamaica. New World groups are spreading rapidly throughout the Anglophone region. They help to publicize in regular popular forums the Caribbean's problems in production, environmental management, economic management, the schools, the media, the lawcourts, and parliament, and they discuss innovative solutions that are being attempted in several countries. These forums, drawing on community mobilization traditions that had experimented with processes of social change in Jamaica, Grenada, and Guyana in the 1970s and 1980s, are important strategies in organizing local communities to think deeply about Caribbean problems and experiment with solutions.

Community leaders emerge from this process, among them women and men who know what it is like to struggle with the injustice of being marginalized. They coordinate the hard work of facilitating community initiatives and of systematically pressuring governments to support these initiatives, in recognition that the key task is to increase the "human development index"(HDI), conceptualized as comprising health and longevity, literacy/schooling, and per capita purchasing power.[12] Most Caribbean governments had spectacularly failed in the 20th century in their responsibility to increase that index; failed to redistribute an adequate proportion of the nation's resources to social uses that enabled poor people to become more productive. The new community groups know that unless this is turned around, societies cannot achieve equitable socio-economic growth.[13]

As a result of highly organized collective action gathering momentum from around 2006, a new kind of radical political change sweeps through the region. The road is hard; the movement has to try to alter the colonized values of many people who are blind to the contradictions and dangers of the model of unsustainable consumption and social fragmentation, which the Caribbean had so deeply internalized.[14] But by 2010, this popular movement has put into office in most Caribbean countries new-style governments that have:

- The courage to "speak truth to power";
- The foresight to encourage citizens to intensify their alliances with strong progressive movements for peace, environmental wholeness, and cultural and gender equity in other countries of the world;[15]
- The commitment to tackle seriously the task of building up the HDI; and
- The guts to be accountable.

Expanding university access is an urgent task. The problems and hurdles facing the region make it increasingly clear "that the Caribbean is in great need of sophisticated technical human resources in the area of economic, social, and public policy analysis and management."[16] University access in the region is still immensely disparate. It ranges from 2,220 places per hundred thousand population in Cuba to 600 in Jamaica and Trinidad, to 60 in Haiti.[17] Cuba, faced with the economic crisis of the collapse of its socialist bloc trading partners in the 1990s, had been forced to downscale its high proportion of university students,[18] but it still had large university capacity and an excess of graduates compared to the rest of the region. It is logical for the English-speaking Caribbean to turn to Cuba for assistance in improving higher education.

Scholar activists help the new-style governments to negotiate this role, and they also help in expanding links with the universities of the Dominican Republic and Haiti. These scholars also lead the way in linking universities into open-learning, high-tech academic networks that span Latin America and the Caribbean. Scholar activists in UWI's School of Education, with their specialist knowledge of educational options and delivery, play an important role in helping to develop the policies underlying this expansion of tertiary education, as well as in assisting the Ministry of Education with the cultural transformation of the inequitable and inefficient neocolonial school system. All of this feeds into the process of restructuring higher education so that it is far more accessible to growing proportions of the region's population, and therefore more relevant to the needs of sustainable development.

THE ROAD TO TRANSFORMATION OF CARIBBEAN
HIGHER EDUCATION IN 2050

We are in the middle of the 21st century. By the year 2050, the Caribbean has at last, after much striving, improved its integration in trade, facilitated the movement of peoples into each other's countries for temporary or permanent work, and developed more sophisticated educational standards and foreign language skills in a greater proportion of its population. The region's universities have contributed greatly to this breaking down of neocolonial barriers that had kept the societies fragmented and insular, trapped in the language and educational traditions of the former colonizing powers. The higher education sector is well on the way to being transformed in terms of expanding access, research and leadership, and offering creative and flexible degree programs that blend a strong Caribbean character with a sophisticated ability to incorporate suitable global trends.

A Glimpse of the General Picture

The proportion of the 20 to 28 age group accessing higher education in 2050 has increased to 30 percent, and numbers of postgraduate researchers have quadrupled. The universities are working closely in many fields with their counterparts in Cuba, the Dominican Republic, and Haiti, and Caribbean business is helping governments to finance them. Applied research developed by Caribbean universities is helping to improve significantly many aspects of the region's economy and society. For example, researchers in agriculture are helping to change and expand the sector significantly. Old crops are forming the basis of new, value-added industries—for example, sugar cane is the basis for fuel and building materials, and banana leaves and tree stems are the basis for new textiles and clothing. Agriculture is linked to food processing, and more extensively serves the local market, including the hotel sector. Horticulture, mariculture, and other nontraditional fields have been systematically expanded and are thriving because of effective marketing. Applied research has helped the tourism sector to achieve greater sustainability and attract more customers by the development of better local cuisine, beverages, and entertainment, and by expanding ecotourism and inter-island travel.

The University of Fine Arts, established in 2015, has 18,000 students by 2050. It trains high-quality performers and artists in music, drama, film, and dance, and as a result, artistic output is much greater and the entertainment industry is fulfilling its potential to bring Caribbean expressive culture in all its uniqueness to other countries across the globe. This multifaceted change process has grown out of the new vision of society that was born of collective dialogue between scholar-activists, politicians, and worker/peasant intellectuals. They have combined the "different categories of sensibility . . . of the historian, the poet, the student of philosophy and the social sciences, the economist, and the theatre director"[19] to create an enriched regional culture.

All the universities use a mix of open learning through the Internet, CD ROMs, television and correspondence, and on-site classes, to deliver their programs. This means that many people can study from home at times convenient to them, coming into the university occasionally for special week-long workshops, to interact with other students and enjoy those features of campus life that are a necessary complement to "virtuality" in education.[20] The universities are assisted in developing skills in organizing open learning by special government departments located in several Caribbean countries. These have a concentration of expertise and of audiovisual and electronic equipment, and this is put at the service of regional educational development. Some students live on campus in dormitories, no longer in the luxurious single rooms, which had absorbed large sums and which meant that fewer students could have on-campus accommodation.[21]

A Personal Scenario

The higher education system in the Commonwealth Caribbean is providing students of the mid-21st century with the opportunity to assemble parts of their degree program from a variety of universities both regionally and globally. Some choose to integrate subjects offered by metropolitan universities in North America and Europe into their Caribbean degree. Others, seeking more knowledge of the newer postcolonial societies and cultures, are opting for subjects in universities in Africa, Asia, Australia and New Zealand, Latin America, and/or the Spanish- and French-speaking Caribbean. Fees are charged, and they have to negotiate with their university to accredit these subjects within their overall degree program. For example, 25-year-old Keisha Hunter, a Literature and Communications student at the University of the West Indies in 2040, assembles this suite of courses for her part time B.A. degree, to be done over six years while she works as a part-time producer in a television studio:

- Caribbean Literature in English–UWI
- Language and Linguistics: English and Creole Studies–UWI
- Postcolonial Literatures of Africa–Makerere University, Uganda
- Literatures of the Spanish Caribbean–UWI with the University of Santiago de Cuba
- Spanish–UWI with the University of Santiago de Cuba
- Media and Society–UWI
- Film Studies–UWI and the Open University, UK
- Communications Planning–Boston University, USA

Keisha studies her program both on-line and on-site. For the subjects in Cuba, she attends two five-week residency programs at the University of Santiago de Cuba, where she is able to develop her Spanish speaking and listening skills and a day-to-day appreciation of Cuban culture. She is able to do the subjects from Africa, the United Kingdom, and the United States through the Internet. This is an expensive way of doing an undergraduate degree, but Keisha is able to finance it from her savings and from a loan, which she undertakes to pay back within 10 years. Her part-time salary at the television station covers her living expenses (and makes her ineligible for one of the government scholarships available to the very poor). After graduating, she decides to take two years leave from her job to do her Masters in filmmaking at the famous Film and Television Institute of the Three Worlds in Cuba.[22] Here she gets the opportunity to participate in teams making short films in both Spanish and English, practices the roles of directing, producing, scriptwriting and editing, and gains experience in working with teams that specialize in writing subtitles and dubbing Spanish to English films and vice versa. This university education prepares her to carry out her lifelong ambition of becoming a film director and scriptwriter to help improve the Anglophone Caribbean film industry, which had started on a small scale in the mid-20th century. Critical, creative work in film and television is a vitally important role, helping to counter the intolerable situation in the late 20th century of reliance on imported television which, as Lamming had put it, was "(the) garbage of another world, unloaded on a mesmerized and uncritical populace . . . intended to ensure and reinforce the underdevelopment of our people."[23]

The Anglophone Caribbean now has a systematic work-study element in its undergraduate programs. This is developed by combining the work-study approach practiced in Cuba during the 20th century, with the work experience model utilized by Jamaica's University of Technology. Teams of undergraduate students are attached as workers for a few weeks each year to different workplace and community sites, both inside and outside the Caribbean. The sites have relevance to possible careers as well as to continuing community involvement. Language learning is added as a vital element of the university degree, and students get the opportunity to live for several weeks in the Spanish and French-speaking Caribbean. So attractive and useful are these Caribbean-immersed university programs that most students choose to study in their region—proportionately fewer are migrating to study in North America than was the case in the second half of the 20th century.

KNOWLEDGE FOR TRANSFORMATION:
THROUGH SOCIAL PRACTICE

This chapter has painted a narrative scenario of the future of Caribbean universities in order to contribute to dialogue about what needs to be changed and how it can be changed educationally in countries of the "South." Far from being merely wishful thinking, scenarios can be anchored in reality by analyzing problematic social patterns, considering how people can tackle the problems, and envisaging, step-by-step, the process that could experiment with solutions. Using this approach, the chapter puts forward the position that the foundation of change in Caribbean higher education in the 21st century will be the strengthening of the "soul" or essence of the university through the commitment of its scholar-activists to the development of communities, and the restructuring of politics and the education system. The main strategies of change are the expansion and upgrading of universities through regional collaboration, and the systematic application of research to improving regional economy and culture. The Caribbean university of the 21st century goes beyond producing graduates who are simply in hot pursuit of a personal career. It produces graduates who put knowledge in the service of social practice, and who see "disciplines" as instruments that aid the process of sustainable development and sociocultural change.[24] Knowledge is no longer "locked up in an enclave of scholars and research workers, consultants, and technocrats," but is becoming the shaping influence on the consciousness of the folk roots which made it possible in the first place.[25] The university sector reshapes its organization and culture, and prepares students in such a way that they graduate able to use local and global opportunities to creatively meet Caribbean cultural/economic needs within the difficult context of future change.

NOTES

1. Havelock Ross-Brewster, "Tributaries and All Their Legacies: The Politics of Poverty," in *The critical tradition of Caribbean political economy: the legacy of George Beckford*, Kari Levitt and Michael Witter, eds. (Kingston: Ian Randle Publishers, 1996), 183.

2. See Philip Sherlock and Rex Nettleford, *The University of the West Indies. A Caribbean Response to the Challenge of Change* (London: Macmillan, 1990), Chapter 17; and *Strategic Plan 1997–2002, University of the West Indies* (UWI: Canoe Press, 199), 5–9.

3. *World Bank, Caribbean region: access, quality and efficiency in education* (Washington DC: The World Bank, 1993: 152–56); and *Strategic Plan 1997–2002* (University of the West Indies) op cit.: 9–10.

4. Between 1978–1985, Jamaica lost to migration 78 percent of doctors who had been trained at the University of the West Indies, World Bank, Caribbean (1993), op cit.: 12.

5. See Trevor Farrell, "The Caribbean State and Its Role in Economic Management," in *Caribbean Economic Development: the First Generation*, S. Lalta and M. Freckleton, eds. (Kingston: Ian Randle Publishers, 1993), 200–14; Peggy Antrobus, "Gender issues in Caribbean development," in ibid.: 68–77; K. Levitt and M. Witter, eds. (1996).

6. Brian Meeks, "Saving the Soul of the University." Paper presented to symposium at the Mona campus of the University of the West Indies, June 1998, to celebrate UWI's 50th anniversary. From an audiotape recording, Radio Education Unit, UWI, Mona.

7. George Lamming, "The Caribbean Intellectual and Western Education," in *Crossroads of Empire: the Europe-Caribbean Connection, 1492–1992*, Alan Cobley, ed. (Barbados: University of the West Indies, 1994), 78–93. See also Rupert Lewis, "Ideological Aspects of the Writing and Reception of 'How Europe Underdeveloped Africa,'" in *Before and after 1865: education, politics and regionalism in the Caribbean*, B. Moore and S. Wilmot (Jamaica: Ian Randle Publishers, 1998), 351–62.

8. See Douglas Hall, *The University of the West Indies: a Quinquagenary Calendar 1948–1988* (University of the West Indies: The Press, 1998), 115–30.

9. Michael Witter, "Conference Overview," in K. Levitt and M. Witter, eds., op cit.: 57–67.

10. Brian Meeks, "Saving the Soul of the University," op cit.

11. The Sistren drama group writes and produces plays based on the lives of Jamaican women, as well as working in communities to help people develop problem-solving dramas. See Joan French, "Organizing Women Through Drama in Rural Jamaica," in Miranda Davies, *Third World, Second Sex* (London: Zed Books, 1987), 147–54.

12. UNDP, Human development report. (New York: Oxford University Press, 1990.)

13. Havelock Ross Brewster, "Tributaries and All Their Legacies: The Politics of Poverty," in K. Levitt and M. Witter, eds., op cit.: 181. See also C. Deere et al., *In the Shadows of the Sum. Caribbean Development Alternatives and U.S. Policy* (Boulder, Colorado: Westview Press, 1990).

14. Norman Girvan, "Economics and the environment in the Caribbean: An Overview," in *Caribbean Ecology and Economics*, N. Girvan and D. Simmons, eds. (Barbados: Caribbean Conservation Association, 1991), xi–xxiv; George Lamming, "George Beckford and the Predicaments of Caribbean Culture," in K. Levitt and M.Witter, eds., op cit.: 19–28; Lloyd Best, "Independence and Responsibility: Self-Knowledge as an Imperative," in K. Levitt and M. Witter, eds., op cit.: 3–18.

15. See Medea Benjamin and Andrea Freedman, *Bridging the Global Gap. A Handbook to Linking Citizens of the First and Third Worlds* (Washington D.C.: Seven Locks Press, 1989); and Jerry Mander and Edward Goldsmith, eds., *The Case Against the Global Economy and for a Turn to the Local* (San Francisco: Sierra Club Books, 1996).

16. Don Robotham, "Focusing and Developing Graduate Education in the UWI System: A Report to Strategy Committee." (Jamaica: University of the West Indies: unpublished report, 27 November 1997): 1.

17. *Unesco World Education Report 1993* (Paris: Unesco, 1993).

18. In the 1980s, Cuba had about 40,000 university graduates a year. By the mid-1990s this had been reduced to 30,000. Many students who formerly gained university access are now being placed in technical institutes. See Anne Hickling-Hudson, "Cuba's University Scholarships to its Neighbors and National Development in the Caribbean," *Centro: Journal of the Centro des Estudios Puertorriquenos,* City University of New York, IX, 4 (1997), 99.

19. George Lamming, "Beckford and the Predicaments of Caribbean Culture," in K. Levitt and M. Witter, eds., op cit.: 19–28.

20. Dennis Gibson and William Hatherell, "Reflections on Stability and Change in Australian Higher Education," in *Australia's Future Universities*, J. Sharpham and G. Harman, eds. (Armidale: University of New England Press, 1997): 121–36.

21. In catering for mass higher education, Cuban universities utilize dormitory-style arrangements, which make the individual rooms in UWI halls of residence seem relatively luxurious.

22. Cuba's international Escuela de Cine y Television is popularly known as the "School of the Three Worlds." The Caribbean and Latin America, Africa, and Asia represent the three worlds.

23. George Lamming, "Beckford and the Predicaments of Caribbean Culture," in K. Levitt and M. Witter, eds., op cit.: 27.

24. Anne Hickling-Hudson, "Cuba's University Scholarships to its Neighbors and National Development in the Caribbean," op cit.: 99–114.

25. George Lamming, "The Caribbean Intellectual and Western Education," in Alan Cobley, ed., op cit.: 90.

14

Internationalizing the Curriculum: For Profit or Planet?

──────────────────────────────── *Patricia Kelly*

Universities are under increasing pressure to respond to the connected issues of student diversity and globalization.

The globalization of our communication and transport systems, and the growing interdependence of countries and regions, create the need for people who can operate across national boundaries, outside familiar environments. . . . [T]hose students . . . will be the leaders in tomorrow's world.[1]

The OECD defined globalization as "a set of conditions in which an increasing fraction of value and wealth is produced and distributed worldwide through a system of interlinking private networks."[2] The rush of businesses and organizations to put their products and services on the Web exemplifies this global network. However, globalization is problematic. Not everyone benefits. In 1996, James Speth, the Administrator of the United Nations Development Program gave alarming statistics about declining standards of living in many countries. He warned that "if present trends continue, the defining concerns of international affairs in the next century will resolve around the struggle for equity—equity among nations, equity within nations, between the sexes and for future generations."[3] The leaders of such a world will need a new order of skills. However, "little attention is paid to the idea of conscripting the acquisition of metaskills or metacommunication into the service of creating a more just and equitable social order in which capitalism is placed under critique on moral and political grounds."[4] Most Australian universities have responded to this pressure with an official commitment to, or at least an expressed interest in, internationalization.

One effect is that many faculties are being required to "internationalize" their curriculum by a given date. This is rarely a welcome message, because most academics have been given few opportunities to understand the context or terminology and less support to put these into practice.

This chapter uses an Australian context to explore internationalization of the curriculum in higher education, within the context of a post-development vision of the future. There is no one "ideal" model for internationalization. It may be best seen as a "continuous cycle, not a linear or static process."[5] The phases in this cycle integrate an international dimension into the university and both depend on and create the supportive culture needed for successful change. Definitions also vary. A useful Canadian example sees internationalization as a "process that prepares the community for successful participation in an increasingly interdependent world . . . our multicultural reality is the stage for internationalization."[6] An Australian group concluded, "Internationalization includes teachers and students learning from each other, meeting the needs of overseas, offshore and local students, creating interdependence between students, viewing our professional practice from diverse perspectives, using culturally inclusive teaching practices, accessing teaching and learning resources that reflect diversity, and offering high-quality courses that are internationally relevant."[7]

In practice, much of the internationalization discourse is based in educating for profit. This is expressed in policy meetings and documents as a combination of attracting full-fee-paying overseas students; exporting ready-made courses to any country that will buy them; sending a tiny minority of wealthy or scholarship students to study abroad; setting up off-shore campuses and importing overseas staff. It also assumes that the mere presence of international students and staff will create an environment that, as one document put it, is "palpably international in flavor." The evidence actually suggests that "unless intercultural contact is engineered as part of formal study, social cohesion will not happen and all students will miss out on critical learning opportunities."[8] Head counts alone should not be accepted as convincing evidence of successful internationalization of the curriculum.

Because profit has made internationalization attractive, it has renewed interest in and support for policies and programs similar to those that should have been happening in response to the social and cultural diversity of the Australian community. Too many educators still regard diversity as a temporary annoyance, a problem for someone else to "fix," rather than as a cultural, economic, and intellectual resource that they should nurture. The deficit approach to diversity is so entrenched that many local and international students have internalized it. Even when academics informally invite students to use examples from their home countries or home cultures in assignments, the students are understandably apprehensive. If it isn't official, why would they risk failure? Academics who do encourage students to include multiple "knowings,"[9] often discover that there is a dearth of library resources to support such research. Others are embarrassed when they realize they don't know what is available. For these and many other reasons, many current approaches to internationalization of the curriculum in higher education are ad hoc, tokenistic, and inadequate.

THE BIG PICTURE

Few university courses help students to fit their learning into a societal and global context. This may be one cause of what Richard Slaughter calls the "mismatch between the deteriorating world picture and inadequate human responses."[10] There are alternatives to humanity's apparent "rape, loot, and pillage mission on planet Earth."[11] Italian futurist Danilo D'Antonio suggests globalism, defined as "a vision of an interconnected world in which the actions of few influence outcomes for all. There is a need to cooperate, justly, for global goals of: good ecology; sustainable society; population control; and the fair distribution of tasks, opportunities and gains."[12] He believes that globalists and globalizers can complement each other and that the visions and reflections of the globalists could be brought to fruition by the concrete action of the globalizers. In practice, "the importance we place on common humanity could provide the spring for the political will to challenge 'market logic' and explore alternatives."[13]

Without this globalist dimension, higher education technological futures may also fall into the trap of "aiding the domesticating and corporatizing of the future instead of the corporation becoming futurized or transformed."[14] Take the common scenario of a lecturer who works from home via a network and teaches through a variety of electronic methods, including on-line text, graphics, voice and video formats. The same questions arise whether the teaching is face to face or on-line. For example, what support in terms of personal and professional development do lecturers need and get, to acquire the skills to teach diverse students in this new medium? Interaction between students, or between students and lecturers, can go awry on e-mail as easily as in person. I have been told of off-campus overseas students who resist e-mail communication with their Australian lecturers because they have not been given a chance to develop a personal connection. International, joint student projects can also fail if students have not been prepared for the sensitivities this new field of cross-cultural communication requires. The resulting glitches are cultural, not technological. Moreover, how do the writers decide appropriate content? Who chooses the visual images? What input is there from voices of diversity, within and between cultures and through what consultation process? Readings and resources are usually Anglo-American. Indigenous and non-English speaking background perspectives seem absent. No amount of "flexible" delivery or technical gadgets compensates for irrelevant or poorly chosen information, inappropriately delivered. A technically well-produced presentation may be an even more effective tool for excluding voices of diversity, precisely because it looks so professional. Technology needs not just a human face but the faces of humankind.

In reviewing courses that are trying to "internationalize," from a variety of disciplines, I keep noticing similar shortcomings, many of which have been carried over from the original. The first and most obvious is the lack of a "human" voice. In proposed off-shore courses, the course writers and deliverers rarely introduce themselves, or answer implied student questions such as: Who is teaching me? Why would I want to learn from this person? What interest do they have in teaching me? How do they perceive me? How does this course recognize and include my context and ways of knowing? This gap is often widened by the accepted academic written style, using the passive voice, which seems cold and almost intimidatory. "All students will . . . ," "Students are expected to. . . ." In dealing with any diverse student cohort, and particularly in the absence of face-to-face contact, clear and appropriate language styles are essential preconditions for successful learning. Some of the gaps could be bridged by slightly differently worded questions and by input from people of diverse backgrounds. Another deficiency lies in the common expectation that students will work collectively, yet few courses build in activities to help students develop these skills, which include effective oral presentation. Academics seem to believe that students have somehow already acquired these skills or that they will gradually acquire them by trial and error. This is an inefficient and stressful method for most students. Another explanation is that many lecturers and tutors lack training, experience, and confidence to teach group skills.

Encouraging lecturers to acquire new perspectives is not easy. As part of an assignment for a course I teach, a lecturer described a common response. Her offers to help fellow lecturers work with diversity in the classroom were met with "resistance and excuses that there was not enough time." She concluded "[C]hanging mind frames in relation to cultural awareness of fellow staff and students is a long-term goal." Even a greeting can be a political act. If I begin a workshop for academics by acknowledging the traditional Aboriginal owners of the land, I know it will alienate some participants and make them resistant to anything else I say. Developing cultural awareness needs personal commitment and continual, high-level, institutional support and encouragement. In the haste to get courses out into the "marketplace," professional development and support are the most easily ignored and dispensable aspects of the process. Open Learning researcher Hilary Perraton warns that while "globalization and the information revolution . . . are making education more international . . . we lack mechanisms of governance to guide or regulate the process."[15]

A CRITICAL ALTERNATIVE

Inayatullah's "post-development, linear, progressive, and cyclical vision" of the future provides an alternative basis for internationalization of the curriculum in higher education.[16] He has developed this alternative approach as a way to rescue the future from the dominant paradigm of development and globalization. A curriculum developed on this basis will not use the language of certainty—"a path," "the way"—but will ask, "what are the particular social costs for any approach or view of the future."[17] This approach widens assumed universal knowledge into many possible 'knowings.' It offers a "prospective" view of history, which values the past, present, and future. Thus, it opens the door to a diversity of views of time and cosmology. One of the great oppressions of the current centrality of the machine and the technocrat in education is that many students believe they have to devalue or even discard their cultural knowings in order to succeed. Moreover, multiple, oppressive devaluing can occur within any society, in terms of gender, indigenous rights and sexual politics, among others. We need an approach that can work confidently but respectfully with the challenges of alternative paradigms. The nine characteristics of Inayatullah's vision appeal because they challenge neoliberalism and nationalism as well as tradition:

* The spiral
* Ecological sensitivity
* Gender cooperation
* Growth and distribution
* Epistemological pluralism
* A range of organizational structures
* Transcendental social theory
* The individual and the collective
* A balance between agency and structure

I address some implications of the first five.

The Spiral

The spiral (progress with history) metaphor challenges both the linear (continued growth) model and alternatives such as a cyclical—return to an idealized past model. Internationalization of the curriculum based on this metaphor could prepare students to be able to create the "new visions of development"[18] we need. Being free to draw from many traditions would enable students to find ways out of the "straitjacket of the dominant paradigm of development"[19] which underpins so much of the current, unquestioned content base; the way it is taught and the way students accept it. It also addresses the "poor fit between the language, culture, and beliefs of many nonwestern students, and the cultural meanings embedded in the (Western language) of science education."[20] Nigerian research suggests a complementary teaching approach in which "old view" analysis is followed by "new view" learning. This is combined with a harmonization process in which the science being taught is related directly to the indigenous culture.[21] The authors suggest this as a successful strategy to provide more effective science education in "nonwestern" societies, but it has wider relevance. All students would benefit from being introduced to indigenous attitudes to the natural world in science (and any other) courses. For example, I contrasted two differing views toward the land for some engineering students: one is part of the narrative from a 1925 film, the second from an Aboriginal elder from Kakadu in northern Australia. These have been cleverly juxtaposed in a recent Australian documentary history series.[22]

Man has come to stay. His conquest has begun. . . . Fences must be put up. Trees must be ringbarked, scrub must be burned and the earth yields to the dominion of man. (1925 narration)

This ground . . . and this earth like brother and mother. They cutting its body off us. They cutting our mother's belly. (1997 Bill Neidjie—Kakadu Man)

The inherent differences across time, cultures and gender attitudes in these texts challenged Australian and international students alike and produced thoughtful written reflections. Two responses from students from different backgrounds follow:

We have become more aware of the fact that we are responsible to protect the environment and not above it so that future generations have the chance to appreciate it.

This shows that ethics has change (sic) through times and technology. From the Kakadu man's quote, we can feel the "softness in human" (sic). . . . with technology being more advanced every day, we as engineers can help to rebuild the environment.

Inayatullah's vision is "progressive" as opposed to "progress" based. This is relevant because we rarely challenge "progress" by asking progress toward what, for whom, defined by whom? "Progressive" allows choices. It respects the past but also challenges its oppressions, inside and outside of the society. "The world of many selves asks: 'Which world is this? What is to be done in it? Which of my selves is to do it?'"[23] By teaching in ways that include such spaces, "intellectual and spiritual resources presently being wasted will become valuable inputs into economic development,"[24] providing the competitive advantage for "productive diversity."[25] Most students are studying courses based on linear, unlimited development and profit-based models. This shows short-term thinking. Professionals who have been educated to exploit and not to sustain are no use to societies with economies and ecologies facing increasingly severe crises.

Ecologically Sensitive

Equally crucial in the vision is the notion of ecological balance. How can tertiary courses encourage "the new ethic of life"[26] implied in this principle? We will be really taking seriously the question of sustainability when we see that our social frameworks are inevitably constructed within an ecological reality."[27] All cultures need to demonstrate that they can be reflexive and self-critical. Traditional practices may also work against ecological sustainability. For example, the demand for traditional medicine, combined with large markets, threaten extinction for creatures on land and in the sea.[28] This clash between cultural practices and ecological sustainability is a legitimate topic for university courses. Creative alternatives may be found but great knowledge, skill, and sensitivity are required to discuss and teach such issues without seeming judgmental and confrontational. The Institution of Engineers, Australia (IEAust), and international professional engineering bodies are already providing the vision and leadership needed, by requiring engineering graduates to demonstrate effective communication skills and an understanding of social, cultural, global, business, and environmental responsibilities, as well as the principles of sustainable development.[29]

The best academics already model critical reflection as a transferrable and desirable skill. Many others need professional development in order to learn how to teach this way and to understand why it is important. They can then explain it to students, many of whom have been convinced by previous education and experience that unquestioned and restrained development is a desirable end in itself. Other students are taking the lead to demand change. One concerned lecturer told me that students had challenged him as to why environmental issues were not included in a particular business subject. He gave the honest response that he hadn't thought about it and didn't feel confident to teach it. He set a question on it for the exam anyway and despite the fact that he had not formally taught the topic, a quarter of his students chose this question in the examination.

Gender Agenda

Gender is another area where culture, power, and structures intersect. "[A]ny individual student's voice is already a "teethgritting" and often contradictory intersection of voices constituted by gender, race, class, ability, ethnicity, sexual orientation, or ideology."[30] Any preferred vision of an internationalized curriculum would embrace this challenge. However, international conferences dedicated to responding to the challenges of internationalization, still make little attempt at gender inclusion, even at a token level of workshop leaders and chairpersons. Conferences I have attended in Europe and Asia in 1998 have been set up on the "sage on the stage" model, which discourages dialogue and interaction. Delegates are somehow meant to get to know each other by being in the same space. It takes a very confident female or young person to speak from the microphones set up for audience feedback on such occasions or to bring the issue of inclusion to the attention of the organizers, who are usually of higher status. The issue is complicated for visitors, who are reluctant to offend the host culture. Conferences should encourage and support communication through a variety of genuinely participatory forums, rather than being platforms for restating and reaffirming the views of those with power. The public support of senior (usually male) colleagues is critical in bringing about structural, not cosmetic changes in this situation and it is lamentably long in coming.

A globally portable graduate will have the confidence to question her/his values and how they impact on their own lives and those of others.[31] A Muslim colleague who has chosen to wear the hijab (head-covering) was asked by a young Australian student, "Are you a nun or something?" She had the maturity and personal skills not to be offended, but it is an example of cultural ignorance that should not happen at tertiary level. Universities are keen for lecturers to earn money through teaching courses in other countries, but few require or offer professional development courses to prepare them for a successful experience and to build on their knowledge.

Cultural blinkers are a global issue. International students, post-graduates in particular, may be in their 30s and older. They may come from high-status positions to being students again. This is not an easy transition. At my university, some middle-aged, male, international students attending a short-term course refused to attend academic support sessions if females conducted them. Everyone loses in this situation. The students felt pressured. The female lecturers felt devalued. The students are not acquiring the cultural flexibility they need to function effectively as professionals in the international arena or to expand their own learning. Moreover, their behavior is seen by the host culture as reinforcing negative religious and cultural stereotypes.

Any course that aims to prepare students for a rapidly changing world would include the building blocks for cross-cultural communication and lifelong learning. A recent Fourth Congress of the Asian Planning Schools' Association (APSA) Conference in Bandung, Indonesia, attended by over three hundred participants from Asia, Africa, the United Kingdom, the United States, and Australia, identified their major planning issues as: "globalization; decentralization; public/private ownership; sustainable human development; cross-cultural education, and gender issues."[32] This is the kind of evidence I must seek and use in order to persuade academic staff and university managers that these are issues in the "real world" for which they believe their courses are preparing students and from where they seek students.

Growth and Distribution

All courses should consider ethical business—the impact of culture on doing business and the impact of business on culture. This engages with the economic growth and distributive justice dimensions of wealth creation. It is business and globalism, rather than just global business. Dr. Selim Jahan, the deputy director of the United Nations Human Development Program, at the Australian launch of the 1998 report, stated that 26 percent of the world's people account for 86 percent of spending for personal consumption. The wealthiest 20 percent consume 45 percent of meat and fish, use 58 percent of total energy, own 74 percent of all telephone lines, and 80 percent of the world's vehicles.[33] How many lecturers use such statistics and engage with their implications? As part of a first-year engineering module, a colleague and I try to address this by inviting professional engineers from a diversity of backgrounds to share "critical incidents" with first-year engineering students. They present the facts of a real incident from their working lives. Most incidents involve a combination of business, cultural, and ethical issues, which students have time to identify and discuss before hearing the actual solution.

Business and globalism, as defined above, involve more than token sessions at the beginning or end of courses. One-off sessions can lead to simplifying and stereotyping. At the beginning, they may set up high expectations that need to be fulfilled throughout the course. The last lecture of a course is often reserved for the "Other," whatever or whoever that may be. Many students do not attend since it is too late for it to be assessed. If it isn't valued enough to be assessed, why bother? Placing knowledge on the margins keeps it marginal. Moreover, relying on guest "experts" to provide this perspective also avoids the regular lecturer having to learn about it, incorporate it, or resource it.

Epistemologically Pluralistic

We are preparing students for a world that desperately needs successful cultural dialogues. Such dialogues need a basis in knowledge and human rights. It will take great skill, support, and understanding to reconcile some cultural practices with human-rights imperatives. Some cannot be, but customs and values are deeply and sincerely held. Students and staff are unlikely to share or discuss such issues if they feel they are in an unsympathetic or critical environment and yet we need such discussions in order to challenge and change ideas. Cultural practices are also often linked to power. This is not yielded easily. Critical discussions on values and beliefs are often easier to have outside the pressures and expectations of one's home culture. They may also stimulate new, creative interpretations of the cultural practices of all concerned.

When cultural interaction is given priority, the effects can be cathartic. I attended a conference held at the Auckland Institute of Technology in Aotearoa/New Zealand (1998). A Powhiri/welcome was organized for conferees in the meeting-house which has been built as part of that institute's commitment to successful education for Maori students. Almost three hundred delegates, mainly from Oceania, were welcomed into the meeting hall for a two-hour ceremony. The Maori elders explained the significance of the ceremony, and spoke and sang in Maori. The ceremony ended with an invitation to hongi. What I had previously seen as a "nose-pressing" greeting took on its profound significance as an exchange of trust and sharing. This was very different from Maoris "performing" as exotic "others" for an alienated and insulated audience. It was a moving experience and changed the atmosphere of the conference through to the end. It added a spiritual and human dimension missing from most of our busy lives and was a true learning experience. For the non-Maoris, it was a privilege to be allowed to share this rich culture, while the Maoris said it was affirming to have such a strong and valued presence. A Maori elder shared a proverb that summed it up. If you share your basket of food and I share mine, together we have a feast. It was a salient comparison to the crumbs offered by the Australian One Nation Party's mean-spirited idea of "one" culture. Conferences like this happen when organizers make conscientious efforts to build cultural exchange into their official agenda. "It is men and women who must act courageously, who must bring about preferred visions, who must with their intellect develop new scientific possibilities and societal futures and thus develop the new human in the new world."[34] "Courage" is not an exaggeration. Several participants apparently complained later to the organizers that the welcome ceremony described above had taken up "too much time."

The very cultural aspects that have given cultures stability in the past may not be appropriate in rapidly changing situations. Those in power can misuse traditional respect for status to avoid being held accountable in the present, with dire economic and social consequences. When I was an Academic Adviser for overseas post-graduate students, some students told me how difficult it was to share their hard-won knowledge and expertise in their home countries. Their suggestions were often ignored or not even sought, because as new graduates, they lacked the necessary status to be heard.

ROLE MODELING CHANGE

"[T]ertiary institutions have a social responsibility to design learning environments which foster students' development of intercultural adaptability as one of the major aims of the internationalization of higher education."[35] The students from an effective system would be globally portable graduates,[36] world-class professionals, a kind of 'Globo-Sapiens.'[37] They would be interculturally competent in their personal/professional lives, show openness to differences and similarities in cultures other than their own, and be able to identify the major limitations and problems in their personal and professional lives that arise from ethnocentrism.[38] Universities can use internationalization to achieve these ends and to prepare effective professionals and future leaders. However, we have to ask what skills lecturers and tutors need to prepare such students, whether they already have them and what commitment universities are making to professional development for staff to acquire and maintain them. We are either role models for change or maintainers of the status quo: part of the problem or part of the solution.

Working with staff and students in this area isn't easy. "Even among those . . . who cannot be considered reactionary, there still exists a certain anxiety and insecurity engendered by the appearance in the university of pedagogies which take issues of race, gender and sexuality seriously and locate such issues within a praxis of social justice." [39] In my work, this attitude manifests in comments such as "no one asked me if I wanted to be multicultural!" or "bit heavy on equity!" Meanwhile, the world is burning. We have little time left to choose sustainable paths. What more will it take to make us change what we teach and the way we teach it?

NOTES

1. Fay Gale, "Where Does Australian Higher Education Need To Go From Here?", in *Australia's Future Universities,* J. Sharpham and G. Harman, eds. (University of New England, NSW 2351, 1997): 107.

2. Organization for Economic Cooperation and Development (OECD) *Technology and the Economy: The Key Relationships* (1992), 210, cited in Leo Maglen, "Globalization of the World Economy and its Impact on Employment and Training in Australia," *Australian Bulletin of Labor* (National Institute of Labor Studies, The Flinders University of South Australia) 20, 4, (1994): 299.

3. James Speth, *"Economic Growth and Equitable Human Development,"* the launch of the 1996 Human Development Report, UNDP (16 July 1996.)

4. Peter McClaren, "Critical Pedagogy in the Age of Global Capitalism: Some Challenges for the Education Left," *Australian Journal of Education* 39, 1 (1995): 10.

5. Hans De Wit, ed., *Strategies for Internationalization of Higher Education: A Comparative Study of Australia, Canada, Europe, and the United States of America* (European Association for International Education (EIAIE), in cooperation with the Program on Institutional Management in Higher Education (IMHE) of the OECD and the Association of International Education Administrators (AIEA), (Amsterdam, 1995): 25.

6. A. Francis, (1993) Facing the Future: The Internationalization of Postsecondary Institutions in British Columbia, British Columbia Centre for International Education, Vancouver, cited in Jane Knight and Hans De Wit, Strategies for Internationalization of Higher Education: Historical and Conceptual Perspectives. In *Strategies for Internationalization of Higher Education*, H. De Wit, ed. (1995), op cit.: 15.

7. Gursewak Aulakh et al. (1997) cited in Kate Patrick, ed., *Internationalizing the University: Implications for Teaching and Learning at RMIT.* A Report on the 1996 Commonwealth Staff Development Fund Internationalization Project conducted by RMIT. (Melbourne: RMIT, 1997) 6.

8. S. E. Volet and G. Ang, "Culturally Mixed Groups on International Campus: an Opportunity for Inter-cultural Learning," *Higher Education Research and Development* (HERD) 5, (April 1998): 219.

9. Professor Brenda Dervin introduced me to a critical view of noun-based cultures. See Brenda Dervin, "Verbing Communication: Mandate for Disciplinary Intervention," *Journal of Communication*, 43, 5 (Summer 1993).

10. Richard Slaughter, "Futures Concepts," *Futures*, (April 1993): 307.

11. Ian Lowe in Fay Gale and Ian Lowe, *The Boyer Lectures* (Sydney, ABC Books, 1996), Chapter 6.

12. Danilo D'Antonio, "Globalism and Globalization," E-mail posting to *FUTURES.L,* (22 Oct. 1997), dasa3000@mondrian.sgol.it

13. D. Ransom, "Globalization—an Alternative View," *New Internationalist* 296, (November 1997): 10.

14. Sohail Inayatullah, "Deconstructing the Future," *Futures*, 22, 2 (March 1990): 115–41.

15. Hilary Perraton, "The Virtual Wandering Scholar: Issues for International Higher Education," in *Learning and Teaching in Higher Education: Advancing International Perspectives*, R. Murray-Harvey and Halia Silins, eds., HERDSA Conference, Special Edition, School of Education, Flinders University (July 1997): 174.

16. Sohail Inayatullah, "Framing the Shapes and Times of the Future: Toward a Post-Development Vision of Futures," in *The Knowledge Base of Futures Studies, Vol. 3*, R. Slaughter, ed. (Media and Futures Studies Centre, Melbourne, 1995), 118.

17. Ibid., 114.

18. Ibid., 123.

19. Ibid., 124.

20. David Baker and Peter C. S. Taylor, "The Effect of Culture on the Learning of Science in Non-Western Countries: the Results of an Integrated Research Review," *International Journal of Science Education* 17, 6 (1995): 702.

21. Ibid.

22. *Rewind*, a 26-program (x 5 minutes) compilation of Australian history (1997). Available as two videos from Film Australia. See www.filmaust.com.

23. Michel Foucault, cited in Sohail Inayatullah (1990), op cit.

24. Sohail Inayatullah (1995) op cit.: 124

25. Mary Kalantzis and Bill Cope, "Why Culture Will Win Out Over Markets," *Management, Australian Institute of Management Journal* North Sydney, NSW (July 1997): 33.

26. Sohail Inayatullah (1995), op cit.: 124.

27. Ian Lowe, "Sustainability: Principles to Practice." In *Fenner Conference on Environment 1994, Proceedings*, Canberra, 13–16 November, Strategic Policy Unit, Department of the Environment, Sport and Territories, ACT 2600, 182.

28. R. Parry-Jones, "Can We Tame Wild Medicine?," *New Scientist* 2115 (3 January 1998): 26–29.

29. IEAust, *Policy on Accreditation of Professional Engineering Courses*, The Institution of Engineers, Australia, National Office (1997), Canberra.

30. Elizabeth Ellsworth, "Why Doesn't This Feel Empowering? Working Through the Repressive Myths of Pedagogy," *Harvard Educational Review* 59 (3 August, 1989): 312.

31. Sid Morris and Wayne Hudson, "International Education and Innovative Approaches to University Teaching," *Australian Universities' Review* 2 (1995): 70–74.

32. John Minnery and Bishnu Bajracharya, *Report on the Visit to Indonesia*, School of Planning, Landscape Architecture and Surveying, Queensland University of Technology, Brisbane (30 August–26 September, 1997), 3.

33. J. Ellicott, "Gadgets Leave Us Poorer," The Courier Mail, Brisbane, Queensland (9 October 1998): 3.

34. Sohail Inayatullah, e-mail communication (1997).

35. S. E. Volet and G. Ang (1998), op cit.: 21.

36. Sid Morris and Wayne Hudson (1995), op cit.

37. I first heard the term "Globo-Sapiens" at the Futures Conference in Brisbane, 1997. I would be grateful to know who coined it.

38. From Tom Whalley, *Best Practice Guidelines for Internationalizing the Curriculum* (Centre for Curriculum, Transfer and Technology, Victoria, British Columbia, 1997), 15. Available on the World Wide Web at http://www.ctt.bc.ca.

39. Peter McLaren (1995) op cit.: 14.

Part 3

Alternative Universities

15

The Crisis of the University: Feminist Alternatives for the 21st Century and Beyond

———————————————— *Ivana Milojevic*

Why is it that every time women enter a certain profession or institution in significant numbers we start talking about the "death" of that very profession or institution? For centuries, women were among those excluded from entering institutions of higher education: the universal fact, throughout history and throughout cultures. It is only in the last 50 years that women were enabled and encouraged to enter universities and other institutions of higher education in great numbers. However, it seems now that women's efforts were slightly misdirected as the university itself has become "under scrutiny" and is "in ruins."[1] Dator claims that in the future universities will become a "theme park" from the past, as they have lost the purpose for their existence.[2] Apparently, their purpose for creating a certain profile of workers and passing on a particular culture is being outdated. Indeed, global capitalism has reduced the importance of national institutions, and is making higher demands for the immediate connection between knowledge and usefulness. At the same time, the Web has dramatically transformed our access to information, creating a culture where human contact becomes more and more redundant and mediation through machines acceptable. But this attitude toward university is, however, fairly recent as the review of literature on higher education historically shows. As recently as thirty years ago, the approach toward higher education was entirely different than it is today. While the need for reform and the university's transformation has been widely discussed, in general, the optimistic attitude and belief in the liberating potential of higher education has prevailed. The main issues, then, were: accessibility, quality, and democratization of higher education. These issues were also the main issues within feminist writings on higher education, with the exception of radical feminism, which seeks to dismantle all hierarchies and institutions. Throughout past centuries and through the greater part of the 20th century, mainstream feminist research, writings and actions have focused mostly on efforts to:

* Make higher education accessible to women;
* Increase women's proportion throughout university's ranks (raising the "glass ceiling") and different areas of study (especially in science and technology);
* Fight sexism and prejudices in university settings (environment, research, knowledge); and
* Transform knowledge to be less gender biased and more inclusive of women's perspectives.

Today, we have succeeded up to a point in many of those goals. We have a majority of women amongst students in several countries, higher participation of women in "masculine" occupations and fields of study (such as engineering and science), and a female dean shows up once in a while. Activists and academics have created women's studies courses that are attempting to create knowledge about, by, and for women. Lately, some universities have accepted affirmative action programs and are trying to change the atmosphere and environment where it is hostile to women. This has helped to improve some women's personal lives by giving them varied skills for competing in the job market, or giving the opportunity and "excuse" for young girls to move away from their parents. But today's rules have changed. While we are still struggling and trying to succeed within, and even transform one of the previous fortresses of masculine gatherings, our efforts can be compared to the swimming of a fish in a pond next to the sea. Interests, "usefulness," "relevance," and consequently money and jobs, have been shifting somewhere else, to other areas of the knowledge economy.

So, what really happened to one of the oldest institutions? How can we make some sense of all these changes and transformations? More importantly, how are current changes going to influence women's education in the future? And where should women (with or without feminist consciousness) direct their efforts in the area of higher education in the future?

In this chapter, I make several arguments:

* The current downfall of the universities is the consequence of the dominant ways of thinking within our patriarchal societies;
* Gender is not an accidental but crucial factor for how we think of and define education;
* The current crisis of the university is creating an opportunity for a paradigm shift in regard to education in general, and institutions of higher education in particular; and
* Feminist writings on education, and feminist educational practices offer a viable alternative for the times to come.

THE CURRENT TRANSFORMATION OF THE UNIVERSITY

The current situation with the institutions of higher education, particularly with the university, is the consequence of a worldview (sometimes recognized as male, patriarchal, or Western) that favors, amongst other things, greed, competition, usefulness, ranking, and hierarchy. There is a great deal of pressure for today's universities to start performing better or perish, to act as a successful corporation and reach as many consumers as possible. As government funds dry up, marginal groups, as always during turbulent changes, are the first to go. Women especially lack the resources—in time, money and energy—to be able to compete success-fully. Unfortunately, our dominant worldview does not allow thinking about long-term consequences and distant future. What is important is what is happen-ing today or next year, since an investment without bringing immediate revenues means failure.

The Corporate University

The university as a corporation is increasingly becoming the reality of many of today's universities—where deans and directors concentrate mainly on acquir-ing means for further functioning. The university as a corporation is just another business, possibly an independent and autonomous bureaucratic organization, or a place for vocational training. Of course, this scenario is based on the reality of globalization, and cuts in government support. Many universities, especially in the West, are pressured to turn toward this model, if they are to survive in the future, or at least that is what they believe.

While concentrating on globalism and economic rationalism, "the realities" of our present societies, there is one thing we often forget. The university as a cor-poration is just one of the possible scenarios for its future. Furthermore, even if it is the most likely one, it can also be just a transitional phase, and a temporary process. The university in the future can be what we want it to be. However, often, we are trying mostly to "catch up" with the future, instead of trying to create more positive visions and images. The most important question then is not whether the university will become a corporation in the future but whether that is what we want it to become.

Do we really want to see a future university where the main intellectual activ-ity is grant writing? Do we really want to see the university where our thinking would be a priori limited within the eligibility and guideline criteria? As for women, it is almost certain that the corporate university, with its focus on com-petition, profit, vocationalism, and immediate usefulness would dramatically reduce not only the number of women, but political and educational gains for women as well. Yes, potentially, the corporate university could increase women's chances at the job market, although the correlation between women's education and access to jobs has always been much more problematic and much less linear than the one for men. As potential customers at the future corporate university, women would probably still have some say. At best, the future corporate univer-sity would respond to women's needs by making studying more accessible and more flexible for women, allowing re-entries, providing child care, and address-ing sexual harassment issues. Maybe it would even be shifting curricula toward inclusion of women and women's perspective and simultaneously trying to diminish gender bias in most disciplines. However, it would fail to radically transform gender relationships, the nature of education, and the way we think about our society. While the future corporate university might include some feminist perspectives (similar to the ways current universities are) its main purpose would be to create competent information workers.

Before we look at the alternatives, let's first look at the other most often discussed future scenario for the university: the global electronic university and discuss it from a woman's point of view.

The Global Electronic University

The emerging global electronic university is another main preoccupation when discussing the futures of the university. This model raises many issues such as: costs, access, distribution of services, quality, place or space, inclusion/exclusion, globalism, multiculturalism, communication and connection, flexibility, and information/knowledge. In the best case scenario, it will mean the creation of webs of knowledge with unlimited access to information, informal faculty–student relationships, and learning based on cooperation. It will overcome the "tyranny of the disciplines," replace hierarchy, and through reduced costs and flexible access, reach an enormous number of people. It has the potential to become what universities should be about: access to "everything"—all the knowledge and all the existing information. In the worst case scenario it will further implement a one-dimensional view of reality, replace knowledge and wisdom with fragmented information and data, and exclude the majority of the people, especially from marginal and disadvantaged social groups and countries/peoples.

While the discourse of the new worldwide electronic university mostly focuses on democratization—the way universities are becoming less costly, more accessible, and more in tune with current technological achievements, for women this change raises once again the issue of access. This time, it is less an issue of direct (legal or customary) exclusion, like it was in the past, but more an issue of structural exclusion.

The creation of a global (worldwide) electronic university is happening within the context of the vast majority of the world's women being "illiterate." This illiteracy is, of course, computer illiteracy, and is unequally distributed among women, being influenced by our class, age, wealth, and country of residence. Computer illiteracy of women in certain areas of Asia and Africa, among older women, among certain national and religious minorities and indigenous populations is as high as nearly 100 percent. Those lucky to be able to access the Net discover that computing is not so gender-neutral as it is alleged to be.

Feminists critique the Net for being prone to cyber-pornography and cyber-exploitation of women, pedophilia, and continuing the further alienation of individuals in society. The difficulties women face in juggling work, family, and the time they like to spend on the Net, and the already-mentioned inability of certain groups of women to "join the fun" are also problems. The picture is, of course, not totally bleak as there are many positive dimensions of current trends for women: flexibility, higher access to information, ability to work from home (with a catch: as women are simultaneously expected to manage the household and take care of children), creation of global sisterhood, and informal women's networks, to name just a few. And while certainly "the power (computer offers those with knowledge and access, the power to define many aspects of their lives) . . . is not equally available to men and women, nor will it be in the future,"[3] future women academics will have to also concentrate their efforts in the utilization of computers for creation of women's own information databases, "taking back the power to name categories of knowledge that are important to us."[4]

While it is certainly important to discuss these two very likely scenarios for the future of the university, it is equally important to remember that they are just that: scenarios. As such, at least one of them can even be "the worst case scenario" for academic freedom or for academics of the female gender. Such an interpretation is absolutely crucial for our future actions. Seeing the corporate or global-wide Web university as future realities means adopting "coping with" strategies. Seeing them as less desirable scenarios means adopting "fighting against" strategies. While this repositioning might seem too naïve, we should not forget that even the very idea of what the university is changed throughout space and time. The current university as we now "universally" understand this word is a western creation that began some thousand years ago. During that time, its purpose for existence, position in society, and access by minority groups (including women) has been radically changed. So why should we then concentrate on future images of the university, if we do not see them as very desirable, just because they are the dominant theme of our times?

We can also create other ideas of the university and advocate for their future to be realized; for example, the idea of the university as a place of/for academic leadership, acquisition of knowledge, and the search for truth. This is the traditional idea of the university where the main focus is on teaching—passing of acquired knowledge to students, and research—the expansion of the knowledge base of university disciplines. Or we could focus on the more recent idea of polyversities and multiversities instead of universities[5]—the idea of the university where the search for universal knowledge, instead of being exercised through the implementation of the dominant group's view of reality, would shift toward universal acceptance of difference, especially in the humanities and social sciences. Or we could cherish the idea of a community-based university, whose main function is in public service, as proposed by Rooney and Hearn in this volume. Or even develop and advocate for the image of the women's university. While some authors such as Rahman would see this, in its Islamic fundamentalist form, as retrogressive, the following vision is more utopian.

THE VISION OF THE FUTURE WOMEN'S UNIVERSITY: THE UNIVERSITY FOR, ABOUT, AND BY WOMEN

Having another look at the way we situate and contextualize education we can see that gender plays a crucially important role. Traditionally we are taught to accept the model in which the educational system is like a leech depending either on mecenas, sponsors, governments, or business. They set the terms, educators play by the rules. It is interesting to remember how the rules for women, during just one century, have changed significantly. First women were supposed to be educated in order to become better wives and mothers. Then, to become qualified information and service workers. And now, to become competent information workers. On the other hand, what if we shift the focus and see education as one of the most important institutions in society, with corporate, state, and military (if still existing) sector focusing on the needs of the education system. How about if we believed that child-care workers and teachers in early childhood education should be one of the highest (rather then lowest) paid professionals? What implication would this have to the institutions of higher education? Would universities still be "elitist" institutions, or would they lose such characteristics in a society in which everyone would get the opportunity to study?

As we can see from feminist fiction writings, they bring radically different images of future societies. For a start, education, together with parenting, is put at the center of social life and everyday activities. Furthermore, education and parenting are seen as the very purpose of the existence of those future societies. Most feminists believe that education is an extremely important social institution and as such should receive more attention in society. Such focus, on parenting and education, and primarily on future generations, would not only transform education but also society in general. The rush to obtain more money and more power, and the urge to dominate would be replaced with a more sustainable approach, focused on cooperation. If we put the future of our future generations on the top of our priority listing we would not be able to justify many of our current practices, including the degradation of our educational system.

Apart from this major shift in how we situate education, women's studies and feminist theory have also developed more detailed characteristics of a desirable educational system. While there are many differences between many feminists and many feminisms, both policy (women's studies) and future visions (feminist writings, actions and strategies) evolve around certain ideas of what this desirable model might look like. This model is probably not the most ideal one for our long-term future (everything ages with time), but it is the best we have so far. At least, it is the best for most women and it is definitely better than the current ones. I call this model the future "women's university."

THE EMERGING FUTURE WOMEN'S UNIVERSITY

The Difference between Women-Friendly and Women's University

The women's university[6] has its beginnings in efforts to unlearn the lie, the lie which "asserts that white people [of male gender] are innately superior morally, intellectually, and culturally to other racial/cultural groups."[7] While most recent feminist efforts are concentrated on breaking the rule by which men are "the norm" and women are "the other," it is extremely difficult to deny the reality in which women are, and have been for most of our recorded history, second-class citizens, "the other" or on the margin. Most attempts to envision modes of education which evolve around women's lives, realities, interests, and perspectives start with a critique of existing institutions and ways of education. But as feminism is also a social movement and concerned with social change, it is at the same time futuristic in its efforts not only to change and transform but also envision far ahead as well.

There are two main lines of feminist envisioning. One is partial and limiting as it is locked into present realities and institutions of higher education: this is the idea of *a women-friendly university*. The other one has a very different idea as to what the university should be about, how it should look and be organized, and where it should be situated within society: this is the idea of *a women's university*.

While working toward the same goal of reaching equality for women in the future, there is a significant difference between women-friendly and women's university. The first one exists within the future mainstream university but is more inclusive of women's needs and perspectives, while the other one is an *authentic women's university*, where women's experience is the norm. The first model is usually criticized as not being radical enough and the other for its difficulties in finding *authentic women's experiences* and the tendency to universalize the particular (the category of woman). However, both are important, as both are alternatives and are attempts to transform an institution that drastically omits, distorts, marginalizes, and trivializes women's experiences.

Women's university, on the other hand, has a much more radical agenda. As previously said, it would be situated within a social context where education, together with parenting, is a central social institution. Furthermore, education and parenting would be the main purpose of the very existence of society. Business, science and technology, military, and so on, would concentrate on serving the first two, and not the other way around. Therefore, there would not be so much concern over the costs for education, nor nagging complaints about educational expenses as their reduction would come after reducing all other costs, but before reducing costs necessary for sustenance of the lives of people (especially children), their health, and well-being. It is important to note that not only education, but also other aspects of society, would be defined differently from how they are today. For example, security would then mean security of income, health care and freedom from domestic violence, rather than security from attack by "alien forces." This is how most of today's women see their personal and family security and this is how security would be defined if women had their say in policy and decisionmaking.

Community, Ethics and the Atmosphere for Learning

Women's university is very much community based and the main question is not so much the pursuit of truth but how to attain better health, happiness, and

quality of life for present and future generations. The boundaries between
university and community are obliterated, and community members participate in
deciding the university's main issues, agendas, and teaching and learning priorities. Academics would still have the freedom to pursue their interests but their
research areas would not be seen as "objective," apolitical, and value-free. The
women's university is concerned with ethics: Medical research would always
have to respond to moral issues and very much justify (if not totally abolish)
experimentation on nature, animals, and people. Ideally it would nurture respect
toward all life and would be based on a philosophy that would see us (nature/
people) all as one and therefore advocate love and respect for all beings, animate
and inanimate. Consequently, this perspective would reduce the need for models
based on power, control, and the domination/subordination polarity. The atmosphere at the university would reflect this approach by concentrating on transcending notions of hierarchy, through cooperation instead of competition, and
through equalizing power between resource persons and students.

When considering the atmosphere at the women's university, most women
envision the future women's university as a place that would be nurturing and that
would deal with the emotions—emotions like the fear, anger, anxiety, and pain
women experience when they "first face their own feelings of being oppressed,
powerless, and immobilized."[8] It would also promote the values of community,
communication, equality, mutual nurturance, shared leadership, participatory
decisionmaking, democratic structure, interdependence, and the integration of
cognitive and affective learning. While these visions might be dismissed as essentialist and not challenging enough of existing gender stereotypes, these themes are
rather genuine women's concerns, which are repeated consistently. These visions
are also some of the goals for future women's university where the development
of an environment offering both emotional and intellectual support and a place for
growth and change is seen as one of the basic preconditions for learning.

Approach to Learning

Within the women's university one of the guiding principles of teaching is that
we are all "learners" and all "teachers." The women's approach seeks to incorporate emotional and personal learning (instead of just cognitive and impersonal
models) and to personally involve students, challenging them into developing
their own ideas and into analyzing the assumptions behind their actions. Other
characteristics of learning and teaching emphasize "connection over separation,
understanding and acceptance over assessment, and collaboration over debate";[9]
respect for and allowing time for "the knowledge that emerges from firsthand
experience"; and "instead of imposing their own expectations and arbitrary
requirements,"[10] encouragement of students to "evolve their own patterns of work
based on the problems they are pursuing."[11]

Perspectives

One of the main features of the women's university is the shift from a masculinist perspective to feminist or feminine one. This does not necessarily have to mean "women only" groups. I believe future societies will differentiate people's gender on a larger scale, and locate them within multiple gender identities. Therefore thinking about the women's university in the context of emerging future multiple gender diversities should be a more useful tool than still thinking in terms of female-male bipolarities. Although the issue of "women's only" versus coeducation model will remain as a tension, in concrete terms, women's university might seek to form parallel separatist occasional groups as well as gatherings together within a more inclusive setup. This will allow further development of a feminist/feminine perspective that is inclusive of traditional women's ways of knowing, feminist theory, feminist and women's political activism and grassroots activities, as these are central to a women's university.

However, such a university cannot justify its demands for inclusiveness within dominant ways of organizing knowledge if it remains exclusive of other perspectives, especially those coming from peripheries, people from the margins as created due to their race, nationality, age, sexual preference, (dis)ability, and class. While the women's university should also be inclusive of dominant, "malestream" knowledge paradigm (only if that one is being perceived as the other rather than the norm), the main direction is in constant efforts to include the perspective of the powerless at all levels of the university. Inclusion of this perspective in knowledge, organization, membership, and curricula would enable transformation toward "multi-diversity" (instead of "uni-versity"), fluid relationships, and a constant shifting of the center toward the periphery (margins).

Global Sisterhood and New Technologies

The Women's university would seek to create a university of "global sisterhood," and this will be possible with simultaneous inclusion of other perspectives and equal representation of different social, cultural, and national groups, among students and among faculty. This is where using new technologies can particularly help connect women all over the world, and enable women's "own information networks, computerized mailing lists, and political alert systems."[12] The women's university might try to encourage teachings from intellectuals and activists coming from the not-so-developed world. For example, teachers on issues such as ecologically and economically sustainable futures, or consumer reductionism, should preferably come from countries and areas where industry has not done so much damage, from societies in which the balance between nature/culture/technological developments have been relatively preserved. Virtual space can have an enormous potential for inclusion of women who are normally excluded in physical space, for example nonresidents or illegal immigrants.

While current universities, which are "going on the Net," still keep the traditional division of students (those who belong to the nation-state where the university is located and those who do not), a virtual women's university could be truly international (therefore, for example, fees should be based on individual wealth rather than "belonging" to a particular country or region). While new technologies do have certain inherent characteristics, which have the potential to silence women's ways of knowing, they would redeem themselves through being a medium of creation of an international women's network and "global sisterhood" and through direct and indirect ways of empowering women. They could also help courses being concentrated at mostly one place, reduce the need for going "all over town" in search for learning material and therefore greatly respond to one of the most serious limitations when it comes to women and learning—time. If new technologies can help maximize womens' resources in time and money, which are, apart from cultural values, the two main variables preventing women's enrollment at higher education levels, they could truly start fulfilling their promise for the further democratization of education.

The Purpose

The main purpose of the women's university is not so much to provide the skills for survival within existing and future patriarchal (industrial) informational society, although they are important, but to transform and change the very societies within which learning takes place. While the traditional model of education concentrates on the modeling of character, the passing of culture, and the development of vocational skills, the women's university seeks to be useful in improving the conditions of women's lives and teaching activities aimed at changing (patriarchal) characters and cultures.

Knowledge, Research Methods, and Curricula

In order to achieve this goal, the women's university has to transform some aspects of knowledge, research methods, and learning curricula. In the women's university, there would be no separation between knowledge and politics, theory and practice, mind and body, or public and private and wherein new inter-, multi- and transdisciplinary frameworks are being built. The methodology would be anti-essentialist (seeing gender as social practice), multicultural, with prioritizing "issues," and being problem-oriented. This university would also encourage an eclectic approach in the choice of research methods that are adapted to the specific demands of each individual research project.

The women's university would probably be initially based on feminist theory and would go back and forth in description, analysis, critique, visioning, policy, and strategy. Curricula should also be interdisciplinary, flexible, problem-oriented, knowledge-based, holistic, and practical (knowledge *for* instead of just *about*), and the university should be simultaneously involved in social activism and politically "autonomous" (having autonomy to choose political positions). Throughout each discipline one of the crucial foci would be gender. For example, curricula might incorporate issues of dystopian images—such as visions and realities of extreme forms of patriarchy, rise of the religious and political right, loss of women's control over their bodies and reproductive ability, persecution of minorities, loss of women's recent political gains, destruction of the environment, loss of individual freedom, extreme polarizing of women's and men's gender roles, and rise of male aggression—and discuss them from various perspectives (biological, scientific, technological, educational, or sociological).

While in traditional educational models different problems get classified throughout different disciplines (for example, the amount of pesticide in food is in the jurisdiction of chemistry, and cloning in the jurisdiction of genetics), in the women's university, disciplines would be transformed into perspectives and used as approaches to problems, with the goal of solving them in accordance with the best interests of today's peoples and future generations.

TOWARD A WOMAN'S UTOPIAN VISION

The aforementioned image of the future women's university is just one of the possible models written from a woman's perspective. It is heavily influenced by feminist theory and, as such, has all the limitations (Western) feminism has. However, within this context, its main purpose is not so much to propose the blueprints of the perfect educational system, but rather to contextualize current discussion and start the process of seriously questioning where higher education is going and where we want it to go. This is a contribution to the debate where one particular "we" wants it to go. Its main intention is to question current and future dominant images of the future of education, mainly those that are still not seriously questioning our dominant (patriarchal) knowledge paradigm. While probably still radical, even within the 21st century, this model is outlined with the hope that our great-granddaughters will transcend it.

NOTES

1. Bill Readings, *The University in Ruins* (Cambridge, MA, USA: Harvard University Press, 1994).

2. Jim Dator, "The Futures of Universities: Ivied Halls, Virtual Malls, or Theme Parks?," *Futures* 30, 7 (1998).

3. R. R. Sims and S. J. Sims, eds., *Managing Institutions of Higher Education into the 21st Century* (Westport, CT: Greenwood Press, 1991): 157.

4. Ibid.

5. Paul Wildman, "From the Monophonic University to the Polyphonic Multiversity," *Futures* 30, 7 (1998).

6. These ideas have previously been outlined in I. Milojevic, "Women's Higher Education in the 21st Century: From 'Women-Friendly' to Women's Universities," in *Futures* 30, 7 (1998).

7. J. Zimmerman, "What are Rights without Means? Educating Feminists for the Future," in *Learning Our Ways: Essays in Feminist Education*, C. Bunch and S. Pollack, eds. (New York: The Crossing Press/Trumansburg, 1983), 5–9.

8. S. Sherman, "Women and Process: The Sagaris Split, Session II," in C. Bunch and S. Pollack, ibid. 132.

9. R. Iskin, "Feminist Education at the Feminist Studio Workshop," in C. Bunch and S. Pollack, ibid., 183.

10. Ibid.

11. Ibid.

12. H. Tierney, ed., *Women's Studies Encyclopedia*, Volume II (Westport, CT: Greenwood Press, 1990).

16

Homo Tantricus: Tantra as an Episteme for Future Generations

─────────────────────── *Marcus Bussey*

Institutions reflect the minds of those who create them. Change the mind and you change the institution. In this essay I explore such a change to try and foresee what kind of university might emerge if we were to shift as individuals and as a culture from a model of mind based on the Western sapientia of Homo sapiens, to a model of mind founded on the consciousness inherent in the Tantra indigenous to central Asia and the Indian subcontinent.

Currently most cultures have submitted to the educational model based on the vision of people as Homo sapiens, being possessed of a distinctly Western rationality that dominates and exploits its environment. This form of instrumental consciousness is trapped by its own internal necessity and cannot escape from the force and form of its own logic. The time is ripe for it to cross-pollinate with other nonwestern epistemes to build into our consciousness the flexibility and vision needed to reinvigorate our emergent global civilization.

Tantra, in the form of Homo tantricus, offers such a fusion. Human consciousness enriched by a tantric episteme offers to us a chance to explore new ways of educating based on an ethic of relationship and integration that will act as an antidote (what a wonderful Western metaphor) to the alienation and instrumentality that has impoverished the educational landscape.

Many who follow this article may say, to quote the poet Wallace Stevens, "but you do not play things as they are."[1] And you will certainly be right when looking at the "story" from our current social and economic setting, but then this is not what futures is about. Rather it is about finding, and playing, the "tune beyond us, yet ourselves."[2] Paul Wildman and Sohail Inayatullah's work on causal layered analysis gives us a clue here. With this method we can go beyond conventional framing of issues. Each layer is an authentic strand within our experience of reality, and used as a tool of analysis we can, by "[m]oving up and down layers . . . integrate analysis and synthesis, and horizontally we can integrate discourses, ways of knowing and world views, thereby increasing the richness of analysis."[3] Tantra fits comfortably into this description as it offers multiple realities, embraces various (often conflicting) ideas, and situates these within a discourse that is fundamentally metaphysical and unifying.

Tantra is usually relegated to the esoteric domains of book stores and libraries. Books on the subject will be found along with indigenous American shamanism, Australian Aboriginal myth, Celtic astrology, and esoteric sex. I want to argue that though some aspects of Tantra are certainly esoteric, it is also intensely practical and methodical. Tantra is not a religion, but an ethical and spiritual approach to life that is rooted in a resurgent indigenous consciousness. It is both ancient and modern, possessing the deep wisdom of its traditional eastern roots, while being energized with a liberatory ethic aimed at physical, social, and spiritual emancipation from exploitative ideologies.

Homo tantricus is a creature of the future. He or she will possess the skills of the present but will apply them with love and an appreciation of humanities' existence within a dynamic and beautiful whole. In this essay I will look at how such a being may be reflected in an institution of higher learning. Perhaps the term university will no longer be used but, judging by Tantra's respect for tradition and continuity, I think it will. First, we must briefly look at the state of universities today in order to contextualize how they might be different, or to quote Stevens again, how we might better play that "tune beyond us, yet ourselves."

TODAY'S UNIVERSITY

At the present time, universities have become large corporations producing and selling knowledge. As the postmodern philosopher Jean-Francois Lyotard wryly notes: "Knowledge is and will be produced in order to be sold, it is and will be consumed in order to be valorized in a new production: in both cases, the goal is exchange."[4] This is a natural development that reflects our culture's commercial obsession with capital. The knowledge-power nexus transforms information into a commodity that can be exchanged in the university marketplace in the form of bundles of "information." Knowledge is exchanged for power and vice versa. In this system, knowing and its product knowledge that does not translate into information that can be observed, measured, controlled, and easily exchanged, is excluded in favor of docile forms of knowledge that are more amenable to transaction.[5]

The significance of this development is that as power has shifted from the hands of those with an investment in culture, the liberal elite, to those who create capital, the managerial elite, the emphasis of the university has shifted to reflect these changes. Thus the university acts as a repository of socially valued knowledge forms and we can track the fortunes of ideologies by following the appearance, popularity, and disappearance of subjects on the timetable. So today, we see that the liberal project has come on hard times and that it is being eclipsed by a technical and managerial rationality, which has close links to capital and its production, and is distant from what that arch-liberal Cardinal Newman described as a form of learning that "refuses to be informed (as it is called) by any end."[6] This definition is of course suspect in that all institutional learning founded on this principal at least has the desired end of what the educational philosopher Paul Hirst describes as "personal development by initiation into a complex of specific, substantive social practices with all the knowledge, attitudes, feelings, virtues, skills, dispositions and relationships that that involves."[7] Lyotard describes such initiates as "heroes of knowledge"[8] and Michael Peters sees them as "trained in the great task of pursuing good ethico-political ends . . . leading their countries toward social progress."[9]

Such postmodern thinkers have disturbed the neat liberal narrative of education leading to the good life, not only by questioning its underlying benevolence, but also by offering a discourse of discontinuity and fragmentation. But such postmodern critique can hardly be held responsible for the shift that we have seen in the very substance of universities. No, these shifts owe more to the liberal project itself than to any ideological critique. The creative Marxist thinker Antonio Gramsci foresaw the seeds of this shift years ago when he described how the middle class, the architects of liberalism, had constructed an organic route through education and law that allowed all entry to its world. "The bourgeois class poses itself as an organism in continuous movement, capable of absorbing the entire society, assimilating it to its own cultural and economic level."[10] Thus the state became the educator, opening the doors of hallowed institutions to any who sought them out. With this opening up, learning had to become more utilitarian because the focus of the majority has, within the modernist paradigm, to be on "ends." And also with this opening up foreseen by Gramsci there comes a point of saturation at which the class itself starts to disintegrate and the State too ceases to be a useful unit of organization.

This is where we find ourselves today. Modernism appears to be on the point of collapse. The powers of the State have been eroded by the global marketplace and the individual has been cloned. Cultural critic John Ralston Saul describes this development as "a hijacking of Western Civilization."[11] His concern is that the West as a civilization has made no real progress over the past two and a half thousand years. Indian philosopher and mystic Prabhat Rainjan Sarkar has made the same assertion. Progress is illusory and should not be measured in technical terms.[12] Saul argues that we are in the grip of unifying narratives that blind us to reality; we are in fact an unconscious civilization in which "we are actually teaching most people to manage not to think."[13]

Without a doubt universities are in trouble, since all they do is reflect the dominant mind-set of a culture that has ceased to dialogue with itself. They have ceased to create culture, to offer safe havens for dissent, to create their own future. They are now tied to the purse strings of fearful governments more worried about being returned at the next election than about the long-term effectiveness of these institutions as generators of a learning culture that might help us enter the next millennium with vision and dignity.

RECONTEXTUALIZING LEARNING

It is not my intention to chronicle the parlous state of universities in the late 20th century. Rather, it is to chart a course of vision and hope into the next millennium by looking at the reasons for the system's failure, and recontextualizing learning within an episteme that allows for human potential to be expanded to include new ethical and spiritual dimensions. Central to this new episteme is the thinking of Prabhat Rainjan Sarkar. But his is not a lone voice as many people from many traditions are turning away from material rationality and its managerial and hegemonic agenda by seeking to chart alternatives that are creative and more fully attuned to human aspiration and spirit.

Earlier this century, Rabindranath Tagore started a university, and more recently William Irwin Thompson and a group of English intellectuals founded the learning community of Lindesfarne in the United States. Sarkar is, however, a seminal thinker, and it is his vision of a Tantra University, embedded in a spiritualized education system, which will be examined here as an example of how different universities of the future may be from their lackluster ancestors.

A REAWAKENED DISCOURSE

In the mid-1950s, Sarkar began laying the philosophical foundations for his educational agenda. Central to this project is his recognition that we, as a global civilization, are rapidly approaching a crisis—the positive resolution of which will only come about through a shift of consciousness. The new consciousness will be holistic, having its roots deep within an indigenous appreciation that it is consciousness, not humanity, that is central to the drama of existence. Because this reframing greatly expanded the humanist mandate that placed human consciousness on center stage. Sarkar called this new awareness of our interconnection with the universe *Neohumanism*.

In a recent reappraisal of the New Age movement, David Spangler pointed directly to the fundamental issue of our times: the birth pangs of a new consciousness. Such an immense shift has not been seen since the emergence of civilization itself thousands of years ago. "We are in the midst of a process of reimagining and reinventing ourselves and our world."[14] But this shift is not occurring without pain and disruption. In fact, forces are amassing to contest the emergence of this new ethic:

- The massive escalation in the dominance and penetration of managerial and corporate psychology;
- The hunger to possess and control that drives all agents within society from the individual to the vast corporation via nuclear family and nation–state;

- The fear of difference and the need to silence dissent through a wide range of media from the bullet to the universalization of the unreflective consciousness of television and cyberspace; and
- The total disregard for the integrity of the natural world and our own bodies, which we poison and pillage at will.

It must be remembered that power never willingly surrenders to change. It intensifies its means of control through the technologies that penetrate deeply into everyday life; the visual, oral, and print media along with education and an economic system that binds it all through the linking of personal autonomy and happiness with economic success. This escalation cannot be sustained indefinitely. Modernism relies on the concept of indefinite progress to maintain its own momentum, but progress that is synonymous with cultural, environmental, psychological, and spiritual exploitation cannot last. Ziauddin Sardar points to this when he asserts that "the innate and powerful desire for meaning and identity in non-Western societies cannot be eradicated."[15] Sardar calls this desire "traditional idealism"[16] and it is in this nonwestern critique of the West, to which Sardar belongs, that lies the creativity and depth to accomplish the reimagining of ourselves and our future.

THE "TRADITIONAL IDEALISM" OF TANTRA

Sarkar's civilizational discourse also emerges from this space. In reimagining the future he weaves stories of continuity and discontinuity. Tantra is essentially a worldview rooted in indigenous pre-Aryan Indian culture.[17] Its historical roots go at least as far back as the peaceful Dravidian peoples who lived on the Indus river and gave rise to what archaeologists call the Indus Valley civilization that flourished about 2500 B.C. and was swept away by the Aryan invasions of Northern India about 1700 B.C. The warlike Aryans brought with them the earliest Vedas and wove into their own culture the cosmology of Tantra.

This perennial tantric tradition of India has permeated many other cultures, particularly in its Buddhist and Jain manifestations. Today, Tantra is alive and well and has made successful inroads into popular Western culture through the modern fascination with the "spiritual treasures of the orient," hence the success of Vivekananda and Yogananda in the United States earlier this century and more recently of Maharishi Mahesh Yogi, who began the university initiative described in Grant's chapter, and Shrii Satya Sai Baba. These ideas are not unique, and corollaries are found in all spiritual traditions drawing on the deep collective myths of the human soul.

What is unique about the way Sarkar has redefined Tantra is that it gives very clear form to these popularized images and fuses them in a spiritual and social agenda that generates the energy and vision to begin the project of social reconstruction. Being deeply rooted in the indigenous experience of reality, Tantra has a broad metaphysical base, which allows for ways of knowing, feeling and processing that go far beyond the limited rationality that informs the post-Western

Enlightenment project. Priorities are different as Sarkar notes because, "spiritual life controls all other arenas of human life."[18] This perspective generates a synthetic outlook steeped in what Sarkar calls "spiritual vision."[19]

So in Sarkar's tantric worldview, the individual can only exist within a collective to have meaning, with individual and collective consciousness working together in striving to overcome the physical obstacles that arise on the path of evolution. Consciousness is seen as an infinite and eternal entity of which we are a spark.[20] While "reality" is both relative and very real from our position within its unfolding story, in Sarkar's view, we have a sacred relationship with everything and are thus responsible for the maintenance of the whole by serving the parts. In this way we maintain our mythic connection to the whole. So in this tantric view the personal drama of life is also mythic and reflects our relationship with the sacred.[21]

Most indigenous cultures have found their purpose to be in maintaining cosmic balance and working in harmony with others and their environment.[22] In many ways traditional Tantra also followed this pattern. Modern Tantra, as Sarkar has defined it, has a more dynamic agenda. It is specifically liberatory and therefore political. Tan in Sanskrit means "bondage," and tra means "to liberate from."[23] Traditionally this was interpreted to mean the individual transcending the limitations of their own ego. Sarkar radically shifted the emphasis from the individual to the collective by linking the two so that neither could progress without the other. Spirituality ceases to be selfish and becomes a collective act. Within this construction of Tantra the individual works for their own liberation by following specific physical, social, and spiritual practices, while at the same time struggling to free others from physical, social, and spiritual bondage. This brings to spirituality an ironic tension in which the individual must engage with the world in many ordinary and extraordinary ways. Thus "spirituality is both a grand project and an everyday task,"[24] as the bioethicist Jennifer Fitzgerald points out. The poet David Rowbotham summed the situation up nicely when he wrote, "Pray, speak beauty, but dust first spoke."[25] Much of the energy and dynamism of Tantra lies in this ironic tension.

Sarkar has based his educational philosophy on this expanded definition of Tantra. Sarkar is offering a meta-narrative of power, which is deeply attuned to the yearnings of the human soul, what Fitzgerald calls the "innate desire to expand one's potential."[26] Yet Saul rails against the dominance of meta-narrative in the form of ideology in the 20th century,[27] but his complaints are directed at materialistic and mechanistic ways of interpreting and acting upon life. Neil Postman states that the deeper "gods" are dead and that education has died because we now only educate in self interest. He argues strongly that the human "genius lies in our capacity to make meaning through the creation of narratives that give point to our labors, exalt our history, elucidate the present, and give direction to the future."[28] Sarkar shares this opinion and offers deep spiritual tantric narrative as the way to establish education and culture in a future that weds material reality with deeper readings of life.

Tantra's Key Concepts

As Peter Scott reminds us, universities are capable of "ceaseless adaptation."[29] They possess a dynamism that ensures their relevance for future generations. Sarkar's concept of Tantra is certainly dynamic but it shifts the emphasis of the university away from its traditional base. In earlier liberal constructions of the university, knowledge was often an end in itself, the possession of which endowed its owner with significant cultural capital. Later the most privileged knowledge came to be linked with mastery over technology, either institutional or real. Sarkar appreciates the cultural value of knowledge and its technical importance but he places these discourses, the liberal and managerial, within an expanded metaphysical framework. His agenda directly involves the university in activities that will take those engaged in them, the Homo tantricus of the future, into the community in a facilitative and participatory way. The origin of this shift lies in an episteme rooted in an ethical relocation of purpose from individual aggrandizement to social responsibility situated in a spiritual worldview.

The key concepts[30] that underpin this relocation include:

- The theory of PROUTist[31] economics—provides the understanding of the social process needed to promote justice and equity taking into account the forces of capital, human ambition, and ecological responsibility;
- The philosophy of Neohumanism—a holistic philosophy situating all human activity in intimate and reverential relationship with the universe, spiritualizing the educational mission;
- Microvita theory—subtle energy waves affecting matter and thought, changing our foundational assumptions about science, learning, and consciousness;
- Theory of mind—the mind has many layers of which academic discourse acknowledges only one, reframing what constitutes knowledge, intelligence, and communication;
- Theory of prama—describes all individual and social structures in terms of physical, psychic, and spiritual balance, along with Prout, makes much of what universities do start with the practical, such as ecological degradation and economic disparity;
- Concept of aesthetics as a liberatory (that is, purposeful) activity—the arts are drawn into the center of human learning and experience as an important way to develop intuitional intelligence;
- Reconceptualization of history—history is cyclic and evolutionary, redrawing our understanding of human progress and of the function of education;
- Linguistics—a science that is spiritualized with introduction of Tantric theory of vibration and form, reflecting intent and also psychology. This is essential in understanding human mind and cultural expressions;
- Sadhana, meditative practice—research is also redefined as an intuitional science, consciousness needs to be plumbed through systematic meditative investigation, the results of such work make sense of the economic, social, aesthetic and ecological functions of the university;
- Concept of ecology—situates universities as part of projects designed to heal, protect, and nurture the earth as extensions of their community.

These concepts provide the organizing principles for the Tantra University. Growing out of traditional structures, they empower the human agency well beyond the limits offered by those structures. Agency vivifies structure, which in turn locates agency within a cosmology that promotes universalism instead of the entrenched individualism of Western culture. In this way, Sarkar escapes both the traditional passivity associated with indigenous expression and the dynamic but selfish individualism that typifies the West. Thus freed from its cultural moorings, tantric episteme, as encapsulated in these key concepts, has applicability well beyond India and Asia. By introducing dynamic universalist ethics to Tantra, Sarkar has created the conditions for a breaking down of barriers relating to culture, class, gender, and species. The result is potent indeed and has great significance for all explorations of culturally relevant alternatives to the dominant Western model of education.

In this way dissent emerges from the periphery to recover what the Indian futurist Ashis Nandy calls the "other selves" that nonwestern cultures have written out of their own stories in order to fit into the dominant categories of the West. Sarkar's revitalizing of Tantra offers resistance to what Nandy calls the "dominant politics of knowledge."[32] Thus Tantra resists the structural violence of colonization, those "monocultures of the mind," which according to peace educator Frank Hutchinson have lead to the "domestication or impoverishment of social imagination."[33]

It is important to realize that Tantra represents an epistemic shift that critiques and expands all practices, both Western and nonwestern, in the light of universalist ethics. By asserting that Tantra is rooted in an indigenous Indic episteme is not to assert that such an episteme is accepted uncritically or that Tantra will colonize in the name of this episteme. Tantra seeks to create universal culture based on generally shared values inherent in the key concepts previously described, yet it is sensitive to local and regional variations. Sarkar laid great emphasis on this fact. The nature of epistemic shifts is, as feminist futurist Ivana Milojevic observed, to "help bring about new resolutions, policies, and actions."[34] From such resolutions, policies, and actions emerges the new, informed by its past. In this sense Tantra is no longer indigenous, but transdigenous[35] as it no longer has regard for traditional boundaries. This disregard for boundaries fits well within the context of our emergent global culture, which has scant regard for many of the divisive practices that constitute earlier forms of cultural expression and oppression. But globalism needs to be tempered by concepts such as those inherent in the episteme of Tantra because, as the Islamic cultural critic Ziauddin Sardar has observed, it is becoming synonymous with the extension of capitalism and Western culture and is therefore perceived to be inimical to all nonwestern peoples.[36]

The Tantra University in India

The experiment is already under way in India where the organization Sarkar established in 1955, Ananda Marga, has started the first Tantra University at Ananda Nagar in West Bengal. This project, which is part of a broader educational movement called Ananda Marga Gurukula that ranges from kindergarten to university, has already attracted much interest amongst India's intellegensia who are looking for ways to escape the dominant model of learning that was imported into India by the British, as discussed in greater depth by Rahman in this volume.

The project places the Tantra University alongside a number of other tertiary institutions. The Gurukula, an ancient Sanskrit term denoting the residence of a realized teacher (that is, a place for deep learning), as the entire campus is called, offers courses that include the staple university threads such as the sciences and humanities, but stretches far beyond them in an attempt to embrace the deeper mythic and cosmological realities that are part of the Indian consciousness. The Tantra University is one institution amongst many on this campus, its focus being on "the application of Tantric precepts to contemporary problems facing society—political, economic, social, educational, environmental, and the rest." Its stated mission is to "foster social changes based on justice to all beings."[37] Some interesting developments within this university are its determination to sponsor poor and tribal peoples and the way it breaks down disciplinary boundaries to allow for rich rereading of old discourses. Thus they bring spiritual philosophy to bear on political theory as part of their Proutist Economics course, also we find homeopathy, ayurveda, and other indigenous medical practices being taught alongside, and interacting with, Western allopathic medicine.

A BROADER VISION OF IMPLEMENTATION

The curriculum of any Tantra university would reflect a transcendence of conventional divisions of knowledge. This is because in Tantra knowledge is rooted in deeper epistemes of meaning in which discrimination and wisdom are valued over "information retrieval." Conventional disciplines only have relative meaning in this broader discourse in which, as Rick Slaughter commented, "we are all and always immersed in a stream of knowing in a world brimming with immanent meaning."[38] This loosening of the stranglehold of "disciplines" on the mind of Homo tantricus allows for a great unleashing of creativity. What this means to us now in a world still dominated by the compartmentalized worldview it is hard to say, but we can certainly indulge ourselves here with a little educated guess work.

Links between the arts and science could become real as scientists and artists discover that what they are both dealing with is microvita, those subtle energy waves that both generate life and influence thought and emotion. Historians too can bring an understanding of microvita into their work, once again in collaboration with scientists and artists, and perhaps we will see courses like Microvita and Revolutions, and Microvita and the History of Ideas on campuses of the future. Similarly the Tantric theory of the mind as a many-layered system may have great implications for psychology, medicine, and the humanities. The introduction of this concept of layers, called koshas, may lead to the birth of courses like Criminology and Kosha Theory, or Kosha and Language Groups—Explorations in Cross-Cultural Linguistics. These courses may sound strange to modern ears but the real power of these ideas to transform our understanding of current disciplines should not be underestimated.

Take another example using Proutist economic theory. Here we can imagine courses like Proutistic Strategies for Agrarian Reform in Papua New Guinea and Proutistic Business Management. Education will be transformed with the appearance of neohumanism shifting the emphasis from discipline and control to neohumanistic learning strategies. Subjects will appear like Neohumanistic Child Development and Neohumanistic Curricular Development. Teacher training may involve subjects like Ethical Mathematics and Overcoming Learning Blocks: Reincarnation Theory and the Developing Mind.

The possibilities are endless and fascinating to explore, even with our limited consciousness. Playing like this fills me with a sense of pathos at the suffering we endure because of our isolation within a rationalist framework. "If only . . . " I keep whispering to myself. But all the signs are here that change, major change is on the way. The presence of thinkers like Sarkar confirm this. Too much is already giving way for the old boundaries and constructs to last.

HOMO TANTRICUS

In choosing to play with a term like Homo tantricus I have deliberately combined two very different cultural traditions, the West's deductive and rational narrative with the East's synthetic and mythic consciousness, to suggest that unlikely partners may generate fruitful insights into the future.

Although much about a Tantra University remains speculative, the creative potential of such a concept cannot be denied. The value of a rich tradition like Tantra for the problems of our day—ecological degradation, social and economic disparity, individual alienation, and spiritual impoverishment—is that it is not bound to play by the rules of the dominant paradigm that has created these problems. And, although such a proposition raises as many questions as it seeks to solve, I have no doubt that Homo tantricus will have a lot of fun answering them.

NOTES

1. Wallace Stevens, "The Man with the Blue Guitar," *The Collected Poems* (New York: Vintage Books, 1982): 165.

2. Ibid.

3. Paul Wildman and Sohail Inayatullah, "Ways of Knowing, Culture, Communication and the Pedagogies of the Future," *Futures* 28 (1996): 735.

4. Jean-Francois Lyotard, "The Postmodern Condition: A Report on Knowledge" (Minneapolis, U.S. University of Minnesota Press, 1984): 4, quoted in Michael Peters, "Legitimation Problems: Knowledge and Education in the Postmodern Condition," in *Education and the Postmodern Condition*, Michael Peters, ed. (London: Bergin and Garvey, 1995): 28.

5. R. Usher and R. Edwards, *Postmodernism and Education* (London: Routledge, 1994): 105.

6. Quoted in D. Cowan, *Unbinding Prometheus: Education for the Coming Age* (Dallas: The Dallas Institute Publications, 1988): 77.

7. Paul Hirst, "Education, Knowledge and Practices," in *Beyond Liberal Education: Essays in honor of Paul H. Hirst*, R. Barrow and P. White, eds. (London: Routledge, 1993), 197.

8. Lyotard, as quoted by Peters, op cit.: 29.

9. Peters, op cit.: 29.

10. Antonio Gramsci, *Selections from the Prison Notebooks*, Q. Hoare & G. N. Smith, ed. and trans. (New York: International Publishers, 1980), 260.

11. John Ralston Saul, *The Unconscious Civilization* (Melbourne, Australia: Penguin, 1997), 2. It is interesting to note that Saul does not seem all that concerned with the West's hijacking of nonwestern civilizations.

12. Prabhat Rainjan Sarkar, "Human Search for Real Progress," *Supreme Expression: Discourses on Social Philosophy* (The Netherlands: Nirvikalpa Printing, 1978), 103–13.

13. Saul, op cit.: 15.

14. William Irwin Thompson and David Spangler, *Reimagination of the World: A Critique of the New Age, Science, and Popular Culture* (Santa Fe, New Mexico: Bear and Co., 1991), 25.

15. Ziaddin Sardar, "Terminator 2: Modernity, Postmodernism and the 'Other,'" *Futures* 24 (1992): 504.

16. Ibid., 504.

17. Prabhat Rainjan Sarkar, "Tantra and Indo-Aryan Civilization," Shrii Shrii Anandamurti, *Discourses on Tantra, Vol. 1* (Calcutta: AM Publications, 1993), 141–75.

18. Prabhat Rainjan Sarkar, "The Rule of Rationality," in P. R. Sarkar, *A Few Problems Solved*, Pt. 8 (Calcutta: AM Publications, 1988), 45.

19. Shrii Shrii Anandamurti, "Desire and Detachment," *Subhasita Samgraha*, Pt. 3 (Calcutta: AM Publications, 1992), 104.

20. Prabhat Rainjan Sarkar, "The Creation of the Universe," P. R. Sarkar, ibid., 15–20.

21. Shrii Shrii Anandamurti, op cit.: 105ff.

22. A. Voigt and N. Drury, *Wisdom from the Earth: The Living Legacy of the Aboriginal Dreamtime* (Simon and Schuster, Australia, 1997).

23. P. R. Sarkar, "Tantra and its Effect on Society," in P. R. Sarkar, *Discourses on Tantra*, Vol. 2 (Calcutta: AM Publications, 1993), 22.

24. Jennifer Fitzgerald, "Reclaiming the Whole: Self, Spirit, and Society," *Disability and Rehabilitation* 19, 10 (1997): 407.

25. David Rowbotham, *New and Selected Poems:1945–1993*, (Melbourne: Penguin, 1994), 62.

26. Fitzgerald, op cit.: 408.

27. Saul, op cit.: 19.

28. Neil Postman, *The End of Education: Redefining the Value of School* (New York, Alfred A. Knopf, 1995).

29. Peter Scott, "The Idea of the University in the 21st Century: A British Perspective," P. Raggatt, R. Edwards, and Nick Small, eds. In *The Learning Society: Challenges and Trends* (London: The Open University, 1996), 236.

30. Prabhat Rainjan Sarkar, *Proutist Economics: Discourses on Economic Liberation* (Calcutta: AM Publications, 1992). P. R. Sarkar, *The Liberation of Intellect: Neo-Humanism* (Calcutta: AM Publications, 1991). P. R. Sarkar, *Microvita in a Nutshell* (Calcutta: AM Publications, 1992). Avadhutika Ananda Mita Ac., *The Spiritual*

Philosophy of Shrii Shrii Anandamurti: A Commentary on Ananda Sutram (Denver, USA: AM Publications, 1981), 148–55. P. R. Sarkar, *Prama* (Calcutta: AM Publications, 1989). P. R. Sarkar, "The Practice of Art and Literature," in P. R. Sarkar, *A Few Problems Solved, Pt. 1* (Calcutta: AM Publications, 1987), 1–57. J. Galtung and S. Inayatullah, *Macrohistory and Macrohistorians: Perspectives on Individual, Social and Civilizational Change* (Westport, CT: Praeger Publishers, 1997). P. R. Sarkar, "Acoustic Roots," Shrii Shrii Anandamurti, *Discourses on Tantra, Vol. 1* (Calcutta: AM Publications, 1993), 74–82. P. R. Sarkar, "Self-Realization and Service to Humanity" Shrii Shrii Anandamurti, *Ananda Vacanamrtam* 30 (Calcutta: AM Publications, 1996), 38. P. R. Sarkar, "Prout and Neo-Humanism," P. R. Sarkar, *Prout in a Nutshell, Pt. 17* (Calcutta: AM Publications, 1991), 43–48.

31. PROUT—Progressive Utilization Theory. Spiritual economics based on the Tantric principle that all human activity, including economic activity, should be directed toward liberation from poverty, ignorance, and injustice so that every human life can be spent working toward spiritual realization.

32. Ashis Nandy, "Shamans, Savages and the Wilderness: On the Audibility of Dissent and the Future of Civilizations," in R. A. Slaughter, *The Knowledge Base of Futures Studies, Volume 3: Directions and Outlooks* (Melbourne: Futures Study Centre, 1996), 145.

33. F. P. Hutchinson, *Educating Beyond Violent Futures* (London: Routledge, 1996), 34.

34. I. Milojevic, "Learning from Feminist Futures," D. Hicks and R. Slaughter, *World Yearbook of Education 1998: Futures Education* (London: Kogan Page, 1998), 85.

35. Here I display poor etymological sense (I should have said trans-genus) but this word-play makes the point that Tantra transcends its own roots and is no longer concerned with the inward self-reclaiming of indigenous movements today, but rather with a reclaiming of the transcendent global self.

36. Sardar, op cit.

37. Acharya Shambhushivananda Avt, "Tantra Vidyapeetha," *Gurukula Network* 1, 2 (New York: AM Publications, 1996), 5.

38. R. Slaughter, *The Foresight Principle: Cultural Recovery in the 21st Century* (London: Adamantine, 1995), 172.

17

Universities Evolving: Advanced Learning Networks and Experience Camps

—————————————————— *Patricia Nicholson*

The course of the university's evolution is charted by the institutional overseers who continually respond to core context questions: "What is the university's mission?" "To whom does the university belong?" "Who are its clients?" "On whose behalf do the trustees of a university hold their trust?" "Does the university exist to serve its enrolled students, a subset of the society, or society as a whole?" "Is the university itself a change agent or are its graduates the change agents?"

CONTEXT AND LEADERSHIP

Higher education institutional overseers (president, board, accrediting board, key members of state government) are the true navigators, and those who adhere to a mission and make sure it is well articulated are the most skillful among them. Stakeholders such as taxpayers, faculties, and student bodies continually exert pressure for changes in direction in a given institution. The navigator-leaders, who revisit the aforementioned questions frequently and who answer them consistently over time, can fortify an institution for its journey into the next millennium.

Some Universities Experience Insurmountable Difficulties

Prognosticators depict a world economy during the coming decades that is extremely volatile, if not utterly depressed. With scarcity of resources as a backdrop, taxpayers and consumers will feel entitled to closer scrutiny of private and public higher education institutions in the future. Commercial concerns will gain influence. In other words, higher education will be subjected to the same "resource management forces" that have changed and rationalized health care systems in the developed nations.

Many universities will disappear. Today, particularly from the vantage point of the world of commerce, some universities are true ivory towers—"monastic" institutions that have survived due to inertia more than due to vital academic programs. Their leadership may be weak. Those with vague missions, no matter how venerated they were in the early 20th century, are decidedly at risk. In the next few decades, institutions with heavy expenditures on curricula that are unaligned with practical paradigms (that is, those that promote intellectual discourse in disciplines that have no pragmatic application), will be branded as wasteful.

As elements of waste are identified, overseers will be hard pressed to defend some time-honored features of the university. These include expansive, high-maintenance campuses, and book libraries, overheads which involve the cost of student recruitment, administratively burdensome athletic programs, and a plethora of "pure research" endeavors. Institutions that do not check unbridled expansion, and do not prune their programs appropriately, will see funding from both public and private sources gradually dry up. This outcome is hardly surprising: practical problems have always had profound influence on higher education financing.[1]

Other Universities Thrive

The universities that survive and emerge as innovators in the next century will have the following three essential assets:

- A curriculum that is directly relevant to educating the labor force
- A mission that is unequivocal regarding the institution's specific, measurable contribution to societal progress and societal benefit
- Firm, unbiased leadership

Those institutions that foster the education of an enlightened modern citizenry, that offer relevant instruction in the survival tools of the millennium, and that boast leaders who can recognize vital breakthroughs for the betterment of society, will survive and thrive.

Paths of Transformation

In order to best illustrate possible university transformations, we might envision two thriving institutions in the year 2030. What are their characteristics, and what decisions ensured that they could meet 21st century needs and carry out a 21st century charge? Let us proffer two institutions at different ends of the spectrum of academic disciplines: "Enterprise University" and "Communiversity." Enterprise University's graduates are primarily found in the technical fields such as computer engineering and medical research. Communiversity's alumni are primarily politicians, social workers, ambassadors, and teachers.

Over time, both institutions undergo shifts in their income base. As the source of revenue begins to shift, overseers of each institution examine curricular strengths and reassess their missions accordingly, parlaying strengths with strategic partnerships while making radical changes in their methodologies of instruction.

EVOLUTION OF ENTERPRISE UNIVERSITY

At the beginning of the 21st century, Enterprise was a well-respected, private research institution conferring both undergraduate and graduate degrees in a broad spectrum of disciplines. Recognizing the unique strengths of its engineering and physics programs, the trustees honed Enterprise's mission, rearticulating the university's purpose as an institution dedicated to enhancing society's knowledge via exploration in the physical realm.

Collaboration with corporations took on huge significance in the early 21st century,[2] and Enterprise's increasing income stream from partnerships and joint ventures was noteworthy. The disciplines offering opportunities for technology licensing and sponsored research began to thrive. As departments with commercial enterprises and joint venture research projects increased, additional representation from the corporate sector on the university's board increased as well. Since educating the labor force became the primary value, there came to be less emphasis on the awarding of degrees and more emphasis on the awarding of licenses to practice.

The focus by the overseers on the university's curricular strengths was tightened further by the institution's increasing utilization of technology in instruction. Efficient and far reaching, courses, which formerly had to be delivered in person, could now be taught on-line. The advantage of distance learning modules for the institutions themselves was the instant growth of the "market" for their "product." Students were able to enroll from around the world.

In classroom-free cyber-arenas, courses in medicine and physics, for example, which were formerly taught via lectures, textbooks, and experimentation, were gradually written for delivery via the World Wide Web. The advent of Web TV and the development of easy-to-use conferencing software (which could handle audio and video files in addition to text files) helped bring this form of instruction into the mainstream.

Emergence of the "Advanced Learning Network" (ALN)

The combination of the convenience of instruction, the efficiency of research that the Internet facilitated, and the infusion of resources from commercial sponsorships catapulted Enterprise University into an "Advanced Learning Network." Now, in 2030, Enterprise Advanced Learning Network is free from the burden of maintaining costly classroom buildings and libraries, and it enrolls 40,000 students compared to the 15,000 students it served in 1999. The reduced cost per student makes the advanced learning network easily accessible to the middle class.

The governing entity is a council of private industry leaders, whose role is to hire faculty and determine required competencies. Facilities are minimal. A single administrative building now houses all of the high-speed hardware and technical staff.

Sites for courses are password-protected so that only paying students may access them. The conferencing component of on-line courses may be either synchronous or asynchronous, depending on subject matter and the number of students enrolled. With a file scanner not unlike a unique bar code used in supermarkets, students easily locate the relevant class on the Net. Both faculty and students appreciate the fact that the content of the interchanges are permanently archived.

While no grades are given, the ALN awards certificates of competency and licenses to students when they complete a module. Students who are not licensed the first time they take an on-line course are considered enrolled until they master the subject matter.

The Advanced Learning Network Faculty

While the role of administrators and facilities managers has shrunk comparatively to their roles when the Enterprise was a university, faculty roles have expanded. The Advanced Learning Network faculty-affiliates perform at least one of three distinct functions.

- The first role is that of *admissions/assessment specialist*. This role involves determining the eligibility of applicants to participate in learning modules based on test results and on-line interviews.
- The second role is that of *courseware author*. These course designers are generally highly regarded experts in their fields; they contract with their employer to design interactive academic modules for Web-based delivery. Module authors prepare and organize lectures, conferences, and bibliographic resources for various learning modules, and are compensated with a courseware development fee. For Enterprise ALN, course development contracts specify how frequently new material is to be added to courseware. Generally, courseware developers and sponsoring ALNs share copyright on Web-based material equally, and cannot publish it independently without the permission of the other party. When original research and extensive collaboration are involved, the intellectual property rights for the modules reside primarily with the faculty authors and secondarily with the sponsoring ALN.
- The third function, that of *on-line facilitator*, is carried out by para-faculty. These specialists moderate all on-line discussions for a particular course or module, pose questions, measure student competencies, and provide detailed feedback They issue certificates of competency, recommend combinations and sequences of modules for particular students, and grant permission for students to advance to new modules. They also play a role in diagnosing technology/connectivity problems.

EVOLUTION OF COMMUNIVERSITY

The overseers of Communiversity also chose to revisit and focus its mission. Recognizing curricular strengths, its rearticulated mission emphasized its role in the exploration of the political realm and the effect of humans on the planet. Degrees in environmental sciences, public policy, psychology, and law from Communiversity were highly prized.

Unlike Enterprise ALN, which saw an increasing income stream at the beginning of the 21st century from the *corporate* sector, Communiversity began reporting significantly increasing revenues from the *public* sector. Government funding (which had formerly come in the form of financial aid and loans for students) began to come increasingly in the form of grants for community work. The bulk of these grants were not for research but for the establishment of programs that had a distinct social agenda. Large grants were received, for example, to evaluate public policies, to establish new programs for arbitration and dispute resolution, and to develop "service learning" curricula (secondary school students receive academic credit through community service).

The overseers of Communiversity, experiencing the same burdensome administrative overhead that had plagued Enterprise (high maintenance campuses, and so forth), applied foresight in recognizing the value of partnerships. Communiversity began to enter into formal partnerships with nonprofit and government agencies to carry out its mission.

Emergence of the Experience Camp

As Communiversity began to utilize other sites to carry out its instructional charge—churches, military sites, churches, hospitals, libraries, and farms—it evolved away from a degree-granting university to a different type of institution: an Experience Camp. Thus a hybrid emerged from the many creative partnerships; Communiversity evolved into a sophisticated system of internships for students interested in the "human" disciplines.

Now, in 2030, Communiversity Experience Camp has features of both a service agency and a university. Its board of directors has equal representation from the academic side and the community. (In other words, board seats are split evenly between local government officials, who had no direct contact with students, and faculty, who serve as licensed teacher-mentors to students in the Experience Camp). The Experience Camp is selective in its admissions process. Students must score well on entrance exams, have a record of high academic achievement, and demonstrate community awareness/service experience during the secondary school.

Academic content is drawn directly from the service activities the students engage in. Students receive "on-the-job training" in the discipline of their choice from the first day they enroll. Mentors team with faculty to help create and guide a two-year curriculum for each student. Faculty, who have an advising but no formal "teaching" load, also have administrative roles within the Experience Camp.

Students follow a curriculum of independent study at the site of their internship, with the regular approval of their main teacher and mentor. For example, an aspiring social worker might produce entertainment for convalescing seniors or care for handicapped children and be mentored by a filmmaker. An aspiring urban planner might plan and build a waste disposal site for a community and be mentored by an environmental scientist. An aspiring school administrator might serve as an interpreter in a multilingual school district and be mentored by a pastor in the local church.

Most study and service plans require an initial three months of preparatory research in the field by the newly enrolled student (for purposes of gathering and studying best practices). Following the preparation phase, students work on their project for a minimum of two years. They do not attend lectures, take tests, or experiment in laboratories. They are not graded for their work. Upon successful completion of the internship, the Experience Camp awards a "Certificate of Leadership," which requires specific competencies in a defined academic arena as well as demonstrated and measurable leadership skills. To qualify for certificates, students must document progress or success in their area of inquiry based on originally stated parameters. Government and nonprofit employers value the certificate of leadership highly.

SCENARIOS ENCOURAGE REFLECTION

One of the benefits of describing future universities is the deeper probing that the snapshot visions engender. While the two courses of evolution are certainly plausible, the described scenarios give rise to some important questions: Do these institutions' utilitarian missions leave any room for pure academic inquiry? How are spiritual concerns accommodated in either institution? What are the implications (particularly at the expensive Experience Camp) for equal access to quality education; will there be sufficient financial aid to allow equitable admissions and diversity of student body? And, particularly at the ALN, if distance learning is the key methodology, what has replaced the irreplaceable value of human contact in teaching?

One hopes that Enterprise University and Communiversity undergo their transformations in ways that allow them to develop leaders who have the technical know-how that the rapidly changing world requires and the compassion that the planet's citizens deserve. Yet the questions that the scenarios engender illustrate the complexity of higher education itself. Descriptions of the features of future universities, for all that they illuminate, necessarily leave some aspects of the educational ethos in the shadows. Perhaps through this type of reflection we momentarily experience the role of university leaders; like navigators, we find ourselves in uncharted waters, yet now with a fuller understanding of how very much is at stake.

NOTES

1. Richard Bjornson and Marilyn Waldman, eds., *The University of the Future*. The Center for Comparative Studies (Ohio State University Press, 1990), 3.

2. Clark Kerr, ed., *Troubled Times for American Higher Education: the 1990's and Beyond* (SUNY Press, 1994). See Chapter 5: "The Corporation and the University."

18

Consciousness-based Education: A Future of Higher Education in the New Millennium

—————————————————————— *James Grant*

Educational institutions are products of their culture. As the knowledge, ways of knowing, and values change in a society, educational institutions evolve accordingly. As we look to the possible futures of higher education, we must identify those forces transforming culture. The editors of this book have identified several of these "drivers"—globalization, multiculturalism, technology, and politicization. The premise of the vision of educational futures presented in this chapter is that there is a new driver on the horizon—an expanded understanding of human potential and how it can be promoted—that will transform the conception and content of higher education in the coming millennium.

The concept of human development is fundamental to education. Educational philosophers as diverse as Plato and John Dewey have stated that education is most fundamentally about promoting full human development. As Dewey noted one hundred years ago: "Here individualism and socialism are at one. Only by being true to the full growth of all the individuals who make it up, can society by any chance be true to itself."[1]

Whether one takes the perspective of a hard-nosed state economic planner or an aesthetically oriented humanistic psychologist, full human development is an important educational aim. It is essential both for societies that want to realize their economic potential and for societies that want to reach their spiritual potential. Human development encompasses growth in ability to think and deepening and broadening of one's values. But it also goes beyond these. Human development is important because through human development, we enhance our ability to have in

Dewey's terms "the richest and fullest possible experience"—in other words, to live a full and meaningful life, of maximum value to ourselves and others.

Given the importance of human development as an educational goal, a change in understanding of human potential and how to promote it has great potential significance for education. The understanding that will, I believe, transform education in the next century is that all human beings have the potential to become enlightened, to live life in higher states of consciousness, and that the means to achieve this aim is transcendence—experience of the absolute field of pure consciousness underlying objective and subjective existence.

A NEW BASIS FOR EDUCATION: THE EXISTENCE OF PURE CONSCIOUSNESS

At the basis of this new perspective on education is one central idea—that there is a field of pure consciousness, an unmanifest absolute field of life at the source of all creation, which can be experienced. The understanding that there is an unmanifest field of life at the source of both subjective and objective creation is a very old one. Aldous Huxley has referred to this understanding as "the perennial philosophy" precisely because it is so old and shared by so many cultures. Plato, for example, referred to this field as the Good, Lao-tze as the Tao, Buddhist sages as Nirvana, Vedic rishis as Atma, Aristotle as Being, and Emerson as the Oversoul. This understanding has not gained general acceptance, though, because the experience, which lies at the basis of the perennial philosophy, has not been generally available. In addition, the positivist paradigm underlying contemporary science has not been supportive of the existence of an underlying spiritual reality.

This is changing now, though, both due to the advance of science and the availability of simple, effortless techniques for gaining the experience of pure consciousness. The advance of science has supported the understanding of consciousness as an underlying field in two ways. First, developments in theoretical physics now support the existence of an unmanifest, unified field of natural law supporting all natural phenomena. The spiritual perspective that material creation is based on that which is immaterial is now being supported by modern science. There is still a conceptual lacuna between the existence of a unified field of natural law and the assertion that this field is consciousness, the source of subjectivity, but a number of excellent analyses are now making this claim more plausible.[2]

The advance of science is supporting existence of an underlying field of pure consciousness and the possibility of higher states of consciousness in another way—through provision of objective means of validating this subjective experience. Advances in technology—ranging from EEG machines to sophisticated blood assay devices—now make it possible to monitor fine changes in physiological functioning. Advances in psychological measurement, which make it possible to measure everything from levels of self development and creativity to anxiety and neurosis, further enhance our ability to objectively measure human growth and higher states of human functioning.

This advance in scientific capacity for assessing human functioning is particularly significant in conjunction with the availability of effortless techniques that give experience of pure consciousness. Many different meditative traditions have had experience of pure consciousness and growth to enlightenment as their aim. Most of these traditions, though, have involved arduous techniques and required acceptance of a certain set of spiritual beliefs. This has made them inaccessible to most individuals.

A breakthrough in this area has occurred in the last half of the 20th century largely due to the efforts of Maharishi Mahesh Yogi. Among others, Maharishi, in the last 40 years, has brought out a full revival of the Vedic tradition of knowledge from India, showing its relevance for all areas of life, from education and business to medicine, criminal rehabilitation, and government. He has provided detailed intellectual understanding of pure consciousness and of growth to higher states of consciousness. Most significantly, he has taught effortless, nonsectarian technologies for developing consciousness that have given millions of people from many cultures and religious faiths the benefit of the experience of pure consciousness. Because these techniques are easily learned and require no belief system, they have opened up the possibility of extensive and rigorous scientific testing of the premise that humans can access a field of pure consciousness and that this experience has value for human life.

Research into Pure Consciousness

This scientific research on the Transcendental Meditation and TM-Sidhi[3] programs is highly significant because it bridges the chasm between the great subjective traditions of meditation and the objective paradigm of modern science. This research, begun in the 1970s, is of three kinds.[4]

Psycho-physiological changes

The first verifies that there are unique psycho-physiological characteristics associated with the experience of pure consciousness. Research has verified that subjective experience of transcendence does comprise a unique fourth state of consciousness, characterized by deep physiological rest and heightened mental alertness, different from waking, sleeping, or dreaming consciousness.[5] More recent research in this area has confirmed the existence of unique psycho-physiological correlates of the stabilized state of enlightenment—the state in which pure consciousness is experienced as a reality 24 hours a day.[6] Physiological research of a different sort, but of fundamental significance, has established the profound correspondence between the expressions of pure consciousness, as found in the Vedic Literature, and the structure of human physiology.[7] This discovery, by Dr. Tony Nader under Maharishi's guidance, concretely demonstrates that the total potential of Natural Law—pure consciousness—is lively within the human physiology.

The practical benefit of the experience of pure consciousness for activity

This research has shown profound and wide-ranging benefits consistent with the premise that pure consciousness is a fundamental field of intelligence and orderliness. It has shown that the single experience of pure consciousness leads to significant improvement in all areas of life—mind, body, and behavior. Specific findings on individuals practicing Transcendental Meditation include sharply reduced medical expenditures in all major health categories, improved academic performance, growth of IQ, greater psychological balance, unprecedented growth on measures of self development, and significantly reduced recidivism in prison inmates.[8] This research demonstrating the holistic growth resulting from experience of pure consciousness supports the view that pure consciousness is the most fundamental element of our being, underlying all aspects of our physical, emotional, and cognitive lives.

The environmental influence of practice of the Transcendental Meditation and TM-Sidhi programs

This research consists of dozens of carefully controlled research studies showing that significant positive effects are created in society—reductions in negative tendencies such as crime, violence, sickness, and accident rates, and increases in positive indicators such as political cooperation and economic indices—when a sufficient number of individuals practice the TM and TM-Sidhi programs. This remarkable finding, which is now one of the most rigorously confirmed findings in the field of sociology, is explained in terms of enlivenment of the underlying field of consciousness. When a critical number of individuals are transcending and enlivening this field, the effect is great enough to influence the individual consciousness and physiology of individuals not meditating. The result is that individuals can gain the benefit of transcending without meditating themselves. On an individual level, these benefits include more effective activity, happiness, and positivity, effects that translate on a societal level into less frustration, less violence, and greater cooperation.[9]

EDUCATIONAL IMPLICATIONS OF THE EXISTENCE OF PURE CONSCIOUSNESS

The understanding, based on knowledge of pure consciousness, that there is a state of enlightenment that can be realized, transforms the way education is conceived. The primary transformation that comes from this understanding is the perspective that education should focus on the development of consciousness, not on the amassing of information. In short, education should be consciousness based, not information based. Only through the transformation of consciousness can the full power and dignity of life be realized and the wisdom achieved to use information properly. This understanding transforms the way we understand the goals and practices of education. It is now being concretely implemented in institutions such as Maharishi University of Management in the United States and exists as a real alternative for educational institutions in the new millennium.[10]

Transforming Educational Goals

Within the consciousness-based paradigm, the goal of education, on an individual level, becomes the creation of enlightened individuals. Once the possibility of achieving enlightenment is recognized, all other goals become gross suboptimizations of the educational process. In the words of Plato's famous allegory, one cannot justify the continued bondage of human beings in a cave, where they take shadows as reality, when the possibility of ascent to the sunlit world is possible.

On the collective level, this paradigm opens the possibility for creation of an ideal society. It is not by chance that Plato's Republic, which is the first systematic Western treatise explaining the nature and importance of pure consciousness, is also the first systematic Western treatise on the creation of a utopia. Poverty, war, and violence can all be seen as the products of immature human beings. As large numbers of individuals grow to the state of fulfillment and self-actualization in enlightenment, the collective dynamics of society will change. As Maharishi says: "A few fully educated or enlightened individuals are sufficient to give a new direction to the life of their community and by their very presence bring about an enlightened society, create and maintain world peace, and establish Heaven on Earth."[11] In his *Science of Being and Art of Living*, Maharishi presents this new potential for society in moving terms:

A new humanity will be born, fuller in conception and richer in experience and accomplishments in all fields. Joy of life will belong to every man, love will dominate human society, truth and virtue will reign in the world, peace on earth will be permanent, and all will live in fulfillment in fullness of life in [enlightenment].[12]

On the societal level, education can strive toward this goal based on the knowledge of pure consciousness.

Transforming Educational Practices

The existence of pure consciousness and the ability to achieve enlightenment has significant implications for educational practice, including the introduction of new courses and disciplines, and a transformation in the approach of existing disciplines to their subject matter. Central to the consciousness-based paradigm is a profound new view of human development, which transforms the way we understand the educational process. Currently, development is viewed to be the product of two factors and their interaction: nature and nurture, or maturation and interaction with an external environment. Because maturation is largely out of the educators' control, contemporary educators focus primarily on how to structure students' interactions with the environment—teachers, books, labs— to optimally promote development. The consciousness-based perspective recognizes that there is a third means of development, different from nature and nurture as currently understood—transcendence, the experience of pure consciousness. Experience of transcendence both accelerates growth in the normal range of cognitive and affective development and allows full development of the individual to enlightenment.

Appreciation of the importance of transcendence for development leads to a reconceptualization of the process of education. Students and faculty need to transcend daily as an integral part of education. Because the most important knowledge is knowledge of pure consciousness, the necessary implication for education is that having this experience should be a central feature of the school curriculum.

In addition to this required experiential course in research in consciousness, the new paradigm requires intellectual courses relating to the knowledge of consciousness. Complete knowledge requires both experience and intellectual understanding, and this is as true of knowledge of consciousness as it is of other sorts of knowledge. Without proper intellectual understanding, experience of pure consciousness can be misunderstood and abused, as it has been numerous times throughout history. At Maharishi University of Management, this requirement is satisfied by all students taking a course in the Science of Creative Intelligence— the science of consciousness—as their first course at the University. Further courses in advanced aspects of Vedic Science, as well as a major in this area are available. Topics of these courses range from abstract understanding of the nature of pure consciousness, found for example in the Vedic Literature, to practical understanding of the mechanics of development of consciousness; they cover scientific understanding of the physiological correlates of growth of consciousness as well as investigations into expressions of this underlying reality found in the art, literature, religion, and philosophy of the great traditions of the world.

Acceptance of the consciousness-based paradigm also has implications for the teaching of established disciplines. One general change is the emphasis on wholeness and connection. On the level of consciousness, everything is connected. Wholeness is the ultimate reality and this realization colors the entire curriculum. Understanding of wholeness is fostered experientially through the growth of consciousness produced by meditation—a developed consciousness spontaneously sees life in terms of connections. Intellectually it is fostered through a variety of modalities:

- One is the science of consciousness course that systematically explores the holistic basis of all life, pure consciousness, and how this wholeness manifests in the different relative fields;
- A second is use of large charts in all courses (referred to as Unified Field Charts at Maharishi University of Management) that graphically represent how all areas of a discipline relate to each other and their source in pure consciousness;
- A third is emphasis on common principles that function in all of the disciplines.[13]

Full understanding of consciousness also impacts the content and goals of many disciplines. We have seen this clearly with regard to the field of education. Understanding of pure consciousness changes our understanding of the goal of education, the nature of knowledge, and courses to be taken. This is also true of other disciplines. The arts and literature are transformed by the understanding that the highest aesthetic experience is transcendence, experience of pure consciousness. In light of the understanding of enlightenment, the purpose of art and literature becomes to exalt this experience and promote spiritual refinement.

In the social sciences, understanding of pure consciousness also brings dramatic transformation. Psychology, which has floundered in the 20th century without an adequate understanding of the mind and self, is immeasurably enriched by understanding of transcendence and enlightenment. With this knowledge, growth to higher states of consciousness becomes a major field of study, and the relevance of the experience of transcendence to all the applied areas of psychology is clear. In sociology, the new understanding of collective consciousness transforms the field. The understanding that everyone in society is connected at the level of pure consciousness, and that enlivenment of this field by even a small percentage of individuals can raise the collective consciousness of the whole society, changes the way sociologists approach collective problems. This, in turn, has a significant impact on the field of political science.

This new paradigm recognizes that the greatest determinant of political outcomes is collective consciousness. The collective consciousness of a society is a direct and sensitive reflection of the level of consciousness of its individual members, and in turn becomes a force of its own influencing individual consciousness. When collective consciousness is incoherent—reflecting, and in turn exacerbating, the stress of individual members—conflict dominates and the interest of the individual and group supersedes that of the whole. As collective consciousness rises, harmony grows and values become more enlightened, reflecting a simultaneous respect for the whole and the part. Within this paradigm, cooperation and peace become the emphasis of study, rather than conflict and war. Consciousness is seen to be a key determinant of political behavior on the individual and collective level.

In the natural sciences, the appreciation of the unity of man with nature softens the move of much of 20th century science to dominate and replace nature. This paradigm leads to a deep respect for the environment and for natural approaches to fields ranging from agriculture to medicine. From the perspective of this paradigm, approaches such as genetic engineering and cloning are recognized to be the height of folly; the misplaced attempt to replace nature's intelligence with man's intelligence. Hard disciplines such as physics are subtly transformed by the realization that the laws of nature outside the human being are the same laws that function inside the human being and in all human endeavors from art to politics. This perspective humanizes science.

Making Transitions to Consciousness-based Education[14]

As we sit at the end of the 20th century, still largely embedded in an objective, Western paradigm of information-based education, it is hard to conceive of a transformation to developmentally oriented, consciousness-based education. The seeds of this transformation are with us now, though, and there are positive experiential consequences for educators that will support this evolution. First, it should be noted that the diversity of educational institutions that now exists will not diminish. Gaining knowledge necessary for professional success will always be important, as will studies that promote the understanding of culture, insight into the natural world, and aesthetic development. Institutions will continue to teach this knowledge and approach it in different ways. Within these institutions, emphasis on consciousness will vary. Some, for ideological reasons, might not emphasize it at all. Others, which are highly skills oriented, such as two-year community colleges in the United States, might only offer consciousness-related courses on an optional basis, just as they now offer courses in English literature or philosophy. Many institutions, though, such as those committed to the ideal of liberal arts education today, will have development of consciousness as a central aim of their education, with the educational implications presented.

This transition will be aided, in the early years, by the solutions that consciousness-based education provides to problems faced by contemporary institutions, such as low academic achievement, stress, and binge drinking. Beyond the ability of consciousness-based approaches to help institutions meet challenges they are now facing, there are more subtle changes in intellectual climate occurring that will support this change. One is a growing acceptance and valuing of multiculturalism. Western cultural chauvinism is a big barrier to acceptance of an educational paradigm based on what is widely—although mistakenly—considered exclusively an Eastern tradition of knowledge. The growing acceptance and positive valuing of perspectives offered by other cultures will aid the acceptance of this new paradigm in the coming years.

A second change is greater appreciation of holistic development. Theories of multiple intelligence and emotional intelligence, for example, are broadening the way we conceive the outcomes of education. Recent educational futures research by Jennifer Gidley found that young people having experienced a holistic, imaginative, Steiner education felt empowered to create their own positive futures.[15] As the importance especially of intrapersonal intelligence and self-awareness (the core value of emotional intelligence) grows, techniques for promoting these will naturally have a place in the educational setting. More generally, we are now seeing a greater openness to holistic spiritual perspectives and to the connection of man to nature. Sociologist Paul Ray, for example, has written extensively on the emergence of a major new group in American society, the "Cultural Creatives," who operate on the leading edge of cultural change. The defining qualities of this group, which now constitutes approximately one-quarter of the U.S. adult population, are spirituality and/or ecological awareness. Values held by the "Core" Cultural Creatives (about 10 percent of the population) include serious concern with psychology, spiritual life, self-actualization, enjoyment in mastering new ideas, social concern, use of alternative health care and natural foods, and strong advocacy of ecological sustainability.[16] These values are consistent with those of the consciousness-based approach to education, and as this orientation grows in the United States and other countries, the consciousness-based educational paradigm will gain ground.

The transition to consciousness-based education will also be supported by the positive experience of educators in these institutions. My personal experience, and that of other faculty who have come to teach at Maharishi University of Management from other institutions, is that a consciousness-based environment is significantly better for teaching and working. The first thing one notices here is the alertness of the students—students are awake because of the enlivening experience of practice of Transcendental Meditation twice daily. The heart value is also much more lively. Stress levels in both students and faculty are much lower, leading to a more mutually supportive environment. The cutthroat nature of academics elsewhere does not exist here. The politicization level is extremely low, because the focus is not on power, which is a zero-sum game, but on growth, which is positive sum. The most rewarding aspect of the environment, ultimately, is the holistic development one experiences in oneself and sees in others. One experiences in oneself, and others, growing peace, happiness, creativity, intuition, empathy, strength, and wholeness. The associated fulfillment is extraordinarily rewarding—one recognizes that this is what education should be about. As more academics have this experience—as teachers or students—they will want to recreate these environments elsewhere.

TOWARD HARMONY AND PEACE

The deepest educational thinkers over the ages have recognized that the most important goal of education is to promote individual development. Through realization of this goal, both the individual and society are served optimally. This paper has suggested that a new, although ancient, understanding of human potential is emerging. Based on the existence of pure consciousness, this understanding supports a new paradigm for education—consciousness-based education—with significantly different emphases and practices from contemporary education. Most significantly, the goal of education in this dawning paradigm is enlightenment, the state of fully developed heart and mind where one directly experiences the cosmic status of oneself and others. With this change, meditation becomes the most basic component of education, that component capable of promoting dramatic unfoldment of full potential, and all disciplines are appreciated in the holistic light of their connections based in their collective origin in the field of pure consciousness.

The promise of this new educational paradigm is great: It is both more humane and more profound than contemporary education. Most significantly, it offers the prospect of achieving, in the coming millennium, a new age characterized by lively individuality and universal love, an age free of social problems—in short, an Age of Enlightenment. Such an age would not mark the end of history—it would be subject to the same dynamics of loss and revival of knowledge as other ages—but it would represent the culmination of the quest, expressed in both Eastern and Western traditions, for a harmonious and peaceful society living in tune with nature. This is a goal worth working toward.

NOTES

1. John Dewey, "The School and Social Progress," in *The School and Society*, J. A. Boydston, ed. (Carbondale and Edwardsville, Illinois, USA: Southern Illinois University Press, 1980), 5.

2. John Hagelin, "Is Consciousness the Unified Field? A Field Theorist's Perspective," *Modern Science and Vedic Science* 3 (1987): 3–72. Fritjof Capra, *The Tao of Physics: An Exploration of the Parallels Between Modern Physics and Eastern Mysticism* (Boston: New Science Library, 1975).

3. Transcendental Meditation, TM-Sidhi, Science of Creative Intelligence, and Consciousness-Based are registered or common law trademarks licensed to Maharishi Vedic Education Development Corporation and used under sublicense or with permission.

4. See URL <http://www.mum.edu/TM_Research/TM_research_home> for a comprehensive summary of research on the Transcendental Meditation and TM-Sidhi programs. This site also contains a summary of more than 100 research studies directly relevant to education.

5. Frederick Travis and Robert Keith Wallace, "Autonomic Patterns During Respiratory Suspensions: Possible Markers of Transcendental Consciousness," *Psychophysiology* 34 (1997): 39–46.

6. Lynne Mason, Charles Alexander, et al. "Electrophysiological Correlates of Higher States of Consciousness During Sleep in Long-Term Practitioners of the Transcendental Meditation Program," *Sleep* 20, 2 (1997): 102–10. The following doctoral dissertation is interesting because it contains extensive interviews with individuals experiencing higher states of consciousness: Julia Guttmann, *The Search for Bliss: A Model of Emotional Development Based on Maharishi's Vedic Psychology*, UMI Dissertation Services, Number 9633806, 1996.

7. Tony Nader, *Human Physiology: Expression of Veda and the Vedic Literature* (Vlodrop, Netherlands: Maharishi Vedic University Press, 1995).

8. Following are some representative articles in these areas: David Orme-Johnson, "Medical Care Utilization and the Transcendental Meditation Program," *Psychosomatic Medicine* 49 (1987): 493–507; Charles Alexander, Maxwell Rainforth, and Paul Gelderloos, "Transcendental Meditation, Self-Actualization, and Psychological Health: A Conceptual Overview and Statistical Meta-Analysis," *Journal of Social Behavior and Personality* 6, 5 (1991): 189–247; Robert Cranson, David Orme-Johnson, Jayne Gackenbach, Christopher Jones, and Charles Alexander, "Transcendental Meditation and Improved Performance on Intelligence-Related Measures: A Longitudinal Study,"

Personality and Individual Differences 12 (1991): 1105–17; Charles Alexander, Patricia Robinson, and Maxwell Rainforth, "Treating and Preventing Alcohol, Nicotine, and Drug Abuse through Transcendental Meditation: A review and Statistical Meta-analysis," *Alcoholism Treatment Quarterly* 11 (1994): 219–336; Catherine Bleick, and Allen Abrams, "The Transcendental Meditation Program and Criminal Recidivism in California," *Journal of Criminal Justice* 15, 3 (1987): 211–30.

9. The following URL has references to and short abstracts of more than 40 studies examining the environmental influence of practice of the TM and TM-Sidhi programs: <http://www.mum.edu/tm_research/tm_biblio/socio_c.html> The following two studies have good reviews of this effect: David Orme-Johnson, Charles Alexander, John Davies, Howard Chandler, and Wallace Larimore, "International peace project in the Middle East: The effects of the Maharishi Technology of the Unified Field," *Journal of Conflict Resolution* 32, 4 (1988): 776–812; P. D. Assimakis and Michael Dillbeck, "Time Series Analysis of Improved Quality of Life in Canada: Social Change, Collective Consciousness, and the TM-Sidhi Program," *Psychological Reports* 76 (1995): 1171–93.

10. Maharishi University of Management, founded as Maharishi International University in 1971, is accredited to the doctoral level by the North Central Association of Colleges and Schools, the oldest accrediting agency in the U.S. Information about Maharishi University of Management can be found on the Internet at <http://mum.edu/>.

11. Maharishi Mahesh Yogi, *Maharishi Vedic University: Introduction* (Vlodrop, Netherlands: Maharishi Vedic University Press, 1994), 147.

12. Maharishi Mahesh Yogi, *The Science of Being and Art of Living* (New York: Signet, 1968/1988), xvii.

13. For more discussion of these points see: Susan Dillbeck and Michael Dillbeck, "The Maharishi Technology of the Unified Field in Education: Principles, Practice, and Research," 1987. On-line, Maharishi University of Management Education Department Web page. Available http://www.mum.edu/ed_dept/zpapers/cbeppr_frm.html. November 13, 1998.

14. Consciousness-based education in caps is a trademark term that refers to the specific approach to education offered at institutions founded by Maharishi Mahesh Yogi. However, I am using "consciousness-based" in this article to refer more generally to an understanding that recognizes consciousness as fundamental to education.

15. Jennifer Gidley, "Prospective Youth Visions through Imaginative Education," *Futures* 30, 5 (1998).

16. Paul Ray, "The Rise of the Integral Culture," 1997. On-line, Quay Alliance, Inc. Reading Room. Available <http://www.quantumorg.com/intcult.htm>. November 5, 1998.

Part 4

Transformations of
the University

19

Corporate Networks or Bliss for All: The Politics of the Futures of the University

————————————— *Sohail Inayatullah*

THEORIZING SURPRISE

To begin to approach how the future of the University might be different to conventional trajectories, we need to theorize and contour "surprise," to map likely futures. This is the challenge Peter Manicas poses when he writes that the great promise of pessimistic approaches to the future is that history is full of surprises.

For the university, the most likely configuration is the division of universities into three spaces:

- The elite brand name universities, which expand outward spurred on by globalization and virtualization;
- Convenience mega universities, which through flexible delivery, capture the majority of the world's students; and
- Smaller niche universities that focus on multiculturalism or regional and local concerns.

We can thus assume that in the long run Harvard/Oxford and other elite universities will buy up leading universities around the world—that is, the victory of the multinational corporatist vision of the university. Of course, given the politeness of traditional academia—the pretence that it is the accumulation of knowledge that matters—it will not be done so crassly. But like other American institutions such as the Peace Corps, it will be developmentalism that provides the ideological framework and repressive tolerance that will be the long-term outcome. Thus, there will be a slow but decisive shift in the political economy of the university. While elite American and British universities already define what is to be researched and what is legitimate knowledge, what is significant for the future is that soon (and, of course, this will be franchised) they will write courseware for universities all over the world. This is more than having dominating textbooks, it is about making a cleavage between professor/teacher and content designer—with the professor/teacher more and more the soft/fuzzy facilitator (although more likely the bored-stiff robot) and the content designer shaping knowledge delivery through the Net. The Harvard/Oxford stamp will be the seal of approval, allowing their Net courses to flourish, giving some discipline to "wild west chaos" that is the Net.

However, if elite institutions do not do this, believing that they will retain their marketshare, irrespective of the virtualization and the impact of globalization, new players like the convenience University of Phoenix or the International Management Centers or the multitude of other university "wannabes" (primarily in the North but also in the South) will step in. Yet if they do dilute their brand name, in the very long run, the eliteness of such institutions will disappear.

This will occur for several reasons. First, as already underway in the South, such brand names can be easily copied. For example, in Islamabad, the American University of London uses the brand name of American University of Cairo/Beirut to promote itself.

Second, courseware content developers over time will lose the sense of alle-giance—the ego-gratification of working with an elite university. They will sell themselves and their content to whomever will provide them best conditions. Best conditions for courseware developers will be, of course, content control; profits over many years will be more important than the ego-gratification of working with an elite institution. They might prefer to sell their wares from Tahiti, or places certainly more beautiful than the East Coast of the United States. Eventually, content designers will create their own virtual universities. Like Microsoft has done for personal computers, these content designers will provide the new operating system for the future of pedagogy, as was done earlier through the structure of the book.

Third, the Web does create the possible conditions for a university on every street corner, following the "wise man in every ashram" model, or the Greek philosopher intimately linked with the people (in more ways than the obvious). What this means is that once the distinction between professor/courseware con-tent designer begins, once the monopoly of the academy over knowledge—accreditation—begins to explode, there is no turning back. In the very long run, of course, power will centralize again and larger systems will emerge from the chaos of the Net. In the short- and mid-term, publishing, to begin with, will decentralize, allowing any academic to, if not compete with larger multinational publishers, at least create their own niche markets.

Finally, there is a fourth crucial possibility that does not point to a bright future for the elite scenario: students. While many desire university degrees that lead to jobs, it is relationship or connection with others that is equally important. Universities are not only sites of information, they have been, in the modern world, sites of politics and dissent. They have also been places where partners are discovered, lifelong friends created, and where the world comes to be known through relationship. This is the feminist, ecological, and spiritual argument—that it is connection with the other—be it gender, nature, the spiritual, or other human beings—that is most important. The university still offers an alternative to how to organize life and provide self and group identity outside the cold model of the corporatist organization or the bureaucratic state system. Globalization and virtualization have been unable to speak to this level of reality. Indeed, the tools they bring to it are part of the problem. As Raimundo Pannikar has put it: "Applying logos to the myth, amounts to killing the myth: it is like looking for darkness with a torch."[1] That is, cyberspace and postmodernity create even more fragmented selves, fragmented disciplines.[2] Once the illusion of cyberconnection is discovered (and the Net, as with books, is seen primarily as an informational tool and not as a process that enhances communication), pedagogy based on inter-active relationships, and sharing and learning will become even more important, more of an issue. Information will be ubiquitous, the challenge in the alleged postindustrial future will be communication—creating a dialogue among civilizations, cultures, genders, disciplines, and colleagues. Essentially this is the idealistic task of returning pedagogy to the love of knowledge, love of humanity, and the love of other.

Thus the challenge to the elite university, and as well to the convenience university, might not come from the virtual or the globally elite university but the transdisciplinary university that approaches—in cross-cultural ways—issues of meaning, and provides methods to explore these issues of body, mind, and spirit. William Irwin Thompson's Lindisfarne, the Schumacher College, Sarkar's Gurukul all experiment with knowledge that is practical—in terms of the empirical world—but is approached with critical lenses in the context of self and social transformation. Gidley develops this prospect more fully in her concluding chapter. Thus, while the Net is important, it is transformed consciousness—either in terms of gender awareness, of wisdom or cosmic consciousness—that is far more significant.

THE CONTEXT OF GLOBALISM

Another site of transformation could result from the collapse of capitalism—the failure of postindustrial society to provide jobs—as Neubauer suggested in his chapter. While globalism comes to us a fait accompli if we take a critical view of capitalism it can be argued we are in fact in the last stage of capitalism, and there are signs that we may in fact be shifting to other systems. Either the system has become unsustainable—or instead of providing more jobs, massive unemployment is the likely scenario—and thus revolt by the masses all over the world is possible.[3] In addition, many argue that the markets have de-linked from the real world of goods and services and thus a giant crash leading to a world depression is about to begin. This could lead to the end of capitalism as a reigning system.[4]

The Indian philosopher Sarkar argues that in the late phase of capitalism or the vaeshyan system, intellectuals or vipras are more likely to take on the perspective or worldview of capitalists. However, instead of creating new wealth or technologies, they became lackeys, or boot lickers, of the capitalist system.[5] These intellectuals are unable to express their idealistic potentials. The ones that do not become lackeys become commodified.

This is exacerbated through virtualization and globalization, which create jobless growth. The future reality is of fewer and fewer jobs for intellectuals (and if Rifken and others are correct about the end of work there will be fewer and fewer jobs for all).[6] Intellectuals, more and more, will become disinvested in the system, except in the United States, where there will always be a market for consultants. They will slowly lose allegiance to the idea of the university since they will be contract workers and not beholden to the mythology of higher knowledge—the good, the true and the beautiful, described by Spies in his chapter. They will also lose allegiance to other faculty. Part of globalization has been disciplining labor everywhere. What this means is that deans and others have selectively eliminated programs through the divide-and-rule method. Faculty members have not united—they have let Adolph Eichmann in the door—instead having sold out other members to save their own program, they have allowed the banality of evil to creep through the system.[7]

Those unable to find any employment will lose allegiance to the larger system. This creates the possibility of a massive global movement of unemployed intellectuals who are fed up with the system, have the consciousness to see through globalization, and are willing to take risks to transform it. While this situation is already at a peak in the South—where intellectuals work largely in the social movements, such as nongovernmental organizations—it is beginning in the West as well. How the global knowledge workers (who are unable to be paid to work full time or gain stable positions) act and react, and what future they create, may be one of history's surprises Manicas refers to. They could very easily cannibalize themselves in chasing the last jobs remaining (or, get bought out by postmodern managerialism with its claims for less hierarchical systems of organization),[8] or they could show solidarity and help create a new system.

WHO ARE THE BEDOUINS?

Ibn Khaldun, the 14th century Tunisian philosopher, is instructive in theorizing the futures of the politics of knowledge. For him, it is the Bedouin outside the city walls—outside of official knowledge centers—who can create the future.[9] The Bedouin has asabiya—or unity created through intense struggle with opposing environmental forces, or in the very late 20th century, with opposing organizational factors. Who then are the Bedouins? Are they the intellectuals who no longer are invested into the capitalist and the interstate system? If so, can they promise a different future for the university than the obvious scenarios of virtualization and globalization?

Perhaps they can create a more communicative postcapitalist vision of what it means to be human, or what the university should be about. The fight will be difficult though. For instance, outsiders, such as myself, a representative of a major transnational telecommunication firm, and political leaders were put in a "fish bowl"[10] at one university conference at an Australian university and asked to comment on the university. The telecommunication executive had one point: the customer is always right. He complained that the university was not run like an efficient business but instead as a disorganized mish-mash of faculty/students/administrators with no lines of clear authority. For the university to survive it had to be corporatized. Efficiency and line command had to be restored. And at the global level, the monopoly universities have had on knowledge and its accreditation had to be eliminated—privatized.

There are two issues here: the first being "is the customer always right?" While students can certainly choose with their minds and their money, a point that went missing was that students are not always right.[11] Even if the professor is action-learning oriented and creates a dialogical space, the student is there to learn new information, to be challenged, to learn new skills, to peel away layers of reality and enter deeper worlds. The student may be right to ask for a computer terminal that works but the student is less right if he writes a nonsensical essay. It is this disciplinary process that the university, as ashrams in India (madrasses in the Islamic world), focused on. How to learn? What to learn? What knowledge is to be transmitted? This was all predicated on the view that one did not know, that life was a journey, and that the university was about facilitating that journey.

Majid Tehranian divides knowledge into additive (science and technology), regenerative (moral), and transformative (spiritual). The telecom representative was unconcerned with these divisions, and, rather, was focused on efficiency itself as knowledge. His question was one of how to get things done in the world, without asking which things should be done and why. However, it is this question of why (that the university can and must continue to ask) that is under attack. The attack is partly from globalization, wherein this question is considered meaningless, with the main issue being that of providing more efficient and effective education. The attack is also from the "Other," from those outside Western knowledge frameworks, who contest fundamentally the categories of knowledge being used to transmit information and who want transformative and moral knowledge to frame additive knowledge, that is, moral science.

This is the multicultural challenge to the future of the university—that knowledge should be taken out of its strict scientific objective stance and located in how different civilizations language the world. From culture studies to gender studies to emerging civilizational studies, there has been a fundamental critique of content, of asking whose story is being told, and how a more inclusive story can be told. Thus the claims that Sardar[12] makes for Islamic science, Goonatilake[13] makes for Buddhist science, and Nandy[14] and others make for nonwestern science in general are not only for moral and transformative knowledge but for additive knowledge as well. This challenge is similar to the economist critique that universities have monopolies. But instead of calling for mass convenience universities that spin out more M.B.A.s and that provide the best value in terms of information bits per dollar, the issue is: "Is what is being taught representative of humanity's history?" Or is it an ethnocentric tale that, by its exclusions, created a world ecumene that is fraught with cultural, gender, and epistemological violence as a reaction to what is not taught?

The second issue is that while it is problematic that universities and disciplinary bodies have monopolies (thus having transformed the intellectual to the academic—or the university to the site of knowledge and dissent to information and efficiency), the solution is not more corporatization but an opening up of alternative ways of knowing—not a further limiting to economism. It is the former that may play a far more important role as the limits to globalism and economic rationalism have become exceedingly obvious. The Net can help with this opening up process but cultural pluralism requires far more than a speedy modem. Thus the Bedouins might not be the "Bill Gates" high-tech Web designers creating the virtual postindustrial university, but instead might be the others on the fringe of history—on the edge, as Wildman puts it, of official knowledge.[15]

However, it is too simple to say that the Bedouins will provide the surprises to the official future, or even to say that it is best not to focus on current problems but on emerging issues. It is as well too simple to argue that those not vested in the current system can dramatically alter the system just because they are not party to its knowledge politics. Remembering Johan Galtung's[16] structural theory of imperialism, the periphery of the periphery at times not only does not represent the new future but in fact is a poor copy of the present. Thus, the periphery instead of being the creative minority can easily be imitative in its responses—it fails the civilizational challenge and either becomes a defeated passive civilization (Aboriginal Australia) or an aggressive defeated nation (Iraq). It does not create difference. Rather, because of its low self-esteem, its inferiority complex, it focuses on imitative structures from the center, from elite institutions. This is the colonized mind, the colonized university—the condition of most Australian, African, South-East, and South Asian universities. Similar are Islamic universities throughout the world, which are only Muslim in the sense of studying the Quran; they have not adopted Islamic epistemological schemes in creating faculties or in rethinking the division of knowledge in the library.[17]

DISSENT

The larger issue is that of dissent. There are many purposes and missions of education generally and the university specifically, including:

- The university as a corporation (run as a business with a powerful administrative staff, which has grown twice as fast in the United States as academic staff);
- The university as a place for academic leadership (teaching and additive knowledge);
- The university as providing the ideological legitimacy of the state; and
- The university as public service (the university that exists for the community).

It is still dissent that is pivotal if the university is about creating an alternative future.

In this sense the university stands, or at least should stand, in the West, in opposition to economic rationalism and in the South, in opposition to the State. It must, as Mojab argues, civilize the State and ensure that the bureaucracy does not use it as a way to bestow favors. The university can, and must be about, limiting the excesses of any civilization or social formation, whether it be the Church/Mosque/Temple or the Prince (state) and Merchant (market). It must provide the third space to reflect on society and civilization; researching it, engaging with students in teaching it, and providing future alternatives to it.

However, dissent, while appearing to blossom in the South, appears to have stalled in the West. This has occurred for several reasons:

- Much of dissent was framed in Marxist class language. Globalization and the transformation of the Marxist professor to the Professor of Marxism have made dissent problematic.
- The language of the Net has bought out dissent as well. As Michael Tracey writes: "the planet is being constructed within the powerful, pervasive, all-consuming logic of the market, there is a second order language, a fairy tale . . . that suggests in utopian terms new possibilities, in particular those presented by the new alchemies."[18] Thus, the Net is offered as the magical solution to an economic process that has gone very wrong.
- Also related to the utopian claims of the Net (the claims of cyberdemocracy), dissent has been focused on attacking particular nominations of history, and creating new departments focused on areas of knowledge that did not fit into modernist knowledge frames (ethnic studies, for example).
- There has also emerged an internal search for truth through nonwestern approaches to self. While there might be some evidence that changes in consciousness lead to changes in institutions and structures, by and large, more important are simultaneous structural and consciousness changes, since they reinforce each other.

Thus faculty in the West have been busy with immediate concerns over self and knowledge territories instead of the larger struggle over who will write the history of the future of the university.

In the South, however, dissent is alive—student riots against Suharto are the latest example, years back in the Philippines against Marcos, and in Belgrade against Milosevic. Dissent in the South is largely against state repression and less about the content of what is to be taught, or the hierarchical relationship between teacher/student. This is quite different in the West where the role of the professor, the structure of learning, and other facets of a university are up for negotiation.

However, for the globalized university, for the Harvard Inc. or the global convenience Inc. model (by "Inc." I mean in some type of relationship with a media giant, such as Sony or Disney) multiculturalism is not about the opening up of knowledge but a strategic advantage used to attract students—multiculturalism then becomes one of the weapons of globalization. The structure remains the same; representation is merely artificially broadened, as Kelly argued in her chapter. Postmodernity as a response to the question of representation is largely about allowing for the many ways of knowing in the Western university, where empiricist and philosophical intellectual traditions are contested, and where all is let loose, the center having caved in. However, the postmodern multiversity is not the vision of the South.

The South vision is partly about dissent, at a deep level contesting modernity/postmodernity, and arguing for the inclusion of the mythic, the spiritual, and the premodern. It is, as Hudson puts it, about speaking truth to power. And in this vision, it is the spiritual that is fundamental, that cannot be reduced. The spiritual is not seen as discursive but as the ground of being. Thus, it is not postmodernity that is sought after, nor is it virtualization. Islamic universities and other alternative universities are aware that even as postmodernity gives spaces for their own perspective, it does so in the context of cultural relativity. It makes their foundational claims discursive instead of authentic and nonnegotiable. At the same time, such alternative pedagogical experiments are often created in the context of realpolitiks, and are funded through particular nominations of culture (one view of Islam, for example). Many like Rahman believe that modernized universities are far more important for the South. According to Mojab, it is this process toward the autonomous university that must be encouraged and not past-oriented civilizational or religious responses.

To argue then that dissent is the norm in the South is problematic. While there are certainly many students and professors who have resisted the brutal state, there are as many who have understood that the state is the provider of jobs—through the Ministry of Education—and have subsequently become guarantors of state oppression. Many of them have played both roles in different parts of their lives; Mahbub al-Haq is a fine example, who was both a henchman of General Zia and the founder and proponent of the Human Development Index, a brilliant contribution to development. The university in the South has essentially played the role of an institutional vehicle for economic development, even if development meant disempowering thousands, or destroying nature, or centralizing wealth, or globalizing wealth.

To summarize, in the North, while the models are that of Harvard, Global Convenience and Regional universities with alternatives coming from the "other" and from the collapse of capitalism or the failure of postindustrialism, in the South the models are different. The first is the civilizationally oriented university—the Gurukul, Islamic University, for example; the second is the modernized university, which resists bureaucratic control becoming authentically autonomous; and the third are the local outposts of the North models.

THE PUBLIC OR COMMUNITY/GLOBAL INTELLECTUAL

Where then in all this is the public intellectual? This is the question asked nationally in the North, with the response always the same: there are none. Perhaps then, instead of asking where is the public intellectual, with the constant answer of nowhere, the question should be: "In which spaces are intellectuals active?" It is in this third space of globally active communities, of nongovernmental organizations or social movements working for ecological responsibility, gender equity, spiritual transformation, and cultural pluralism that intellectuals who desire to play some type of transformative role flock to. To the question, who are the Bedouins and where might the futures of the university lie—it could be in this third space. This is of course Bussey's argument, and the space where Gidley's third scenario arises. This is a far different approach from that of the public intellectual who has to question power in the national realm and then move to international studies, but rather the alternative intellectual who might contest the categories of national and international and seek other ways of rendering the world. Doing so, however, is problematic precisely because universities have been organized in the mythos of public space, which, by and large, has become increasingly bought out by private space. Can we become a public intellectual if McDonald's is running a university or if Disney or other media organizations are buying into a university, or if there is a knowledge center on each street corner, or if the Web defined authenticity? Of course not. That is why alternative knowledge spaces have arisen, to help shape the critical intellectual. Indeed, part of the problem is with the idea of the public intellectual. As Nandy writes: "In much of Asia and Africa . . . the concept of 'public intellectuals' until now is a trivialization of the role played by thinkers from outside the academe, who have not merely influenced public opinion, but have led religious and social reform movements, initiated political campaigns including anti-imperialist struggles, and fought for the oppressed and marginalized within their societies."[19]

Can Harvard Inc. or the convenience model create such transformative possibilities? It is not only unlikely, but exactly the type of transformation such universities would argue against, or more likely, send anthropologists to study.

From this perspective, dissent does not have to be confrontational, it can be about building a new system as the previous system flounders—keeping alive many ways of knowing, while disciplines control; keeping alive the spiritual, while secularism thrives; keeping alive the idea of a fair world, while capitalism reigns.

DRIVERS AND FUTURES

What then are the futures of the university? First let us assess the drivers that were developed in the introductory chapter.

1. Virtualization, while helpful in dissent, cannot capture the dynamism of street revolution, of thousands of students marching. Nor can it capture spiritual dimensions of exchange, nor are Web courses communicative except in the most shallow sense of information transfer. They are not communicative in the deeper sense of idea exploration—of conversation as method, as relationship, as a way of knowing the world—as feminists would remind us. While virtualization might reduce the cost of education, as long as it remains information focused it will not be able to challenge traditional pedagogy. However, virtualization creates the possibility of the decentralization of education, of deschooling society, and of ending the monopoly control

that universities and disciplines have. As Majid Tehranian writes: "If all goes well, the entire human society will become a university without walls and national boundaries."[20]

2. Globalization unleashes economic rationalism on universities allowing them to spread, and at the same time, creates the conditions for the universities' demise, partly through creating a new world intellectual underclass and partly through giving them the technology—the Web and its future evolution—to undercut universities' monopolies.

3. Multiculturalism challenges what is taught, how it is taught, the knowledge categories used to teach, and the way departments enclose the other. Multiculturalism uses postmodernity but rejects its effort to construct the nonnegotiable sovereignties of other civilizations as discursive. Multiculturalism provides a worldview in which to create new models of learning and new universities, which better capture the many ways students know the world. In the extreme, consciousness models of self assert that the main driver is an explosion of inner enlightenment, a new age about to begin.

4. Politicization in the North works through the commodification of knowledge and the creation of Dean, Inc. It makes claims to be transparent but in fact has its agenda: the end of the humanistic university. In the South, it functions to keep power over intellectuals to ensure that they do not dissent. In both cases, intellectuals are forced to move to other spaces to create new forms of knowledge and community.

WHAT THEN ARE THE LIKELY SCENARIOS?

Mileage Plus/Air Points

This scenario is based on the airline partnership model, for example, United Airlines forging links with Lufthansa, Varig, Thai, and others creating a seamless web of world travel routes. This has been followed by its competitor American Airlines creating its own network with British Airways, Qantas, and others.

Within each partnership, academic credits will be transferrable, faculty will have ease of mobility (both physically and virtually), and salaries will be increasingly globalized.

Networks will compete with other networks, a Sorbonne contingent against an Oxford contingent, for example. Each network will have its own course designer. Over time, however, course designers will buy and sell their courses to varied networks, and eventually create the software structure of the new universities.

There will be niches of small universities/colleges that take risks in developing or credentialing new areas of knowledge. But they will be bought out through hostile takeovers, with the best programs being championed and the loser programs being dumped.

There will also be numerous alternative systems—local knowledge cultures, Web cultures—all vying for attention and legitimation by the big players, and there will be many who will just drop out and engage in self learning.

The network will be difficult to maintain because of the paradox the partnerships will find themselves in. Since their culture will be commodified, they will have to seek out alternative local/regional universities for rejuvenation. However, to maintain their profits they will not give anything back to the community, rather they will conduct "idea" and "culture" raids. But once the local is entirely globalized or corporatized, where to next? Where will the sources of inspiration then come from? With all diversity extinguished, will the system collapse?

Virtual Touch

A second likely scenario will be a mix of the virtual university with face-to-face workshops. Face-to-face might ultimately become virtual as well in the very long run, but in the next few decades, the model will be flexible delivery, a mixture of pedagogies.

The professor will become a mix of the knowledge navigator and facilitator, helping students steer through information engines. He or she will also engage in experiential camps, as Nicholson proposed, with short courses being held throughout the world as well as other techniques that include a high-touch dimension to high-tech. Curricula will be based on the participatory action-learning approach where giver and receiver of knowledge learn from each other, mutually creating the research questions, deciding what is important—a true open learning process and university.

Of course, there will be excesses on either side of the equation with some universities being more high-tech and others more high-touch, but by and large the most successful will be the ones that combine the two, creating communication cycles.

On the high-tech side, the dark side of this scenario will be victory of a reductionist information society, and on the high-touch side, a new-age touchy feely approach will prevail with no discipline, no additive or moral knowledge, just experience, feelings, and self-therapy.

Bliss for All

The third scenario assumes a high-tech leisure society, true globalism with the mobility of capital, labor, and ideas (from South to North and North to South) and a stable world governance system (with weakened nations).

Universities in this scenario become the dominant space since they quickly understand that with the issue of scarcity largely resolved (in a post-capitalist knowledge-based sustainable society) dominating issues become how to create a fulfilling knowledge society. This means lifelong learning, learning to learn, learning for transforming society, and learning for ananda—bliss, that is, inner realization.

Knowledge would be complex, based on many variables, not divided into science-culture but far more interactive including the pre- and post-rational, empirical, and idealistic approaches to knowledge. In essence, this would be Pitirim Sorokin's idea of an integrated society.[21] There would be a new episteme. It would be a spiral return to individual self-realization with the institutions of Church (medieval) and State (modern) less dominant.

The challenge will be to stay integrated without becoming functionalist— empirical or worldview—idealistic. The Web and globalizing will end the monopoly of the university and paradoxically place the university simultaneously at the center of society. But of course it would be a very different university without the division of heart and mind or private and public as well as other segmentations.

It would be a university for all of us and the many selves and cultures within us. This would, indeed, be a pleasant surprise.

NOTES

1. Raimundo Pannikar, "Myth in Religious Phenomenology," quoted in James Robertson, *Beyond the Dependency Culture* (London: Adamantine Press, 1998), 18.

2. For more on this, see Zia Sardar and Jerome Ravetz, eds., *Cyberfutures* (London: Pluto Press, 1996).

3. For more on this, see the special issue of *New Renaissance—The Challenge of a new Era* (Summer, 1999). Also see, Sohail Inayatullah and Paul Wildman, *Futures Studies: Methods, Emerging Issues and Civilizational Visions—A Multimedia Reader* (Brisbane: Prosperity Press, 1998).

4. Hazel Henderson points out that 90 percent of the US \$1.5 trillion sloshing around the world's currency markets each day is now speculation-related. The global financial sector has grown by nine times the rate of growth of real goods and services worldwide over the past decade. John Macleay, "Crossing Swords," *The Australian* (December 2, 1998), 34. See Hazel Henderson, *Building a Win-Win World: Life Beyond Global Economic Warfare* (San Francisco: Berret-Koehler Publishers, 1996).

5. See Sohail Inayatullah and Jennifer Fitzgerald, eds., *Transcending Boundaries: P. R. Sarkar's Theories of Individual and Social Transformation* (Brisbane and Ananda Nagar, India: Gurukul Press, 1999). Also see: Ravi Batra, *The Downfall of Capitalism and Communism* (London, Macmillan Press, 1978). First edition. Also: P. R. Sarkar, *PROUT in a Nutshell* (Calcutta: Ananda Marga Publications, 1994).

6. Jeremy Rifken, *The End of Work* (New York: Putnam, 1995)

7. See Jerry Harvey, *Abilene Paradox and Other Meditations on Management* (Lexington, MA: Lexington Books, 1988). Chapter six is of particular interest and titled: "Eichmann in the Organization."

8. David Rooney makes this point. Personal communications, December 12, 1998. See also his chapter with Greg Hearn in this volume.

9. See Sohail Inayatullah, "Ibn Khaldun—The Strengthening and Weakening of Asabiya," in Johan Galtung and Sohail Inayatullah, eds., *Macrohistory and Macrohistorians* (Westport, CT, and London: Praeger, 1997), 25–32.

10. A Conference method where a group of people are put in the center of the room— the fish bowl—and the audience around them, peering in.

11. For more on students and the university, see Greg Hearn and David Scott, "Students Staying Home," *Futures* 30, 7 (1998): 731–38.

12. Zia Sardar, *Islamic Futures: The Shape of Ideas to Come* (London: Mansell, 1985).

13. Susantha Goonatilake, *Toward a Global Science: Mining Civilizational Knowledge* (Bloomington, Indiana: Indiana University Press, 1998).

14. Ashis Nandy, ed., *Science, Hegemony and Violence* (Delhi: Oxford University Press, 1993).

15. For more on this, see: www.others.com.

16. Johan Galtung, *Essays in Peace Research* Vol. 1–6 (Copenhagen: Christian Ejlers, 1988).

17. See Zia Sardar, ed., *How We Know: Ilm and the Revival of Knowledge* (London: Grey Seal, 1991).

18. Michael Tracey, "Twilight: Illusion and Decline in the Communication Revolution," in Danielle Cliche, *Culture Ecology: the Changing Dynamics of Communication* (London: International Institute of Communications, 1997), 50.

19. Ashis Nandy, "Recovery of Indigenous Knowledge and Dissenting Futures of the University," in this volume.

20. Majid Tehranian, "The End of University," *The Information Society* 12 (1996), 446.

21. Pitirim Sorokin, *Social and Cultural Dynamics* (Boston: Porter Sargent, 1957).

20

Unveiling the Human Face of University Futures

—————————————————— *Jennifer Gidley*

This concluding chapter will not attempt to summarize the content of this book but rather to tease out some key threads that have clustered into a meta-theme that needs to be surfaced in order to be transformed. I will also explore how universities might regain their pride of place as centers of real higher learning (as in wisdom) and then offer three scenarios for how the human face of universities might look in 30 years. Finally in this chapter, I seek not to conclude this vital discussion on future universities but to challenge our thinking, our conscience, and our activism in reinventing the futures of universities.

THE DEHUMANIZATION OF HIGHER EDUCATION

From a certain meta-perspective, all the main trends and driving forces, which have been explored in this book for their shaping effect on universities of the present and future, are forces of dehumanization of higher education. The worst offenders in terms of the human, particularly the social costs, are globalization and virtualization.

The massive forces of globalization first highlighted in our introduction and then touched on in almost every chapter, have been largely responsible for bringing the traditional humanistic dimensions of the university to an end. As discussed, the economics of globalism have led university leaders (usually administrators who have effectively appropriated the leadership role once held by professors) to believe that they must sacrifice the very traditions that once defined the core business of university life. In the restructuring process, academic tenure (not to mention freedom), research time (unless commercially funded), and noncommercially viable disciplinary streams (such as humanities), have all but disappeared, in the new "market-sensitive" universities.

The social costs of virtualization may turn out to be even greater. Feelings of alienation, fragmentation, and loss of meaning will undoubtedly continue to increase among students and probably also academic staff. As the human side of face-to-face collegiate collaboration and student-teacher contact diminishes behind the screen (or is it scream), the disempowerment already being felt by many young people about the future is unlikely to improve. And we are yet to see the full extent of human "redundancy" in the higher education sector that will come when virtualization takes its expected place at the table. Based on experience in other industries, it is likely that what we have seen so far is just the beginning.

While outside the ivory walls the world is running out of control, environmentally, economically, politically, and of course socially, to what extent are universities today providing the intellectual, professional, and practical resources to drive a positive transformation of global problems? The answer is negative and circular—universities are no longer providing solutions and the reason is economic rationalism, driven by the forces outlined.

I would argue that the key to breaking such "vicious circles" is inspired human agency. This could occur if universities were centers where humans joined together their skills, knowledge, experience, and wisdom to solve problems, combined with the social conscience to become sites of dissent against dehumanization and the will to become centers of action/praxis. This is a lovely ideal, but how would it happen?

FROM MEGA-TRENDS TO META-MOVEMENTS— TOWARD TRANSFORMATION

The 20th century university model had its rightful place in the context of 19th century industrial and social progress and problems and 19th century Western linear rationality. Centuries of instrumental rationality have led to an atrophying of imaginative vision throughout Western society but particularly within universities that have become obsessed with methodological issues and technical detail. As T. S. Eliot poignantly asked:

Where is the wisdom we have lost in knowledge?
  Where is the knowledge we have lost in information?[1]

And we might add today:

Where is the information we have lost in data?

Looking at the trilogy of methodology, epistemology, and ontology as ideally representing a balance, we must recognize that contemporary universities have all but forsaken the latter two. Universities need to move beyond methodology to encompass the deeper sense of multiculturalism—a dialogue of epistemologies,[2] and beyond that to contemplating their own ontology, as Abeles pointed out—what is their very purpose of being? However, I propose that even this is not enough. If universities are not only to survive the complex political, economic, and social chaos that the mega-trends suggest will occur in the coming decades, but be active in transformation, then they will need more than to know their purpose. I argue that universities of the future, which will be able to rise to the challenge of being agents of transformation, will also need a more extensive, inclusive cosmology—an underpinning system of knowledge comprehensive enough to take in and give meaning to the complex global problems we have unwittingly, and through our greed, created. In the growing complexity of current global crises, such integrated systems/models are demanded. This is what Spies is hinting at with his five aspects needed for a balanced education, and what Abeles refers to when he speaks of long half-life knowledge or ability to synthesize—knowledge underpinned by wisdom. Anthony Judge uses the term *higher coherence* to describe the meta-levels of meaning that are required to solve tomorrow's problems.[3]

Interestingly, it was only in the Alternative Universities section that models such as this have been developed. In particular, in the alternative university models described by Bussey and Grant, the importance of integration, wholeness and meaning are stressed as are application to solving global problems. It is of note that these models are both underpinned by a spiritual perspective/cosmology. In contrast, the modern secular university lacks this larger framework of meaning, the postmodern (corporate or virtual) one, even more so. Reframing T. S. Eliot's point, future universities need more wisdom, not more information, and so do our students.

Unless universities reclaim their core purpose—taking responsibility for higher education in the sense of *higher order* knowing, ability to synthesize and integrate the fragmented pieces of the meta-processes at work in society—the mega-trends of dehumanization will become world destiny. What is needed is the courage of university leaders and faculty generally to reclaim their potentially powerful and central position of providing value-added (or long half-life) knowledge—wisdom—not just bytes of information. It would not be impossible for universities to take up this challenge and become once again the inspired prime movers of society in a meta-movement to transform global problems into constructive directions.

In this event, "offshore" campuses might become mobile "think-solutions" in global hot-spots of need, not just hungry "take-away education stalls," bleeding more resources from already-stricken regions. And foresighting centers might mushroom to foster foresight in potential hot-spots, to help avert tomorrow's disasters—does that forest on Thailand's pristine Phi Phi Island really have to be demolished for Leonardo DiCaprio's next movie?

Academics, administrators, and students alike need to become creatively courageous in reinventing universities if we are to become the creators of transformed futures and not just creatures of the past.

THE POLITICS OF FORESIGHT

Perhaps the aforementioned picture may seem too idealistic, however, with any such attempt to take up the challenges posed there would also be paradoxes and tensions.

- Of course it is understood that foresight in itself doesn't necessarily lead to a more humanistic outcome. In fact many mega-corporations now ride the futures bandwagon in order to make more money.
- In any attempt to solve global problems or to reinvent any of society's key institutions, including universities, there will always be contentious ethical issues that will need to be dialogued.
- For the ideas put forward to come to fruition, there would need to be sufficient numbers of like-minded idealist academics, students, and others to make a critical mass in terms of creating new or transforming old universities.
- How would such ideals be funded, given that the economics of globalism requires its pound of flesh? One suggestion is the redistribution of wealth through a change of conscience in the super-wealthy—the third scenario, which follows, explores this idea.
- Finally, do alternatives underpinned by a spiritual cosmology have to be religion based and if so, how would the tensions of religious factionalism and spiritual arrogance be overcome? Other options do exist in the form of complex spiritually based cosmologies not tied to religious denominations, such as the anthroposophy (wisdom of man) of Rudolf Steiner.[4] Although this comprehensive body of knowledge has been used as a basis for application to such diverse fields as education, agriculture, architecture, medicine, and the arts for a century, and underpins many schools and tertiary colleges throughout the world, as yet no full university has been founded based on this cosmology—perhaps a vision for the future?

THE HUMAN FACE OF UNIVERSITY FUTURES BY 2030

In all the myriad perspectives, discussions, and visions presented in the preceding chapters, most of the content has centered around the types and structures of the institutions themselves. Although it has been hinted that the role of faculty will be extremely different as a result of the changes discussed, very little has been developed about what, if anything, lecturers and professors (if they still exist) might actually be doing. While Skolnik presented the positive and negative responses of the professoriate to the virtualization of the University, and Dator sadly farewelled the privilege of academic freedom, Hudson hailed the hoped-for recovery of scholar-activism in the future of the Caribbean. Milojevic presented a structural/utopian vision of how a women's university might look. On the other hand Manicas and Abeles place responsibility for the future survival and direction of universities firmly in the hands of faculty. Nicholson agrees and develops a scenario for this. My task here is to give some more clues as to how academia might look in the context of some of the futures for universities that have been indicated.

How might the human face of the faculty change in the wake of the tremendous upheavals and transformations discussed in this book?

As the dignity and potential power of the human spirit in the face of adversity (or "human agency") is central to my vision of the future, I have mapped the changes into the following three scenarios depicting possible futures of the roles of lecturers, professors, and other faculty:

- The "broker"
- The "mentor"
- The "meaning-maker"

They relate to some degree, though not entirely overlapping, to the three possible future university scenarios, which have been recurring themes throughout this volume, and summarized by Inayatullah in his concluding chapter. These three broad structural scenarios are

- The corporatized "convenience" mega-university model
- The traditional or "brand name" model
- The alternative, or regional "niche" model (which includes various spiritually based alternatives)

It should be noted here that the "virtual university" model has not been included as a category in its own right because I believe that there are two possible broad options for the virtualization of our futures. Either information technology (IT) and virtualization will continue as current trends suggest and be incorporated to a greater or lesser extent into all of the above models as a ubiquitous part of the 21st century. Or, alternatively, electrotechnology will fail the Y2K test (as recent indicators of global preparedness are beginning to suggest). In this broad scenario we will all, but particularly the "late-comers" to e-technology, be plunged back to what is now called "manualization." The likely benefit of this possibility is that many currently redundant and disenfranchised ex-workers will be working again. However, not withstanding a recent wave of articles in the business pages of Australian newspapers warning of the ill-preparedness of South East Asian businesses to weather this oncoming quake, I am inclined to believe that IT and virtual reality are here to stay. The following scenarios are based on this assumption.

The "Broker"—The Invisible Face of Sub-Academic Futures

It is 2030 and the position of course broker in future universities is common, and is similar in many ways to the positions of insurance brokers or stockbrokers. They are experts in sales and marketing and technical "know-how," without necessarily having any disciplinary or content knowledge. Many work from home or from mobile offices as they primarily need a laptop and e-connection for their operations. Brokers may or may not have university qualifications as the main requirement is being able to "do business." Brokers are paid fees by students for arranging courses for them, as well as commission by hungry providers for students they catch. So it can be a lucrative business for the keen operator, though not without its tensions. Competition in the marketplace is fierce and experienced hackers sabotage many a well-constructed "course." Electronic hijacking of potential students is not unknown. The brokers are mostly private consultants, though a few are employed under short-term contracts to some of the corporate and convenience institutions—though they have to provide enough in revenue to cover their retainer (and more) if they expect to "be renewed"—the new term for what was once called "tenure."

Of course the seeds of this development were already happening in the 1990s, with the casualization of academic staff, who came to be known as "Gypsy faculty,"[5] the expectation for faculty to provide the equivalent of part of their wages through "consultancies," and the emerging demand of students to construct their own courses in a cross-disciplinary and even cross-institutional manner. In addition, already last century there were university brokers, doing deals between traditional universities, industries and private providers; and "stitching together" arrangements "offshore." What is different in the 2030s is the proliferation of these positions as more and more technologically literate unemployed graduates (and retrenched academics) seek new ways of making money through providing a range of services, such as these, for fees, in lieu of other employment opportunities.

This is hardly the chosen profession of young, idealistic post-docs with a passion for pure research, nor does it appeal to mature-age professors seeking to enter "early retirement" with their academic freedom intact. (However, if any of you out there are opportunists looking for a lucrative future in and around future universities, get ready because in 30 years time the universities of the Net will be crawling with brokers.) The following is their catch-cry:

> He barely has a human face
> He lives and thrives in Cyberspace
> . . . Broker.

The "Mentor"—The Last Dance of the Sage

This is the position most closely aligned to the academic of the 20th century, but because of the diversity of offerings that are available in 2030 to students across the global panacopaea of courses, no one *teaches courses* anymore. Academic staff, in order to survive, need to be multidisciplined and also somewhat more in the mode of counselor or guidance officer than teacher or lecturer. Rarely is a lecture given (in real life and real time) to groups of students as very few students opt for straight courses once the barriers that prevented creative course construction came down. While the brokers link the students with their institutions, there is still a recognized need, at least at the preliminary and under-graduate levels, for some mentoring through the information labyrinths in order to arrive at something resembling knowledge, at least in the remaining traditional or elite institutions. (This is far less relevant in the corporate and convenience courses, which are geared more to assessment of competencies or no assessment at all in the case of pure interest courses.) So in the case of students seeking a pro-fessional or broad liberal education, there is a role for a mentor.

Instead of being responsible for a disciplinary subject area or a course, men-tors are responsible for a cluster of students (100 to 200 depending on the size and budget of the institution) who may be doing the widest possible range of courses and course-combinations. They are responsible for mentoring these students through whatever course they construct for themselves. Under the new arrange-ments of cross-institutional study, students are required to undertake at least 50 percent of their studies at their *core* institution in order to be eligible to acquire a mentor. This new role for faculty has the potential for being a highly creative one, promoting much growth on the part of the mentor as it is not possible for them to be an expert in everything their students study and so they too are actively learn-ing at all times.

Unlike academic work of the late 20th century, which was seen by many aca-demics to have become dehumanized and disconnected from its core business of working with students (through excessive accountability, the stress and overload of putting courses "on-line," and the limitations of primitive distance education delivery), mentor positions are considered rewarding. Needless to say, not all the mentor's contact with their cluster of students is in "real time and space." However, part of the commitment of these "high quality futureversities" is that the mentor is required to meet face-to-face with students at least once each semester. Naturally, these mentor positions are highly prized but oddly enough not going to professors who had climbed the specialist ladder of the 20th century, but rather to multifaceted, cross-disciplinary "pracademics" who had also had experience outside the walls of academia.

The seeds of this emerging future profession of undergraduate mentoring was seen in the 1990s primarily in the relationship that was sometimes fostered between postgraduate students and their academic supervisors. When successful, it was a far more empowering learning relationship for the student than the tradi-tional one of passively attending a multiple series of lectures, with the occasional tutorial where the student was allowed to contribute.

The "Meaning-Maker"—The Emerging Face of Tomorrow's Elders

The occupation of "meaning-maker" is still considered a rare privilege by 2030 since it is as yet an emerging role that will continue to grow throughout the 21st century. It evolved out of the mushrooming of new, mostly spiritually based alternative universities that came to be known as "humanversities" for the obvious reason that they valued the needs of human development ahead of other considerations. In their seed form they began in the 20th century as a counterreaction to the harsh, inhuman, economic rationalist policies that underpinned most universities at that time. At first small, private nondenominational initiatives such as the Goetheanum in Switzerland (founded with long foresight early in the 20th century by Rudolf Steiner), Schumacher College in Devon, England, the School of Spiritual Psychology, founded by Robert Sardello in Massachusetts, U.S.A., and others mentioned in earlier chapters, began to sidestep the materialist secular paradigm of "higher education" to offer alternatives that addressed the depth and potential wisdom of the whole human being. In addition, several other spiritually based higher education initiatives also arose with similar concerns. These included the Maharishi University discussed by Grant in this volume, the Gurukula University described by Bussey, and the Naropa Institute in Boulder, Colorado, based on Buddhist principles, to name a few. The trademark of these humanversities is the recognition by their founders that higher education, if it were to be adequate enough to address the complexities of 21st century life, needed to be underpinned by a "higher order meaning system," such as that provided by spiritual cosmologies.

As the economic, social, and political disintegration of the late 20th century continued to gather momentum globally into the early decades of the 21st century, more and more small organically grown and sometimes Net-based institutions of alternative higher education arose. Networking between some of the members of these humanversities began to strengthen both humanly and electronically, until by 2030 a critical mass had developed and this movement to rehumanize higher education had become self-perpetuating. Yet if we could look further into the 22nd century we would see that it was still in its relative infancy at this time. Joining the ranks of initiators and supporters of the humanversity movement were many of the previously retrenched and disenfranchised academics, professionals, and activists. Having worked through their own resultant personal crises and angst at having had to wear the "marginal crown," and then being catapulted into premature paradigm shift and spiritual transformation, they began to network with others and form sort of "post-egoism" communities.

Although these new more organic institutions were as diverse as the individuals and communities who founded them, a fairly typical humanversity of the 2030s would be a kind of hybrid of a regional "niche" university, with a personal growth/healing and arts center, combined with several outreach activity centers engaged in ecological and social work. All this was usually underpinned by a spiritual direction (some single strand denominational, but most being more spiritually eclectic).

The role of the meaning-maker is quite a diverse one and somewhat akin to the role of the elder in traditional cultures. The title arose in a curious way. In the late 1990s the recognition had only just begun to surface from some of the youth futures research that many young people were experiencing a sense of loss of meaning in their lives.[6] It was noted by Frank Hutchinson that these youth were like the canaries down the mineshaft, signaling greater potential distress to come.[7] However, while the World Bank was reporting at that time that the second greatest global problem of the early 21st century would be depression (emotional, not economic),[8] it was not until 2010 that it reported that a highly significant proportion of the world's population was experiencing a "crisis of meaning." Everything had changed so dramatically, so rapidly, that very few were spared severe soul crises as a result. As a reaction to the "overtechnologizing of language during the phase of postmodernity and political correctness," people (even academics) began to use simple language again—language that meant something. The masters of this recovery of the word began to be called the "meaning-makers." Later it became a generic term for the new profession of transdisciplinary "elders" who tried to put the world back together again for the young people and the future's children.

It should be noted that the position of meaning-maker is not like a job that one could apply for—it is conferred by others. There is a natural hierarchy in identifying "meaning-makers" based on recognition of elder status which would relate to degree of breadth of experience and synthesis capability, for example, three meta-spheres of work would be recognized as equally valuable, these being intellectual or what used to be called academic; aesthetic, artistic including visual, performance, literary; and practical, professional, business/praxis. For a person to reach the status of meaning-maker they had to have considerable experience in all three spheres as well as a deep understanding of at least two spiritual disciplines and practice in at least one. It is considered that such breadth of experience not only maximized synthesis capability—a major underpinning paradigm of the humanversities, but also generally led to humility of management style, which overcame the disadvantages of the old narrow academic hierarchies of the 20th century. In terms of meritocracy the values stressed are breadth, experience, and synthesis capability as these are recognized as being carriers of meaning and also openness to learning, for example, the meaning-makers are always students as well as teachers. The best and most popular meaning-makers are usually also talented story or myth makers as foretold by Joseph Campbell, Rolf Jenson, and Hedley Beare some decades ago.[9] The power of the image is beginning to reclaim its central place in the shaping of culture.[10]

Economically these "humanversities" are supported by communities seeking to recover wholeness who, after decades of fragmentation, no longer accept the lie that the information society will be any more successful than the industrial society in restoring the human dream. These communities in turn are supported by the "humanversities" that provide expertise in solving the problems that developed through the last 20 years of the 20th century and accelerated exponentially over the following decades. It should be remembered that the massive global problems that grew during this time went almost entirely unnoticed and without contribution from the late 20th century universities that were then too preoccupied with the frenzy of getting their courses on-line or where their next grant was coming from. Occasionally, the humanversities receive a generous grant from a wealthy patron, a fairly recent development since 2010, the year that is sometimes called "The Billionaire's Disgrace," named after the film by that name. (After decades of effort, Ralph Nader finally convinced Steven Spielberg to risk his fortunes and make a feature movie exposing the obscenity of the global distribution of wealth—both statistically and socially.) A resultant crisis of conscience occurred in sufficient numbers of the then 600 or so billionaires and many of them began to make large grants available to a variety of institutions—the humanversities being highly favored recipients because of their strong record in solving social and ecological problems.

OUR CHALLENGE

While these scenarios are just what my imagination drew from the trends and countertrends I see emerging, they are just a starting point in the creation of many possible inspired, humanly active futures for university academics. We all need to become more creative and agile in our imaginations in order not to accept passively the so-called inevitable trends of dehumanized futures.

This book is a challenge to all of us to develop the clarity of rigorous analysis combined with imagination to see the future coming; the sensitivity of heart to hear and respond to the plurality of its many voices; and the courage and will to shape it wisely.

NOTES

1. Cited in Paul Wildman, "A Note on Mythopoetic Futuring and Strategic Planning," *Futures Bulletin* (December 1995) 14–15.

2. Johan Galtung, *Schooling, Education and the Future*, educational information and debate. Vol. 61. (Malmo, Sweden: Department of Education and Psychology Research, Lund University, 1982).

3. Anthony Judge, "From Information Highways to Songlines of the Noosphere," *Futures* (1996).

4. Rudolf Steiner, *The Evolution of Consciousness as Revealed through Initiation Knowledge: Lectures (1923)* (London: Garden City Press, 1966); Rudolf Steiner, *Microcosm and Macrocosm* (London: Rudolf Steiner Press, 1968); Rudolf Steiner, *The Renewal of Education through the Science of the Spirit: Lectures, 1920* (Sussex: Kolisko Archive, 1981).

5. John Hickman, "The Gypsy Faculty," in *The Australian* (1998): 33.

6. Richard Eckersley, "The West's Deepening Cultural Crisis," *The Futurist* (1993): 8–20; Jennifer Gidley and Paul Wildman, "What are we missing?—A Review of the Educational and Vocational Interests of Marginalized Rural Youth," *Education in Rural Australia Journal* 6, 2 (1996): 9–19.

7. Francis P. Hutchinson, *Educating Beyond Violent Futures*, R. Slaughter, ed. (London: Routledge, 1996).

8. Georgina Safe, "High Anxiety," in *The Australian* (1998): 29.

9. Joseph Campbell, *The Masks of God: Creative Mythology* (Penguin Arkana, 1968); Hedley Beare, "The Beginnings of a New Australian Story," in The Global Scenarios (Macquarie Graduate School of Management: Economic Planning Advisory Commission, 1996); Rolf Jenson, "The Dream Society," *The Futurist* (1996): 9–13.

10. Elise Boulding, *Building a Global Civic Culture: Education for an Interdependent World* (Syracuse University Press, 1990); Jennifer Gidley, "The Power of Imagination: Report on Research with Steiner Educated Adolescents," in *Educare News* (1998): 14; Rudolf Steiner, *Toward Imagination: Culture and the Individual* (New York: Anthroposophic Press, 1990).

Selected Bibliography

Acker, S., J. Megarry, S. Nisbet, and E. Hoyle, eds. *World Yearbook of Education: Women and Education*. London: Kogan Page, 1984.

Altbach, Philip. *International Higher Education: An Encyclopedia*. London and Chicago: St. James Press, 1991.

Appiah, Kwame Anthony. *In My Father's House: Africa in the Philosophy of Culture*. Oxford: Oxford University Press, 1992.

Baker, D. and P. C. S. Taylor. "The Effect of Culture on the Learning of Science in Non-Western Countries: the Results of an Integrated Research Review." *International Journal of Science Education* 17, 6 (1995): 695–704.

Barnett, Ronald. *The Idea of Higher Education*. Buckingham, England: Society for Research into Higher Education and Open University Press, 1990.

Barr, Robert B. and John Tagg. "From Teaching to Learning—A New Paradigm for Undergraduate Education." *Change* (November/December, 1995): 13–25.

Beare, Hedley, and Richard Slaughter. *Education for the Twenty-first Century*. London: Routledge, 1993.

Benn, Denis. *The Growth and Development of Political Ideas in the Caribbean, 1774–1983*. University of the West Indies: Institute of Social and Economic Research, 1987.

Bjornson, Richard, and Marilyn R. Waldman, eds. *The University of the Future*. Columbus: Ohio State University Press, 1990.

Boulding, Elise. *Building a Global Civic Culture: Education for an Interdependent World*. Syracuse: Syracuse University Press, 1990.

Boulding, Kenneth. *Beyond Economics: Essays on Society, Religion and Ethics*. Ann Arbor: The University of Michigan Press, 1968.

Boulding, Kenneth. *The World as a Total System*. Beverly Hills, California: Sage Publications, 1985.

Brown, John S. and Paul Duguid. "Universities in the Digital Age," *Change* (July/August, 1996): 11–19.

Bunch, C., and S. Pollack, eds. *Learning Out Ways: Essays in Feminist Education*, New York: The Crossing Press/Trumansburg, 1983.

Campbell, Joseph. *The Masks of God: Creative Mythology.* New York, Penguin Arkana, 1968.

Carnoy, M., and J. Samoff. *Education and Social Transition in the Third World.* Princeton, New Jersey: Princeton University Press, 1990.

Chandler, Keith. "Modern Science and Vedic Science: An Introduction." *Modern Science and Vedic Science* 1, 2 (1987).

Chitnis, Sama, and Philip Altbach, eds. *Higher Education Reform in India.* New Delhi: Sage Publications, 1993.

Daniel, John S. *Megauniversities and Knowledge Media.* London: Kogan Page, 1996.

Davies, Merryl, Ashis Nandy, and Zia Sardar. *Barbaric Other: A Manifesto on Western Racism.* London: Pluto Press, 1993.

Delanty, Gerard. "The Idea of the University in the Global Era: From Knowledge as an End to the End of Knowledge?" *Social Epistemology* 12 (1998): 3–25.

De Wit, H., ed. *Strategies for internationalization of higher education: A comparative study of Australia, Canada, Europe and the United States of America.* Amsterdam: European Association for International Education (EIAIE), in cooperation with the Program on Institutional Management in Higher Education (IMHE) of the Organization for Economic Cooperation and Development (OECD) and the Association of International Education Administrators (AIEA), 1995.

Dolence, Michael G., and Donald M. Norris. *Transforming Higher Education: A Vision for Learning in the 21st Century.* Ann Arbor, MI: Society for College and University Planning, 1995.

Eckersley, Richard. "Values and Visions: Youth and the Failure of Modern Western Culture." *Youth Studies Australia* 14, 1 (1995).

Eisler, Riane. *Sacred Pleasure.* San Francisco: Harper Collins, 1996.

Galtung, Johan. *Schooling, Education and the Future.* Educational information and debate, vol. 61, p. 91. Malmo, Sweden: Department of Education and Psychology Research, Lund University, 1982.

Galtung, Johan, and Sohail Inayatullah, eds. *Macrohistory and Macrohistorians: Perspectives on Individual, Social and Civilizational Change.* Westport: Praeger, 1997.

Gandhi, M. K. *Hind Swaraj.* Ahmedabad: Navjivan Press, 1908.

Gidley, Jennifer. "Prospective Youth Visions through Imaginative Education," *Futures* 30, 5 (1998).

Gidley, Jennifer. "Adolescent Dreams (and Nightmares) about the Futures: Indicators of Mental Health and Ill-Health." In proceedings: NSW Mental Health Conference— *Making Waves: Country to Coast Expertise, Innovation and Diversity.* Ballina, NSW, 24–27 February: NSW Rural Mental Health Association (1998): 153–59.

Gilbert, Irene. "The Indian Academic Profession: the Origins of a Tradition of Subordination," *Minerva* (July, 1972): 384–411.

Harvey, David. *The Condition of Postmodernity.* New York: Basil Blackwell, 1989.

Hayhoe, R., ed. *Knowledge Across Cultures: Universities East and West.* Toronto: OISE Press, 1993.

Henessey, Alastair, ed. *Intellectuals in the Twentieth Century Caribbean,* Vols. 1 and 2. London: Macmillan, Warwick University Caribbean Studies, 1992.

Hicks, David, and Richard Slaughter, eds. *Futures Education—World Education Yearbook, 1998.* London: Kogan Page, 1998.

Hutchinson, Francis P. *Educating Beyond Violent Futures.* London: Routledge, 1996.

Huxley, Aldous. *The Perennial Philosophy.* New York: Meridian Books, 1945.

Illich, Ivan. *Deschooling Society,* Middlesex: Penguin Books, 1976.

Inayatullah, Sohail. "Deconstructing and Reconstructing the Future." *Futures* 22, 2 (1992).

Inayatullah, Sohail. "The Multi-cultural Challenge to the Future of Education." *Periodica Islamica* 6, 2 (1996).

Inayatullah, Sohail, and Jennifer Fitzgerald, eds. *Transcending Boundaries: Prabhat Rainjan Sarkar's Theories of Individual and Social Transformation.* Maleny, Australia: Gurukula Press, 1999.

Inayatullah, Sohail, and Jennifer Gidley, eds. "The University—Alternative Futures." Special issue of *Futures* 30, 7 (1998).

Inayatullah, Sohail, and Paul Wildman. *Futures Studies: Methods, Emerging Issues and Civilizational Visions.* A Multi-Media CD ROM, Brisbane: Prosperity Press, 1998.

Kerr, Clark, ed. *Troubled Times for American Higher Education: The 1990's and Beyond.* New York: SUNY Press, 1994.

Lawlor, Robert. *Voices of the First Day: Awakening in the Aboriginal Dreamtime.* Vermont: Inner Traditions, 1991.

Leach, Edmund, and S. N. Mukherjee, eds. *Elites in South Asia.* Cambridge: Cambridge University Press, 1970.

Lewis, Gordon K. *Main Currents in Caribbean Thought. The Historical Evolution of Caribbean Society in its Ideological Aspects, 1492–1900.* Baltimore: The Johns Hopkins University Press and Heinemann Caribbean, 1983.

Lucas, Christopher J. *Crisis in the Academy: Rethinking Higher Education in America.* New York: St. Martin's Press, 1996.

Maharishi Mahesh Yogi. *Science of Being and Art of Living.* New York: Meridian Books, 1963–95.

Maharishi Mahesh Yogi. *Maharishi Vedic University: Introduction.* Vlodrop, Netherlands: Maharishi Vedic University Press, 1994.

Manicas, Peter. *A History and Philosophy of the Social Sciences.* New York: Basil Blackwell, 1987.

Martin, Hans-Peter, and Harold Schumann. *The Global Trap: Globalization and the Assault on Democracy and Prosperity.* Pluto Press, Australia, 1997.

McLaren, P. "Critical Pedagogy in the Age of Global Capitalism: Some Challenges for the Education Left." *Australian Journal of Education* 39, 1 (1995): 5–21.

Meeks, Brian. *Radical Caribbean. From Black Power to Abu Bakr.* University of the West Indies: The Press, 1996.

Mehran, G. "Educational Reform in Postrevolutionary Iran: A Shift in Policy." *International Perspectives on Education and Society* Vol. 4 (1994): 135–50.

Menashri, D. *Education and the Making of Modern Iran.* New York: Cornell University Press, 1992.

Morley, L., and V. Walsh. *Feminist Academics: Creative Agents for Change.* London: Taylor and Francis, 1995.

Nandy, Ashis. *Tradition, Tyranny, and Utopias.* Delhi: Oxford University Press, 1987.

Newman, John Henry, and Frank M. Turner. *The Idea of a University (Rethinking the Western Tradition).* New Haven: Yale University Press, 1996.

New Renaissance on "Education for Transformation." 8, 3 (1998).

Ortega Y Gassett, Jose. *Mission of the University.* New York: WW Norton and Company, 1944.

Plato. *The Republic of Plato* (translated by F. M. Cornford). New York: Oxford University Press, 1982.

Rahman, Tariq. *Language and Politics in Pakistan.* Karachi: Oxford University Press, 1996.

Readings, Bill. *The University in Ruins.* Cambridge, MA: Harvard University Press, 1996.

Reich, Robert. *The Work of Nations.* New York: Knopf, 1991.

Rifkin, Jeremy. *The End of Work.* New York: Putnam, 1995.

Rogers, M., and A. Tough. "What Happens When Students Face the Future." *Futures Research Quarterly* (1992), Winter, 9–18.

Said, Edward. *Orientalism.* New York: Vintage Books, 1979.

Sardar, Zia, ed. *Rescuing all of our Futures.* Twickenham, Adamantine, 1999.

Sardar, Zia. "What Makes a University Islamic?" In *How We Know: Ilm and the Revival of Knowledge,* Zia Sardar, ed. London: Grey Seal, 1991.

Sardar, Zia. *Postmodernism and the Other.* London: Pluto, 1998.

Sarkar, Prabhat Rainjan. *The Liberation of Intellect—Neo-Humanism.* Calcutta: Ananda Marga Publications, 1982.

Sarkar, Prabhat Rainjan. *Discourses on Neohumanist Education.* Calcutta: A. M. Publications, 1998.

Schiller, Frederick. *The Aesthetic Education of Man: In a Series of Letters (1795).* New York: Ungar, 1977.

Shorris, Earl. "In the Hands of the Restless Poor." *Harpers Magazine* (September 1997): 50–59.

Slaughter, Richard. *The Foresight Principle: Cultural Recovery in the 21st Century.* London: Adamantine Press, 1995.

Slaughter, Richard, ed. *The Knowledge Base of Futures Studies, Vols. 1–3,* Melbourne: Media and Futures Studies Centre, 1995.

Smith, A., and F. Webster, eds. *The Postmodern University? Contested Visions of Higher Education in Society.* Buckingham: Open University Press, 1997.

Steiner, Rudolf. *The Younger Generation: Education and Spiritual Impulses in the 20th Century (Lectures, 1922).* New York: Anthroposophic Press, 1967.

Steiner, Rudolf. *Toward Imagination: Culture and the Individual.* New York: Anthroposophic Press, 1990.

Steiner, Rudolf. *The Renewal of Education through the Science of the Spirit: Lectures, 1920.* Sussex: Kolisko Archive, 1981.

Takaki, R. *Strangers from Different Shores.* Boston: Little, Brown, 1989.

Tierney, H., ed. *Women's Studies Encyclopedia.* Westport, CT: Greenwood Press, 1990.

Tough, Allen. "What Future Generations Need from Us." *Futures* (1993), December: 1041–50.

UNESCO/BREDA in Africa: Achievements, Challenges, and Prospects. UNESCO/BREDA Press, 1998.

Volet, S. E., and G. Ang. "Bias Issues in the Classroom: Encounters with the Teaching Self." *Higher Education and Development* 17, 1 (1998): 5–23.

Wilber, Kenneth. *Sex, Ecology, Spirituality: The Spirit of Evolution.* Boston: Shambhala, 1995.

Wildman, Paul, and Jennifer Gidley, eds. "Holistic Education: Preparing for the 21st Century." *New Renaissance,* Special Issue 6, 3 (1996).

Wildman, Paul, and Sohail Inayatullah. "Ways of Knowing, Culture, Communication and the Pedagogies of the Future." *Futures* 28, 8 (1996): 723–40.

World Commission on Culture and Development. *Our Creative Diversity.* Paris, Unesco Publishing, 1995.
Http:www.worldbank.org.html/extdr/rmc/guide/africa.htm#2africa

Index

About the Editors and Contributors

SOHAIL INAYATULLAH holds a number of academic positions including Professor and Chair of the School of Futures Studies, International Management Centres; UNESCO Chair, Centre for European Studies, University of Trier (1999), Germany; Tamkang Chair, Tamkang University, Taiwan (1999); Visiting Academic, The Communication Centre, Queensland University of Technology and Adjunct Scholar, Southern Cross University. He is fellow of the World Academy of Art and Science and the World Futures Studies Federation. He is co-editor of the *Prout Review*, *New Renaissance,* and the *Journal of Futures Studies*. Among his authored/edited books are: *Macrohistory and Macrohistorians; Situating Sarkar; Transcending Boundaries; Islam, Postmodernism and Other Futures;* and, *Transforming Communication*. Forthcoming is *Understanding Sarkar* and *Theorizing Futures*. Address: The Communication Centre, Queensland University of Technology, G.P.O. Box 2434, Brisbane, Queensland, 4001. E-mail: s.inayatullah@qut.edu.au, and sinayatullah@hotmail.com.

JENNIFER GIDLEY is an Educational Psychologist and futures researcher in the area of youth visions of the future and empowerment. She has many years experience in psychology, Steiner education, and community learning development, having worked as a teacher, psychologist, and consultant in the primary, secondary, and tertiary levels of the educational domain. In addition, she founded and developed a Rudolf Steiner school in rural Australia. She is currently working as a counselor and consultant to schools (public and private) as well as lecturing in Social Sciences at Southern Cross University, P.O. Box 157, Lismore, 2480, NSW, Australia. She can also be contacted through her private business, Spirit of the Times International Education Initiatives, 5 Palmvale Drive, Goonellabah, NSW, 2480, Australia. E-mail: jgidley@scu.edu.au

TOM ABELES is President of Sagacity Inc., 3704 11th Ave. South, Minneapolis, MN 55407, USA, a knowledge management firm that provides consulting, internationally, on postsecondary education, including virtual learning environments. A former tenured professor, Abeles also consults on environmentally and socially responsible technologies, products, and services.

MARCUS BUSSEY is a writer, teacher, and musician who has spent over a decade working in neohumanist schools. He has published numerous articles on neohumanist education, artistic practice, and tantric philosophy. He can be contacted at 16 Rangers Road, Maleny, Queensland, 4552, Australia.

JIM DATOR is a Professor of Political Science and Director of the Hawaii Research Center for Futures Studies, University of Hawaii at Manoa, 2424 Maile Way, Honolulu, HI, 96822, USA. He was also secretary general and president of the World Futures Studies Federation.

JAMES GRANT is Dean of the College of Arts and Sciences and Associate Professor of Education at Maharishi University of Management at 1000 N. 4th Street, FM 1064, Fairfield, IA, 52557, USA, having been on faculty there since 1987. He received his doctorate from the Harvard Graduate School of Education.

GREG HEARN is an Associate Professor in the School of Communication, Queensland University of Technology, G.P.O. Box 2434, Brisbane, Queensland 4001, Australia. He is coauthor of the book *The Communication Superhighway: Social and Economic Change in the Digital Age*.

ANNE HICKLING-HUDSON is a Deputy Director of the Center for Policy and Leadership Studies in Education, Queensland University of Technology, Kelvin Grove, Brisbane, Queensland, 4059, Australia. Her expertise is in cross-cultural, international, and comparative education and she is president of the Australia and New Zealand Comparative and International Education Society.

PATRICIA KELLY is at the Cross Cultural Curriculum Development, Academic Staff Development Unit, Queensland University of Technology, G.P.O. Box 2434, Brisbane, Queensland, 4001, Australia. She is involved in the professional development of academic staff, particularly in the areas of responding to diversity and internationalization of the curriculum.

PETER MANICAS is Professor of Sociology and Director of Liberal Studies at the University of Hawaii at Manoa, Honolulu, HI, 96822, USA. He has published many books and articles in a variety of areas, including *A History and Philosophy of the Social Sciences* (1987) and *War and Democracy* (1989).

IVANA MILOJEVIC is a Ph.D. student at the School of Education, University of Queensland, St. Lucia Campus, Brisbane, Queensland, 4072, Australia. She has published widely in the area of feminist futures. She previously worked at the University of Novi Sad in Yugoslavia, in the area of sociology.

SHAHRZAD MOJAB is Assistant Professor in the Department of Adult Education, Community Development, and Counseling Psychology at OISE-University of Toronto, 252 Bloor Street West, M5S 1V6, Canada. Her areas of research and teaching include marginalization and resistance in education; globalization and social justice; Islamic fundamentalism and women's rights.

ASHIS NANDY, a political psychologist and cultural theorist, is Senior Fellow and former director of the Center for the Study of Developing Societies at 29 Rajpur Road, Delhi 110 054, India. Among his many books are *Alternative Sciences; At the Edge of Psychology; The Intimate Enemy; The Illegitimacy of Nationalism;* and *Traditions, Tyranny and Utopias.*

DEANE NEUBAUER is Professor of Political Science and Public Health at the University of Hawaii at Manoa, 2424 Maile Way, Honolulu, HI, 96822, USA. He also sits as a member of the regional accreditation body for California, Hawaii, and Guam, and on the Interregional Accrediting Committee, established to review the Western Governor's University for accreditation.

PATRICIA NICHOLSON is Associate Dean, School of Education, Stanford University, Palo Alto, CA, 94305-3096, USA. She is in frequent communication with Stanford alumni who are postsecondary educators at institutions around the world. Her research interests are futures, school reform issues, media and technology issues, and women's studies.

TARIQ RAHMAN is Associate Professor of Linguistics, National Institute of Pakistan Studies, Quaid-i-Azam University, Islamabad, Pakistan. His research focus is on South Asia, the modernization of postcolonial universities and linguistics.

DAVID ROONEY is an assistant Professor teaching communication management at the Graduate School of Management, University of Queensland, St. Lucia Campus, Brisbane, Queensland, 4072, Australia. His interests include the history of technology and knowledge.

MICHAEL SKOLNIK is a Professor in the Higher Education Group, Ontario Institute for Studies in Education of the University of Toronto, 252 Bloor Street W., Toronto, Ontario, M5S 1V6, Canada. His current research interest is on how technology is contributing to the development of linkages between postsecondary institutions, particularly those in different sectors and different countries.

PHILIP SPIES is Director of a private consultancy, Creative Futures Network Cc. He was past director of the Institute for Futures Research (IFR), at the University of Stellenbosch in South Africa. Currently he is a Research Associate of IFR, consultant, and almond farmer.

PAUL WILDMAN is an Independent Futurist and Fellow in Futures Studies, International Management Centers, Pacific Region (Brisbane). He is involved with futures of work opportunities and futures-oriented community economic development. He is coauthor of *Futures Studies: a Multi-Media CD-ROM Reader.* He can be contacted at P.O. Box 74, Nundah, Brisbane 4014, Australia.

ISBN 0-89789-718-8

HARDCOVER BAR CODE